The Rocky Mountain National Park Reader

THE NATIONAL PARK READERS
Lance Newman and David Stanley, series editors

# THE ROCKY MOUNTAIN NATIONAL PARK READER

EDITED BY

**JAMES H. PICKERING**

THE UNIVERSITY OF UTAH PRESS
*Salt Lake City*

The Defiance House Man colophon is a registered trademark of
The University of Utah Press. It is based on a four-foot-tall Ancient
Puebloan pictograph (late PIII) near Glen Canyon, Utah.

19 18 17 16 15     1 2 3 4 5

LIBRARY OF CONGRESS CATALOGING-IN-PUBLICATION DATA
The Rocky Mountain National Park reader / [edited by] James H. Pickering.
    pages cm
  Includes bibliographical references and index.
ISBN 978-1-60781-451-1 (paper : alkaline paper)
ISBN 978-1-60781-452-8 (ebook)

1. Rocky Mountain National Park (Colo.)—History. 2. Rocky Mountain National Park
(Colo.)—Biography. 3. Natural history—Colorado—Rocky Mountain National Park.
4. Rocky Mountain National Park (Colo.)—Description and travel. 5. Rocky Mountain
National Park (Colo.)—Literary collections. I. Pickering, James H.
  F782.R59R627 2015
  978.8›69—dc23

                                2015017687

Please consider page 281, Sources and Permissions, an extension of this copyright page.

Preceding pages: Albert Bierstadt, *Estes Park Colorado, Whyte's Lake*, oil on canvas.
Used by permission Buffalo Bill Center of the West, Cody, Wyoming, U.S.A., gift of the
Coe Foundation, 12.74.

Printed and bound by Sheridan Books, Inc., Ann Arbor, Michigan.

# CONTENTS

*Illustrations follow page 126*

1948 Map of Rocky Mountain National Park, published by the Rocky Mountain Motor Company.

# INTRODUCTION

*James H. Pickering*

Straddling the Continental Divide north and south, Rocky Mountain National Park contains some 415 square miles spread across three distinctive life zones (montane, subalpine, and alpine/tundra). Its geologic history is complex, the culmination of the powerful forces of tectonic uplift and erosion, spanning billions of years. The resulting scenic beauty is one that few places in North America can surpass: rugged and spectacular peaks; U-shaped, glacial-sculpted valleys; crystal clear mountain lakes and snow-fed streams. Ninety-five percent of the park is designated wilderness. Drier on the east than on the west, the park rises in elevation from about 7,500 feet on its eastern boundary to 14,259 feet at the summit of Longs Peak, a magnet for visitors for more than a century and a half. The subalpine region of the park is one of flowering meadows separated by densely wooded stands of ponderosa and lodgepole pine, Engelmann spruce, and Douglas fir, intermixed with aspen and willow—green or golden depending on the season. A full third lies above tree line at 11,500 feet in the harsh and windswept tundra where it is bisected by Trail Ridge Road, the highest continuously paved highway in America. The iconic features of its topographical landscape have long since made Rocky Mountain National Park one of the best known and most visited in the nation. The park with its surrounding region has a long, rich, and varied literature uniquely its own, a literature well worth celebrating and sharing on the occasion of its centennial year. Hence this anthology.

Archaeologists tell us that the park and its two adjacent valleys, Estes Park on the east and Middle Park on the west, have been inhabited by humans, at least on a seasonal basis, for some ten thousand years. Until the late 1700s the Utes dominated the interior mountains to the west, increasingly sharing their territory with others—Comanche, Shoshone, and perhaps the occasional band of Apache. The eastern valleys belonged to the Arapaho, a nomadic people who began to arrive about 1790, pressed west across the northern plains by their aggressive Sioux enemies. Entering the foothills of the Front Range and the area that is now Rocky Mountain National Park, the Arapaho forced the Ute to retreat across the Continental Divide.

Evidence of Native American activity—projectile points, potsherds, broken knives, scrapers, and other tools—have been discovered at various places throughout the park. These include the tundra along Trail Ridge Road where still can be located the remains of low-walled game drives used to herd animals into the arms of waiting hunters. Oldman Mountain, the rocky knob just west of the town of Estes Park, which archaeologists believe served as a spiritual (or vision) quest site, is but the most prominent of the hundreds of suspected sacred sites identified throughout the park region.

What would become Rocky Mountain National Park enters the historical record in June 1820, when the party commanded by Major Stephen H. Long, passing north to south along the Front Range on a scientific reconnaissance mission, first sighted the great peak that would be named in his honor. Though Long and his companions made no attempt to penetrate the mountains of northern Colorado, others already had. By this date, in fact, much of the region's interior had already been explored by Euro-American trappers and traders. Other than a few place names, however, these early visitors left little in the way of written or physical evidence of their comings and goings. Though some historians believe that the travels recorded by mountain man Rufus Sage in his *Rocky Mountain Life* (1846) brought him into or near the future park, the honor of "discovery" belongs to Kentuckian Joel Estes who, in October of 1859, together with one of his sons, stood at the crest of what is now Park Hill and gazed down in wonder upon the empty valley that would soon bear his name.

Their initial stay was brief. It was not until 1863, in fact, that Estes decided to relocate his family of ten from their ranch at Fort Lupton on the South Platte. For the next three years the Esteses made the valley floor their home. Here they supported themselves by carting game they shot down through the foothills to market in Denver while raising cattle and occasionally housing as paying guests those who wandered in to hunt, fish, prospect, or climb mountains. The winters, however, proved to be severe, making cattle grazing difficult. By mid-April of 1866 the Esteses were gone, leaving behind their squatter's cabin and outbuildings that stood in what is now the small arm of Lake Estes. A year later their place was taken by a jovial Welshman named Griff Evans, who moved his wife and young family up from Lyons to occupy and then expand the Estes holdings.

By the early 1870s the number of visitors who sought out the hospitality of the Evans ranch had greatly expanded. They were a varied lot: hunters and fishermen, government surveyors, prospectors, scientists, mountaineers, artists and writers, together with those simply seeking rest, recreation, or improved health away from the heat of summer. Two would leave indelible marks. The first was Windham Thomas Wyndham-Quin, the Fourth Earl of Dunraven, who came up from Denver to hunt during the week after Christmas in 1872. The second was noted English travel writer Isabella Lucy Bird, who arrived a year later, in October of 1873. Both departed deeply impressed by all they found. For the entrepreneurial Earl, Estes Park became a place in which to invest a portion of his not inconsiderable fortune. After having the valley surveyed and opened for settlement in January and February of 1874, Dunraven proceeded to acquire (through means at best suspect) direct title to some five thousand acres of prime real estate to use for raising cattle and as the site of a first-class tourist hotel, both of which he accomplished in short order. The legacy of Isabella Bird's three-month visit was equally important. The publication of her delightful book, *A Lady's Life in the Rocky Mountains*, in 1879 brought Estes Park's scenic wonders and invigorating climate to the attention of the nation and the world.

Dunraven's land grabbing gave him ownership of the best part of the Estes Valley, including choice parcels along its rivers and streams. But there was ample room for others and by 1875 pioneer families had begun to arrive, intent upon making Estes Park a year-round home. Some took time to locate permanently. New Yorker William James and family, for example, had to endure a miserable winter in a dirt-roofed cabin up against

Lumpy Ridge before swapping that property with the Reverend William McCreery for open land along Fall River. Others settled in more quickly: the MacGregors in the mouth of Black Canyon; the Fergusons below the alkaline pond known as Marys Lake; the Hupps in lower Beaver Meadows; the Spragues in Moraine Park; and the Lambs nine miles south in the valley at the foot of Longs Peak. Like Joel Estes and Griff Evans before them, all but one of these new arrivals soon found themselves in the tourist business. Abner Sprague said it best: "The hotel business was forced upon us. We came here for small ranch operations, but guests and visitors became so numerous, at first wanting eggs, milk, and other provisions, then wanting lodging, and finally demanding full accommodations, that we had to go into the hotel business or go bankrupt from keeping free company." Aided by fairly passable new roads linking the Estes Valley to Loveland, Longmont, Boulder, and other Front Range towns, within a few short years Estes Park's future as a destination resort community had been firmly established. All of these early resorts were located either in or close to the area that in 1915 would become Rocky Mountain National Park, quickly establishing a love of place among both residents and visitors that passing years would only strengthen.

The final decades of the nineteenth century were ones of expansion and consolidation, during which these pioneer resort owners and those who followed their example increased the capacities of their establishments, trying without much success to keep ahead of the new and returning visitors who crowded in each summer. Except for the Earl of Dunraven's fashionable Estes Park Hotel on Fish Creek, most of the valley's scattered guest ranches were modest places that catered to those who needed few amenities or were willing to "rough it" out-of-doors in some quiet, sequestered place.

The early years of the new century brought dramatic changes, including a building boom of new lodges, many within the future park. The most important can be traced to the morning of June 30, 1903, when Freelan Oscar Stanley, coinventor with his identical twin brother of the famous Stanley Steamer automobile, negotiated his small steam car up the rough wagon road from Lyons to spend the summer recovering from consumption. That moment, Enos Mills, the community's first historian, would later write, was "the epoch-making event in the history of Estes Park." F. O. Stanley would make Estes Park his summer home and chief beneficiary for the next thirty-seven years. The construction of the magnificent Stanley Hotel, a complex of eleven buildings in all, between 1907 and 1909, was but the beginning.

Stanley's timing was right. By the time that F. O. and his wife, Flora, returned for the summer of 1905, the village of Estes Park had been platted and laid out and building was well underway. Purchasing a half-interest in the holdings of the Earl of Dunraven, Stanley then used portions of that property and his own money to provide the fledgling town with its water, sewerage, and electrical systems, as well as its first bank. Later he would gift Estes Park land for its dump, a new eighteen-hole golf course, a new school, and, finally, the public recreation and fairgrounds that is today's Stanley Park.

There was also the matter of civic engagement. In 1906 Stanley agreed to serve as the first president of the Estes Park Protective and Improvement Association (EPPIA). This organization of local boosters, as its name suggests, sought to increase tourism by protecting the natural resources of the wilderness area west of the new village, including local fish and game, while encouraging the building of new roads and trails. The work of the EPPIA brought Stanley into close and regular contact with Enos Abijah Mills, a young man, not yet thirty, but even then well on his way to building the national reputation as a writer, lecturer, and scenic preservationist that would propel him into the front ranks of America's growing conservation movement. It was, in fact, at a meeting of the association in October 1907 that the "national park idea" was born to preserve in perpetuity the work already so well begun.

The speaker was Herbert N. Wheeler, newly appointed head of the Medicine Bow National Forest, the wilderness preserve that two years earlier had been extended south from Wyoming to include the area that would become Rocky Mountain National Park. "If you want to draw tourists," the chief forester told his audience, "you should establish a game refuge where tourists can see wild life." Wheeler then produced a map on which he outlined an area of more than a thousand square miles, beginning west of the new village of Estes Park and extending across the Continental Divide.

Mills wrote Wheeler the following spring to ask just where the boundaries of such a preserve might be located. It was in the context of this exchange that Mills's own far more ambitious plan for a full-blown national park began to take shape.

The campaign to create Rocky Mountain National Park was not easy. Opposition from entrenched timber, mining, and grazing interests was formidable, and it took seven long years and a broad coalition of powerful civic, business, and political organizations at the state, regional, and national level to make the park a reality. The peripatetic Mills was active on every front, and while others helped, most notably Denver lawyer James Grafton Rogers who drafted and redrafted the needed legislation, without Mills's dogged persistence and determination the "Estes Park Project," as he referred to it, might well have languished and died. In the end it took three separate park bills and five major revisions to get the required legislation through the U.S. Congress, and, even then, the size of the new park had been whittled down from the original Wheeler-Mills proposal of more than 1,000 square miles to 358.5.

The dedication of Rocky Mountain National Park took place on Saturday, September 4, 1915. The site was an open knoll in Horseshoe Park, near today's Lawn Lake trailhead, beneath a banner announcing the event. Despite the gray and threatening weather, it was a festive occasion. Some came by wagon, bike, and on foot. Most came in cars; as many as 267 by one count. "The greatest automobile demonstration," the *Rocky Mountain News* reported, "ever seen in Colorado." Ladies from the Estes Park Woman's Club passed out souvenir buttons and provided box lunches and hot coffee. Their husbands, most of whom were members of the Protective and Improvement Association, dutifully stood nearby dispensing ice cream cones. While guests and dignitaries assembled on a makeshift platform, a twenty-five-piece concert band from Fort Collins serenaded. Those on hand included Colorado governor George Carlson; Colorado congressman Edward Taylor; Assistant Secretary of the Interior Stephen Mather, soon to become the first head of the new National Park Service, together with his young deputy Horace Albright; and Mary Belle King Sherman, chair of the Conservation Committee of the General Federation of Women's Clubs, an organization that had helped galvanize support across the nation. F. O. Stanley, who had generously subsidized Mills's travels and lobbied eastern legislators, was there as well, captured in a memorable photograph holding a small American flag. But the day and hour belonged to Enos Mills, who chaired the afternoon's program. "This is the proudest moment of my life," he told the crowd. "I have lived to see the realization of a great dream come true. It means great things for Colorado and for the nation."

Since that day in 1915, a full century of history has now passed, providing an appropriate, indeed obligatory, occasion for a reflective backward glance at milestone events and achievements. There have been many. One thinks of the completion of Fall River Road over the Continental Divide in 1920, and its successor, Trail Ridge Road, in 1938; of Civilian Conservation Corps days of the 1930s which advanced important park projects, including trail building, by at least a decade; and of the "holing through" of the thirteen-mile Alva Adams tunnel beneath the park in 1944, a key element in the Colorado–Big Thompson transmountain irrigation project. Other, more recent, accomplishments include the opening of the Beaver Meadows Visitors Center in 1967 as part of the Mission '66 project, the last concerted attempt to refurbish and update America's system of national parks; and the completion in 2013 of the reconstruction and relocation of portions of much-traveled Bear Lake Road.

Over the past hundred years Rocky Mountain National Park has grown slightly in size and greatly in complexity. To be sure, it is rather less cluttered than it was in 1915. All of the great resort hotels (those "castles of woods") are gone, as are many of the other, smaller in-holdings once found clustered in Moraine Park and here and there in other places, returning large sections of the park to their natural state. The size of the ranger force and support staff of necessity has also grown (at the time of the dedication there were only three). They are needed to cope with the more than three million visitors who enter the park, mostly by way of Estes Park, each and every year, using a road and trail system that, though well maintained and in some places improved, has not grown materially since the CCC camps were closed by World War II. Protecting the park's resources—physiographic, biological, and cultural—while making them available for use and enjoyment is today the major ongoing concern. Some worry as well that, given the rapid growth of Colorado's Front Range communities, an increased number of visitors may one day, like its much-viewed elk herds, outstrip the park's carrying capacity. Balancing accessibility with the need to protect and preserve the park's fragile ecology is, and will remain, a significant challenge.

What has not changed is the special relationship between Rocky Mountain National Park and its gateway towns. The residents of Estes Park and the Estes Valley continue to regard the mountainous area to the west as their own to use, support, and protect, just as they did in Enos Mills's and F. O. Stanley's time. This is also true of the residents of Grand Lake across the Divide, a community where, as in Estes Park, the summertime population doubles with second homeowners. For both, Rocky Mountain National Park remains *their park*. To promote a game preserve, it was the members of the Estes Park Protective and Improvement Association who in 1913 and again in 1914 pooled their funds to reintroduce elk from the Yellowstone region of Wyoming into an area where they had virtually been hunted into extinction. It was these same residents who, on Halloween evening of 1917, when the park was very young and very vulnerable, left their partying and rushed in costume to fight a fire in Hidden Valley. Four decades later, local commerce-minded citizens would unite once again, this time unsuccessfully, to protest the closing of the ski facilities in Hidden Valley which they had long since come to regard as their own.

As a gateway community and haven for retirees, many of whom came as tourists and returned to stay, Estes Park has long since come to rely on park visitors for its economic well being. For better or for worse, the futures of both are inextricably linked. The same thing is true in an ecological sense, as well, for as Enos Mills and other early park supporters knew all too well, Rocky Mountain National Park and the adjacent Estes Valley share a common ecosystem, a fact that becomes self-evident each fall and winter when herds of elk wander through village neighborhoods.

"No place is a place," Wallace Stegner once wrote, "until things that have happened in it are remembered." Such is true of Rocky Mountain National Park. Engagement with place, often resulting in events that loom large in park history, is, in fact, the underlying theme that connects and animates the narratives in this anthology. Broadly representative, both in subject and approach, they reach back to Arapaho and pioneer times before the park was established; and then move forward to span its first hundred years. The voices that speak to us are equally distinctive. Some tell us about the past, how it once was, recalling personal moments of triumph and tragedy. Other voices are quieter and more polemic. Perhaps the most notable of these are the concluding selections on the white-tailed ptarmigan, elk, and pika whose authors speak directly to realities that define the park's present and that will, in all likelihood, shape its future. All, however, serve a single purpose. They are the attempt to capture and share the rich literary and historical mosaic that helps us understand and better appreciate the national treasure that is Rocky Mountain National Park.

# 1

## PREFACE TO "THE ROCKY MOUNTAIN NATIONAL PARK"

### 1915

*Enos A. Mills*

*No one worked harder for the creation of Rocky Mountain National Park than Enos A. Mills (1870–1922). For those efforts the* Denver Post *and others bestowed on him the title "Father of Rocky Mountain National Park." It had been a long and hard journey. Having arrived in Estes Park from Kansas in 1884 as a sickly youth in search of better health, within little more than two decades Enos Mills had created for himself an attractive new persona. He had become "Mills of the Rockies," a man with a national reputation as mountaineer, lecturer, scenic preservationist, and mountain innkeeper, as well as the author of authentic and highly readable essays on wildlife and out-of-doors adventuring. By the date of the park's dedication, Houghton Mifflin had published three volumes of these essays. Not surprisingly, in the fourth,* Rocky Mountain Wonderland *(1915), Mills chose to devote the final chapter to a descriptive survey of the new park. Today's visitors will have little trouble in recognizing the familiar terrain over which Mills guides them.*

Extend a straight line fifty-five miles northwest from Denver and another line sixty miles southwest from Cheyenne and these lines meet in approximately the centre of the Rocky Mountain National Park. This centre is in the mountain-heights a few miles northwest of Long's Peak, in what Dr. F. V. Hayden, the famous geologist, calls the most rugged section of the Continental Divide of the Rocky Mountains.

This Park is a mountain realm lying almost entirely above the altitude of nine thousand feet. Through it from north to south extends the Snowy Range,—the Continental Divide,—and in it this and the Mummy Range form a vast mountain Y. Specimen Mountain is the north end of the west arm of this Y, while Mummy Mountain is at the tip of the east arm. Mt. Clarence King on the south forms the base of the stem, while Long's Peak is against the eastern side of the stem, about midway.

Long's Peak, "King of the Rockies," is the dominating peak and rises to the altitude of 14,255 feet. There are ten or more peaks in the Park that tower above thirteen thousand, and upwards of forty others with a greater altitude than twelve thousand feet. Between these peaks and their out-jutting spurs are numerous cañons. The Park is from ten to eighteen miles wide, its greatest length is twenty-five miles, and its total area is about three hundred and sixty square miles.

A line drawn around the Park on the boundary line would only in two or three places drop below the altitude of nine thousand feet. The area thus is high-lying and for the most part on edge. About one fifth of the entire area is above the limits of tree-growth. Here and there they are whitened by comparatively small snow and ice fields. From the summits the mountains descend through steeps, walls, slopes, terraces, tablelands, spurs, gorges, and mountain valleys.

This Park is a wilderness. Though entirely surrounded by settlers and villages, it is an almost unbroken wild. Many of its peaks are as yet unclimbed. There are pathless forests, unvisited gorges, unnamed lakes, and unknown localities.

Gray and red granite form the larger portion of its surface. Here and there are mixtures of schist, gneiss, and porphyry. The northwest corner is volcanic and is made up of rhyolite, obsidian, and lava. The Indians have a tradition concerning the volcanic activity of Specimen Mountain, though I doubt if this mountain has been active within a century. It is a dead or sleeping volcano. A part of its old crater-rim has fallen away, and brilliant flowers cover the cold ashes in the crater.

Most of the territory was glaciated during the last ice age, and there still remain five small glaciers and a number of ice-fields. The Hallett Glacier is on the north shoulder of Hague's Peak, the Sprague Glacier on the south side of Stone's Peak, Tyndall Glacier between Flat-Top and Mt. Hallett, and Andrews Glacier in a cirque of Loch Vale, while an unnamed small one is at the bottom of the east precipice of Long's Peak.

There can hardly be found a greater and more closely gathered area of imposing, easily read glacial records than those which centre about Long's Peak. These works of the Ice King, both intact and partly ruined, have attracted the attention and study of a number of prominent geologists and glaciologists. Among these ice works Dr. Hayden and Dr. David Starr Jordan have climbed and wandered. Vernon L. Kellogg has here gathered material for a book, and Dr. Edward L. Orton, former State Geologist of Ohio, has spent many weeks here in study. Within a six-mile radius of the top of Long's Peak are more than thirty glacier lakes and perhaps twice as many lakelets or mountain tarns. Immediately south of the Peak, Wild Basin is literally filled with glacier-records. To the north is Moraine Park; to the northwest, Glacier Gorge and Loch Vale; to the west, lying between the Peak and Grand Lake, there is a wondrous area of the Ice King's topography.

Bierstadt, St. Vrain, and Mills Moraines are imposing deposits of glacial débris. Of these Mills Moraine has been the most studied. It apparently holds the story of two widely separated ice ages. This moraine evidently was formed by the glacier which made the basin of Chasm Lake. It extends eastward from Long's Peak, its uppermost end being at twelve thousand five hundred feet. At timber-line its trend is toward the southeast. It is about one mile wide, five miles long, and in places apparently more than one thousand feet deep.

The ice-stream which piled the enormous Bierstadt Moraine took its rise on the west summit slope of Long's Peak. It flowed first toward the west, and in the upper amphitheatre of Glacier Gorge it united with the ice-stream from the north slope of Shoshone Peak and the stream off the eastern slope of Mt. McHenry. Although a part of this enlarged flow appears to have been thrust across the Continental Divide, the larger portion of it was deflected to the north through Glacier Gorge. Emerging from this gorge and enlarged by the ice-streams from Mt. Otis, Mt. Hallett, and other peaks in the Continental Divide, it flowed on to thrust against the eastern base of Flat-Top Mountain. This bent it to the east, and from this turning-point it began to unload its débris on Bierstadt Moraine. A part of its débris was dropped in a smaller parallel moraine on the opposite side of the Glacier Creek, and finally a terminal moraine was piled against the western front of Green Mountain, where it almost united with the terminal part of the Moraine on the south side of Moraine Park.

The glaciers have formed and distributed much of the soil of this region. Above timber-line there are wide, sedgy meadows and tundras and dry, grassy moorlands. Everywhere on the heights where there is soil there is a growth of Arctic-Alpine vegetation. Above the limits of tree-growth are enormous ragged areas and tiny ledge gardens that are crowded with a variety of brilliantly colored wild blossoms.

The average altitude of the timber-line is about eleven thousand three hundred feet, nearly a vertical mile higher than the timber-line in the Alps. Timber-line the world over is a place of striking interest, but nowhere have I found or heard of a timber-line which exhibits so many telling features as does the forest-frontier on the eastern side of the Continental Divide. The prevailing tree on the drier slopes at timber-line is *Pinus flexilis*, the limber pine. In the moist places Engelmann spruce predominates, and in many of the moister places there are dwarfed and tangled growths of arctic willow, black birch, and aspen.

Among the least broken and most enchanting of the primeval forests of the Park are a few that are grand. One of these is between the head of Fall River and the Poudre; another is in Forest Cañon; one is in the southern part of Wild Basin; still another is on the western slope of Stone's Peak and Flat-Top Mountain. These forests are mostly Engelmann spruce, with a scattering of sub-alpine fir. Around the lower, warmer slopes grows the Western yellow pine, and on the cold lower slopes the Douglas spruce. There are a number of extensive lodge-pole pine forests. These are from thirty to one hundred and thirty years old. Lines of aspen adorn most streams; here and there where the soil is moist they expand into groves.

The wild-flower inhabitants of this great Park number more than a thousand species. Many of these are members of famous families,—famous for their antiquity upon the earth, for their delicate scent, for their intricate and artistic structure, and for their brilliant color.

The gentian family is represented by fifteen species, one of these being a fringed blue gentian, a Western relative of the fringed gentian celebrated by the poet Bryant. There are intricately-formed orchids. The silver and blue columbine is here at its best; it blossoms on the lower slopes in June, on the heights during September. The populous pea family, in yellow, white, and lavender, covers and colors extensive areas. Then there are asters, daisies, mariposa lilies, polemonium, wintergreen, forget-me-nots, black-eyed Susans, and numerous other handsome flower people. These flowers are scattered all over the Park except in places destitute of soil. I have found primroses, phlox, and mertensia on the summit of Long's Peak. In the heights above the limits of tree-growth there are scores of other blossoms.

More than one hundred species of birds nest in these scenes. Among these are the robin, the bluebird, the wren, the hermit thrush, the hummingbird, the golden eagle, the white-crowned sparrow, and that marvelous singer the solitaire. Among the resident birds are the ouzel, the crested and the Rocky Mountain jays, the chickadee, the downy woodpecker, and the magpie. The ptarmigan and the rosy finch are prominent residents in the heights above the timber-line.

Once the big-game population was numerous. But the grizzly has been almost exterminated, and only a few black bear remain. There are a few mountain lions and elk. Deer are fairly common, and in localities mountain sheep are plentiful and on the increase. Specimen Mountain probably is one of the places most frequented by mountain sheep. A number of times flocks of more than a hundred have been seen on this mountain. A scattering of wolves, coyotes, and foxes remain. Conies are numerous in the slide rock of the heights, and snowshoe rabbits people the forests. The Frémont, or pine, squirrels are scattered throughout the woods. Lunch where you will, and the dear and confiding busy chipmunk is pretty certain to approach. The region appears to be above the snake line, and I have never seen a snake within the boundary. The streams and a number of the lakes have their population of rainbow and brook trout. Around the water's edge mink make their home.

The beaver has colonies large and small all over the park up to the limits of tree-growth. Houses, ponds, dams, tree-cuttings, canals, and other works of the beaver are here readily seen. Excellent opportunities are afforded to study beaver manners and customs and to comprehend the influence of his work in the conservation of soil and water.

Big game, and in fact all wild life, begin to increase in numbers and also to allow themselves to be seen from the instant they receive the complete protection which parks afford. This park will thus assure a multiplication of the various kinds of wild life which the region now contains. And this increased wild life, with no hunters to alarm, will allow itself to be readily seen.

There are only a few miles of road within the Park boundaries, but the Fall River Road, now under construction across the Continental Divide at Milner Pass, just south of Specimen Mountain, will be a wonderful scenic highway. Although there are a number of trails in the Park, so broken is the topography that most of the country a stone's throw away from them is unvisited and unknown.

A road skirts the western boundary of the Park and touches it at Grand Lake and Specimen Mountain. Another road closely parallels the eastern boundary-line, and from it a half-dozen roads touch the Park. This parallel road reaches the roads of Denver and of the plains through Boulder, Left Hand, Big Thompson, and two St. Vrain cañons.

The drainage of the western half of the Park concentrates in the Grand River on the western boundary and reaches the Pacific Ocean through the Grand Cañon of Arizona. A number of streams rise in the eastern side. These assemble their waters in the Platte River out on the plains. In their upper course, all these streams start from the snows and come rushing and bounding down the roughest, steepest slopes.

The climate of the eastern slope is comparatively dry and mild. The winters are sunny, but little snow falls, and the winds are occasionally warm and usually extremely dry. Though only a few miles from the eastern slope, the western rarely receives a wind, and its snow-fall is more than double that of the eastern.

Numerous authors and artists have made long visits in this region, and its scenery has received their highest praise. Bierstadt, the artist, came here in 1870. A few years later he was followed by the famous authors Isabella Bird, Anna Dickinson, and Helen Hunt. Frederick H. Chapin visited the region in 1888 and wrote a splendidly illustrated book about it, called "Mountaineering in Colorado." This was published by the Appalachian Club. In commenting upon the scenery of the region Hayden, Father of the Yellowstone National Park, turned aside from scientific discussion in his geological report for 1875 to pay the following tribute to the scenic charm of this territory:

Not only has nature amply supplied this with features of rare beauty and surroundings of admirable grandeur, but it has thus distributed them that the eye of an artist may rest with perfect satisfaction on the complete picture presented. It may be said, perhaps, that the more minute details of the scenery are too decorative in their character, showing, as they do, the irregular picturesque groups of hills, buttes, products of erosion, and the finely moulded ridges—the effect is pleasing in the extreme.

Long's Peak is considered by mountain-climbers an excellent view-point. Standing aside one mile from the Continental Divide and rising above a large surrounding wonderland, its summit and upper slopes give splendid views and command a variety of scenes, near and far. While upon its slope, Mr. Chapin said: "I would not fail to impress on the mind of the tourist that the scenes are too grand for words to convey a true idea of their magnificence. Let him, then, not fail to visit them." It is an extremely rocky and rugged peak, but it is almost entirely free of snow and ice, so that climbing it is simply a day's work crowded with enjoyment and almost free from danger. Though it is two hundred and fifty feet lower than the highest peak in the Rocky Mountains and three hundred and fifty feet lower than Mt. Whitney, California, the highest peak in the United States, Long's Peak probably has a greater individuality than either. Alongside it stands Mt. Meeker, with an altitude of 14,000 feet. These sky towers are visible for more than one hundred miles. The Indians of the Colorado and Wyoming plains used to call them the "Two Guides."

It is possible, if not probable, that Long's Peak was originally one thousand or even two thousand feet higher. The mass of this peak stands apart from the main range and embraces three other peaks. These are Mt. Meeker, Mt. Washington, and Storm Peak. All are united below thirteen thousand feet. They may once have been united in one greatly higher mass. Much of the débris in the vast Boulderfield and Mills Moraines and a lesser amount from the enormous Bierstadt and St. Vrain Moraines must have come from the summit slope of the Long's Peak group. No small part of this may have come from above thirteen thousand feet. An exceedingly small percentage of the glacial débris which surround Long's Peak would, if atop the Long's Peak group, elevate it two thousand feet higher.

The Glacier Gorge region, which lies just to the northwest of Long's Peak, probably has the most magnificent scenery in the Park. Here are clustered enormous glaciated gorges, great glaciated walls, alpine lakes, waterfalls, moraines, alpine flora, and towering peaks.

Wild Basin, a broken and glaciated region of twenty-five square miles, lies immediately south of the Peak. This basin is almost encircled by eight towering peaks, and the enormous St. Vrain Moraine thrusts out of its outlet and shows where the united ice-rivers formerly made their way from this basin. Within this wild area are lakes, forests, waterfalls, and a splendid variety of wild and lovely scenes.

The glacier lakes and wild tarns of this Park are one of its delights. Though most of these water fountains are small, they are singularly beautiful. They are in the middle-mountain zone, in a belt which lies between the altitudes of ten thousand and twelve thousand feet. There are more than a hundred of these, and their attractiveness equals that of any of the mountain lakes of the world.

The best known and most popular of these lakes are Fern and Odessa. These lie about twelve miles west of the village of Estes Park. Chasm Lake, on the east side of Long's Peak, is set in an utterly wild place. Its basin was gouged from solid granite by the old Long's Peak Glacier. Mt. Washington, Mt. Meeker, and Long's Peak tower above it, and around it these peaks have flung their wreckage in chaotic confusion. A glacier almost crawls into it, and the east precipice of Long's Peak, the greatest precipice in the Park, looms above it.

Long, Black, Thunder, Ouzel, and Poudre Lakes have charms peculiar to each, and each is well worth a visit. Lake Mills, in the lower end of Glacier Gorge, is one of the largest lakes in the Park. The largest lake that I know of in the Rocky Mountain National Park is Lake Nanita. This is about one mile long and half as wide, and reposes in that wilderness of wild topography about midway between Grand Lake and Long's Peak. There are mountain people living within eight or ten miles of this lake who have never even heard of its existence. Although I have been to it a number of times, I have never found even a sign of another human visitor. A member of the United States Geological Survey is the only individual I have ever met who has seen it.

As originally planned, the Park was to have more than twice its present area. I hope there may be early added to this region Mt. Audubon, Arapahoe Peak, and other territory to the south. The summit of Twin Peaks on the east would make another excellent addition. A part of the Rabbit Ear Range to the northwest, and Medicine Bow Mountains and the headwaters of the Poudre lying to the north, would make excellent park territory.

But even as it now stands, this splendidly scenic region with its delightful climate appears predestined to become one of the most visited and one of the most enjoyed of all the scenic reservations of the Government. In addition to its scenery and climate, it is not far from the geographical centre of the United States. A number of transcontinental railroads are close to it, and two railroads run within a few miles of its border. The Lincoln Highway is within twenty miles of it, and six excellent automobile roads connect its edges with the outside world.

Each year visitors reach it in increasing numbers. During 1914 there were more than 56,000 of these, many of whom remained to enjoy it for weeks. It has a rare combination of those characteristics which almost every one wants and which all tired people need,—accessibility, rare scenery, and a friendly climate.

# 2

## NATIVE AMERICAN PRESENCE

### The Return of the Arapaho, 1914

*Oliver W. Toll*

*It was part of the publicity campaign for the new park. In early 1914, with legislation stalled in Congress, the nomenclature committee of the Colorado Mountain Club hit upon the idea of researching the original Native American names of landmarks in the Estes Park region. Unable to identify professional anthropologists, CMC members turned to the Indians themselves, raising sufficient funds to bring two elderly Arapaho, Gun Griswold and Sherman Sage, and their young interpreter, Tom Crispen, from the Wind River Reservation in Wyoming for a well-scripted, two-week pack trip that July through the region outfitted and led by veteran guide Shep Husted. Twenty-three-year-old Oliver Toll, the son of prominent Denverites, was recruited to take notes during the journey that followed. These were organized and published in 1962 under the title* Arapaho Names and Trails. *His account, archaeologist Jim Benedict has noted, though not an ethnography, has proven reliable, and brings us as close to Rocky Mountain Park's Native American past as we are likely to get.*

These field notes were written up shortly after a two weeks pack trip with three Arapaho Indians through the Estes Park–Grand Lake region of Colorado in the summer of 1914. Two of the Indians—Griswold and Sage—had lived in that region in their youth, but did not speak English, so Tom Crispin, a younger Indian of partly white blood, came down with them from the Wind River Reservation in Wyoming as interpreter. The trip, arranged in order to learn the Arapaho names for the area, was outfitted by Shep Husted, whose ranch was near Estes Park village, and who was very familiar with the local place names.

We tried to cover as much of the region as possible, especially from the high country. I tried to match the Indian names for the various features of the country, as obtained from Griswold and Sage through Tom, with the local names given by Shep. I also asked about other matters which I thought might be of interest. My notes recorded what the Indians said with little evaluation or selection....

The Indians arrived in Longmont, Colorado, on Tuesday, July 14, 1914, about noon. As they got off the train, Tom Crispin was carrying his suitcase with an air of considerable sophistication. Sage in his blue chief-of-police uniform, rather baggy at the knees, had a roll of blankets under his arm, and Gun Griswold was fanning himself embarrassedly with some eagles' feathers, his share of the luggage.

Of course we became at once public characters to the citizens of Longmont; and in fact throughout the trip were accorded a place in the estimation of the public between that of a governor and a theatrical troupe.

From Longmont we went to Estes Park by automobile, in the machines of Mr. C. F. Hendrie and Mr. F. O. Vaille, arriving at Longs Peak Inn in the latter part of the afternoon. There, with the help of Enos Mills, general plans for our camping trip were made. Our idea was to cover a good deal of the country, and as far as possible to get views from high elevations, so that the Indians could see as much of the geography of the region as possible.

Gun Griswold was the oldest of the Indians, seventy-three years old. He found it a hard trip. He rode in the saddle with the ease and poise of a sack of oats, and about the middle of the trip developed a sore back, so that we made the travelling as easy as possible for him. As Tom said, the people at the reservation would be apt to blame us if Griswold never came back. As we were coming back over the Flat Top Trail, which is pretty hard going, Griswold got discouraged, got off his horse and sat down on a rock, telling us to go ahead, but that he was an old man, it was too hard a trip for him, and he wanted to be left there. It was a natural feeling but not a very practical one. This, by the way, was the only instance on the trip of anything approaching bad humor on the part of the Indians. They were ideal camping companions, jolly and good natured.

Griswold has been a judge among the Arapaho under United States law which was translated into the Arapaho language. Now he is retired on a moderate allowance, taken out in rations, I believe. No one could help respecting him. He spoke little, had a great deal of dignity, and was treated with consideration by the others. They said that his only son had been killed a few months before by another Indian, which accounted for Griswold's lack of spirits.

Sherman Sage, sixty-three years old, was a much more active man, and as jolly as Griswold was quiet. He had been in innumerable Indian battles in his day, a wound on his right hand testifying to his part in the battle of Clear Creek. At present he occupies the office of Chief-of-Police on the Reservation. This is perhaps the most important Indian office there, though the chief activity of the police department is the arrest of Indians who get drunk. (It is against the law to sell Indians liquor.) Sage was evidently a good man for his position, responsible, brave, and cool. He impressed one as particularly trustworthy and honest. Added to this, he was a pretty shrewd old Indian, and a good judge of people....

Sage was distinctly of the old school, while Tom was modern in his attitude. For instance, when we had made camp on the way down from Flat Top to Estes Park, Sage and Tom came into our tent after supper, and we had a little talk. We asked Sage whether he liked things as they are today better than when the Indians used to hunt game in Estes Park. Sage said that he thought things were better now. "In those days," he said, "a man used to be honored according to the damage he could do the enemy, and so all young men were brave; but now a man gets on well if he is pleasant and kind to other people, and that is the better way." The aspect of the present time that seemed to strike Tom most was the greater cost of living. "In those days," Tom said, "a man was always fighting. He was always moving around with very few possessions, camping in bad weather, and was likely to be wounded in some battle and have to lie all night out in the freezing cold weather, with no one to help him. Now a man has an easy time of it...."

Sage took Shep into his especial good graces, would insist on Shep's giving us his version of an Indian war-dance at least once every meal, and grew quite chummy with him. Sage had a better sense of humor, by far, than the average white man, and though he could communicate with Shep only by signs, he managed to put his ideas across, and I believe almost embarrassed Shep once by calling on him for a love song to Squeaky Bob's cook.

When Sage used to live near Denver, fifty years ago, the most substantial building was an adobe house on the lower part of Cherry Creek. Sage's recollection of Denver was of a number of houses standing on sand spits in the creek bottom, resting on posts which kept them several feet above the sand. The settlers asked Bear Claw, the chief of the Arapahos who were camped near Denver, to send the Indian children to the whitemen's school to be educated, and the Indians did so. But at this time Denver was troubled with a good deal of lawlessness, and one night in particular two horse thieves were shot as they were attempting to steal some horses out of a corral. This made a good deal of talk and excitement in the town, and the Indians decided that the whitemen were a rather disreputable lot. Not caring to have their children associate with such people, they took them out of school, "which was too bad," said Sage, "for education is a very good thing."

Tom Crispen, the interpreter, was about thirty-eight years old. He is the official interpreter of the Arapahos on the Wind River Reservation in Wyoming, and interprets very well, as he speaks both good and colloquial English, and is intelligent and accurate. His point of view is entirely that of the whiteman. He has met every president since Arthur, has a daughter who is ready to enter college, and a son, Tom, Jr., whom he calls Buster, so you can see that he is quite up to date. His Indian name is White Horse, and he belongs to a family that is one of the seven leading ones among his tribe. He has considerable property on the reservation. On the trip, Tom considered himself one of us rather than one of the Indians. He would say, for instance, "You couldn't lose these Indians in these woods; they could find their way home from anywhere you could put them, while you or I might easily get lost." Tom slept in our tent, the two older Indians having a tent by themselves.

Tom was an Episcopalian in creed. Sage and Griswold were Catholics.

# 3

## ARAPAHO TALES AND LEGENDS

*Oliver W. Toll*

*As the 1914 Arapaho made their way through the Estes Valley and visited the mountain region that would soon become Rocky Mountain National Park they were encouraged to tell stories particularly in relationship to important land features. Partly as the result of this trip, some thirty-six places within the park now bear Native American names. During their two weeks together, Oliver Toll in his role of scribe simply let the two Arapaho talk, recording as best he could what he understood they were trying to say. Some of what he heard and wrote down can best be described as myth and legend, stories orally passed down from one generation to the next. Such stories, ethnologists tell us, contain powerful truths about place, identity, and heritage, valuable indices of culture that aid greatly in reconstructing the past. Five of the stories told by Sherman Sage and Gun Griswold are included here.*

1. Thatchtop Mountain was called the "Buffalo Climb,"…Griswold says that one winter a herd of buffalo-cows in the Park climbed high on the slope of Thatchtop and were caught there by the snow. The Indians climbed the mountain on snowshoes and killed many of them. (From Trail Ridge it does not look as if it would be possible for buffalo to climb Thatchtop. When this objection was made, Tom replied that he had already said this to Griswold, and Griswold had answered that on the southeast side of Thatchtop the slope was less steep, a fact corroborated by Shep, and that this was the way by which the buffalo had climbed. From where we had been this gradual east slope had not been visible.)

2. In Beaver Park to the west of Hondius Ranch there is a fairly steep rocky hill which has been known in the park as the Indian Fort. The Arapahos volunteered that this had been the scene of a great battle between the Apaches and the Arapahos.

Sage was four years old at the time, and just remembers the wounded from the battle being brought into camp, which was on the west side of Moraine Park. His oldest brother was wounded in the fighting. Some of the Arapahos had old Canadian flint lock guns at this time, but most used bow and arrows.

An Apache war party of perhaps fifty men had come into the park from the southwest, and had been met by the Arapahos in Beaver Park south of the High Drive. Sage found a pile of stones there which certainly looked like an Indian monument. He said that that monument marked the beginning of the battle, and that it was customary to put such a monument where the first man in an important battle was killed. Near the main monument were three or four stones. Sage said that the farthest of these stones showed where the first man who was killed in that battle had been shot with an arrow, the next one was where he had risen and fallen again, and the big pile of stones marked the place where he had finally died. It is rather hard to see how he could have read so much out of a few scattered stones, unless possibly in later years Sage had gone over the scene of the battle with some of the Indians who were in it.

From the point marked by the monument the Apaches had been driven to the southwest, back along the way they had come, and there was quite a battle in the neighborhood of Glacier Peaks. From there the Apaches followed along the glacial ridges to the north, and made a stand for over a day in the Indian fort near the Hondius Ranch....

On the Apache fort there is a place near the south side of the hill, and in the direction of the bench mark, where our Indians said the Apaches laid out the bodies of their dead and burned them, in sight of the enemy. This was said to have been a practice of the Apaches.

From that place the Apaches retreated to the north, skirting Trail Ridge, and leaving the park to the west of the gap between Horseshoe Park and Beaver Park. There the Arapaho chief gave orders to his men to let the Apaches go, so they were pursued no farther.

3. Specimen Mountain they called "Mountain Smokes." Sage said that there was an old Arapaho legend that many years ago this mountain used to smoke. In explaining this, he laid some stones on the ground. The first stone represented Sage's children, the next Sage, the next his father, the next his father's father, and so on. Sage laid out in this way eight stones. "Now," he said, pointing to the last of the stones, "this man, when he was a boy, saw smoke coming out of the mountain." (Specimen Mountain is volcanic in origin and, according to Dr. Orton, formerly State Geologist of Ohio, is said to have been active to the extent of emitting smoke and gasses between 500 and 1,000 years ago. While it could not have been active within eight generations, it seems plausible that there should have been an Indian legend as to its activity. Perhaps in the transmission of the legend the omission of generations was to be expected. So far as I remember, we had not spoken to the Indians of the fact that this was a volcanic mountain.)

We were also told a story of a party of Indians who, at the time when the mountain smoked, tried to go up to see it, but the top of the mountain was so hot that they were unable to ascend. The mountain, they said, used to roar and rumble, and when the rocks from the top of the crater rolled into the creek or onto moist ground, they hissed and sometimes exploded. There are many geodes to be found on the mountain.

4. The Indians' name for Grand Lake was "Big Lake"…; but they also called it "Holy Lake" or "Spirit Lake." …They said that the latter name came from a time when the lake had nearly frozen over, so that only a little patch of water was left in the center of the lake. In the snow on the ice the Indians found many buffalo tracks. The tracks of one especially large buffalo seemed to come from the center of the lake and to return there.

The Indians concluded, therefore, that some enormous buffalo must live in the lake, from which they called it "Spirit Lake."

5. I asked Tom for the Arapaho legend of the creation of the earth, and he gave it to me somewhat as follows:

Once upon a time there was nothing but water over the face of the earth. There was a man who walked upon the water. He had a big supernatural stone pipe, and in the pipe were feathers and bits of fur of all kinds of animals. From these feathers and bits of fur he could make the animals to which they belonged.

So he took out a duck feather, and there was a duck. He told the duck to dive into the water. The duck went down and was gone for a long time, for several days. Finally the duck came up nearly drowned, but he had not struck bottom. Then the man sent other animals down, and they were gone for a long time, and came up nearly drowned without striking the bottom. The fourth one sent down was a turtle. When the turtle came up there was clay wedged under his shell on each side of his head, for the turtle had found the bottom.

The man took the clay and threw it east and west and north and south, and there was land.

Then he took some white clay and made a white man and a white woman, and some red clay and made an Indian man and woman. This is how the world started.

# 4

## THE 1914 ARAPAHO VISIT

Its True Significance

*James H. Pickering*

*In August 2014, in celebration of the one hundredth anniversary of the 1914 pack trip, Rocky Mountain National Park made arrangements to bring back to Estes Park a number of Northern Arapaho elders and their families for a weekend of celebration and remembrance. The present editor made it a point to attend. My reflections on that event were subsequently published in the quarterly newsletter of the Rocky Mountain Conservancy, RMNP's major support organization.*

About noon on Tuesday, July 14, 1914, three Northern Arapaho Indians arrived by train at Longmont. The oldest, at age 73, was Gun Griswold, a rather taciturn retired judge. His younger, and much more animated companion, was Sage Sherman, age 63, dressed for the occasion in his blue-cloth chief-of-police uniform. Accompanying them was Tom Crispin, a much younger man of mixed blood. Crispin spoke fluent Arapaho and English and was there to serve as interpreter. Met at the station by automobiles, by late afternoon the three had been taken to Longs Peak Inn as guests of its owner, Enos Mills.

The Arapaho had come from the Wind River Reservation in west central Wyoming at the invitation of the nomenclature committee of the Colorado Mountain Club, as part of its campaign to gain support for the creation of Rocky Mountain National Park. Earlier that year CMC members had come up with the idea of researching the original Native American names of landmarks in the Estes region. Unable to locate professional anthropologists, the CMC turned to the Arapaho themselves, issuing an invitation for a two-week pack trip that July through the area, outfitted and led by veteran guide Shep Husted. Oliver Toll, a twenty-three-year-old lawyer, was recruited to take notes during their journey. These field notes were organized and published forthy-eight years later, in 1962, by what is now the Rocky Mountain Conservancy under the title *Arapaho Names and Trails*. Thanks in large measure to this trip, some thirty-six Indian names were subsequently affixed to mountains, trails, lakes, and other local land features (as well as names in translation—e.g. Gianttrack, Lumpy Ridge, and Never Summer). Oliver Toll had no formal training as an ethnologist or linguist. Yet, as the late Jim Benedict has observed, though not ethnography in the classic sense, his notes provide "a delightful—often humorous—account filled with information, much of which has proven reliable."

But what was, and is, the real and lasting significance of the visit of the 1914 Arapaho? To be sure there are those place-names, and, even more importantly, the legends and stories that the two elderly Arapaho attached to them: to the Apache Fort in Upper Beaver Meadows, to Longs Peak, Thatchtop, and Specimen Mountain, and to the waters of Grand Lake, as well as to the ancient trails that led up and over the tundra of Trail Ridge. These legends and stories are, as Benedict notes, "all we have."

Until 1914, there had been little or no attention paid to the region's prehistory. In fact, Enos Mills, the area's first historian, in his 105 page, *The Story of Estes Park*, published in 1905, dismissed that past in a single brief paragraph: "When Estes first came to the Park he saw new lodge poles and other recent Indian signs, but, so far as is known, there never was an Indian in the Park since the white man came." Since there had been no frontier-like encounter between Native Americans and Europeans, for Mills their one-time presence had little meaning.

In 1914 the Arapaho were similarly dismissed with little more than wry humor. The *Longmont Ledger* set the stage, telling its readers that their arrival "suggested dream land, fairy land and Leather Stocking Tales." Oliver Toll recalled, somewhat apologetically, that "we became at once public characters to the citizens of Longmont; and in fact throughout the trip were accorded a place in the estimation of the public somewhere between that of a governor and a theatrical troupe." For most, these Native Americans returning home were little more than anachronisms of the Old West, much like the vaudevillians of Buffalo Bill's Wild West Show, a romanticized piece of Americana that lasted until 1913.

I had read Toll's *Arapaho Names and Trails* a number of times, and made frequent use of it in my writings. But its true significance did not occur to me until this past August, when I went down to Bond Park to watch a program sponsored by Rocky Mountain National Park commemorating the 100th anniversary of the 1914 pack trip. On hand were Northern Arapaho elders and their families, who during the day shared their history, stories, legends, and culture, as well as their present-day concerns, with those who came by. The next day they were taken across Trail Ridge to Grand Lake, symbolically completing the pack trip of their ancestors.

That day in Bond Park the Arapaho elders talked about those ancestors for whom the Estes region was once a special place, and about the legends and stories that grew out of their contact with the land itself. It was then that I suddenly understood, in a moment of personal epiphany, the real and lasting significance of the Arapaho pack trip of a century ago. The gift of the Arapaho to us was what historians, sociologists, and psychologists refer to as "a sense of place," a combination of characteristics and meanings that make a particular piece of geography unique and special. Human beings naturally wish to understand the places where they live. A fully developed sense of place involves knowing and understanding the human cultural experience that has taken place in a given landscape over time. It involves not only understanding our own cultural experience in that landscape, but something of the cultural experience of those who have gone before. And it involves our ability to connect the two.

Enos Mills, in describing the world that Joel Estes stumbled upon, saw it only as an unpeopled wilderness upon which the Estes family, without challenge, could superimpose their own kind of civilization. Until Mills populated that world with the pioneers who followed, Estes Park had no history, no "sense of place."

In 1914 Gun Griswold and Sherman Sage told us about the myths, legends, and stories their ancestors attached to the land—myths, legends, and stories which they in turn passed down among their people and which Oliver Toll, in turn, passed down to us. The Arapaho sense of place—the Estes Park–Rocky Mountain National Park region—that they shared so willingly in

1914 was one that their descendants confirmed for us in Bond Park a hundred years later. It was then, as I listened, that I finally and fully understood. Without knowing the cultural experience of the Arapaho, however briefly, my own appreciation of this special place would be a diminished one. That was the Arapaho gift to me that August Saturday morning.

# 5

## FIRST GLIMPSE OF THE ESTES VALLEY

1859

*Milton Estes*

*On October 15, 1859, nineteen-year-old Milton Estes (1840–1913) and his father, Joel Estes (1806–1875), became the first known white men to encounter Estes Park. That day, they stood near the crest of today's Park Hill and looked down in wonder and amazement at the valley below, an experience that has been repeated by millions in the century and a half since. Milton Estes's account was not published until 1939, a quarter century after his death, and its date of composition is unclear. In all likelihood it was written shortly after 1905, for Enos Mills, in his* Story of Estes Park *published that year, notes that he had heard the story from Mr. Estes who "promises to put his Park recollections into writing."*

About the 15th of October, 1859, Joel Estes, Sr., with his son Milton, traveled to the head of Little Thompson Creek, Colorado, near Long's Peak on a hunting and exploring trip. While on this expedition we discovered what is now known as Estes Park, named after my father, Joel Estes, Sr. It is now over forty years since the writer first saw the Park and it is just as fresh in memory as though it happened yesterday. I shall never forget my first sight of the Park.

We stood on the mountain looking down at the head waters of Little Thompson Creek, where the Park spread out before us. No words can describe our surprise, wonder and joy at beholding such an unexpected sight. It looked like a low valley with a silver streak or thread winding its way through the tall grass, down through the valley and disappearing around a hill among the pine trees. This silver thread was Big Thompson Creek. It was a grand sight and a great surprise.

We did not know what we had found. Father supposed it was North Park for that was the only park we had ever heard of in this part of the Rockies. He soon gave up that idea when we looked around in the Park for a few days, and saw no signs that white men had ever been there before us. There were signs that Indians had been there at some time, however, for we found lodge poles in two different places. How long before, we could not determine....

We were monarchs of all we surveyed, mountains, valleys and streams. There was absolutely nothing to dispute our sway. We had a little world all to ourselves. There was no end to the game, for great bands of elk, big flocks of mountain sheep and deer were everywhere. On further exploration in the Park we found the streams or creeks were filled with mountain trout, "speckled beauties." The Park was a paradise for the hunter. Father was carried away with the find, for he was a great lover of hunting and fishing.

# 6

## FIRST ASCENT OF LONGS PEAK

1868

*Lewis W. Keplinger*

*John Wesley Powell is credited with the first known ascent of Longs Peak. Yet on the morning of August 23, 1868, when Powell and his party reached the summit, it was twenty-seven-year-old Lewis "Kep" Keplinger (1841–1928), one of Powell's students from Illinois, who had made it possible. The evening before, while his companions relaxed in camp, he had located the couloir on the south face of the mountain leading to the two-hundred-foot cleft known as "The Notch" that the next day allowed his companions to scramble to the top. They were a party of seven. Besides Powell and Keplinger, there was William Byers, founding editor of the* Rocky Mountain News; *Walter Powell, the major's brother; Jack Sumner, a guide who was Byer's brother-in-law; and two of Powell's other students, Samuel M. Garman and Ned E. Farrell. Keplinger's account was not published until 1917, after he had returned to Estes Park and once again ascended the mountain.*

After the close of the great uncivil war, I attended school at the Illinois Wesleyan University at Bloomington, Ill. Professor Powell, as he was then called, was a member of the faculty in charge of what might be termed the scientific department. Powell had command of a battery during the war and had actively and efficiently participated in the Shiloh fight, where he lost an arm. In 1867 he made a trip to the mountains, accompanied by students of the Illinois State Normal School and of the Wesleyan University.... The next year Powell organized a larger party made up of students from these two schools and I joined it. Different departments of science were represented, including botany,

33

ornithology, geology, and entomology. My part was to determine altitudes and latitudes at various points. I was equipped with sextant, barometers and chronometers furnished by the Smithsonian Institute. That Institute furnished other facilities, but all personal expenses were borne by the members of the party.

We went on the Union Pacific to Cheyenne, where each member of the party provided himself with a horse for riding, and a pack mule....

Our party went in saddle to Denver, then a city of 7,000 or 8,000 people. Thence we went up to Empire City. Here we were joined by W. L. Byers, editor of the *Rocky Mountain News*, a prominent citizen of Colorado and a most estimable gentleman. We crossed the main range over Berthoud's pass into Middle Park and camped at Hot Springs on the Grand River. While in camp there Schuyler Colfax and Samuel Bowles of the *Springfield (Mass.) Republican*, visited us, staying several days. While in Middle Park, Long's Peak was continually before our eyes and in our thoughts. Before leaving Illinois it was understood that whatever else we might or might not accomplish, we would ascend the Peak. That was something that had never been done, though many attempts had been made. The old mountaineers had fun at our expense. They said nothing could get there that didn't have wings. The idea of a bunch of tenderfeet coming out and trying to do a thing like that was ridiculous! Finally we went up and camped at Grand Lake. The city at that time consisted of one log cabin occupied by a trapper. The lake itself, however, was densely populated. I will not subject the faith of those who know me in my veracity by stating the number of speckled trout I saw caught there in an hour on a single hook. Here several of us organized a squad to ascend the Peak. We rode horses and took one or two pack animals. We went along the north side of the lake, through fallen trees, with the utmost conceivable difficulty. After going for two days we camped at the westward base of what is now known as Mount McKinstry, or McHenry, the first peak west and about three miles distant from Long's Peak. From here, the following morning, having corralled and left our animals, we proceeded on foot. After being baffled in various attempts we came to a ridge ascending from the west, which appeared to connect with and lead to the summit. We followed this, stringing along for a distance of half a mile. Jack Sumner, an old mountaineer and brother-in-law of Mr. Byers, was in advance; I was next, at a far stone-throw distance. The ridge grew narrower and narrower. Finally I approached where Jack was sitting down. I called to him, "Hello, Jack; what's the matter?" He replied, "By G---, I haven't lost any mountain." I told him I had, and without hesitation I walked over the narrow place. It was not to exceed eighteen inches in width, and to have fallen on either side would have changed altitude hundreds of feet, though of course the descent was not perpendicular. After seeing me pass he said he could go anywhere I could, and he did, but he got down and "cooned" it. Then we waited until the others came up. They all passed over the narrow place, and we proceeded some way when we came where further progress was impossible. We then retraced our steps, and descending went into camp on the south side of the Peak, in what is now known as the Wild Basin. This was about two o'clock in the afternoon. The "Notch," which is so conspicuous a feature of the Peak, extends down the southerly side as far as and beyond timber line. We camped where there was plenty of timber for fires, intending to make an early start the next morning. As we stood there looking upward and speculating as to the probabilities of our success the next day, a place met our eyes, about a third of the way up, which appeared as though it might not be impassable. I told them that as I was not at all tired, I would go that afternoon in light marching order and reconnoiter. It seemed useless for the entire party to waste its time the next morning if the place on the mountain was impassable. So I set out, leaving blanket and barometer and other impedimenta behind. When I got to the difficult place I found a way around it, but there was another a little farther which seemed doubtful, so I went on and found a way past that also. Then there was the summit, temptingly near. I was closer than any mortal had ever been before! Wouldn't it be a bully thing to go ahead and get a scoop on the other boys? I went ahead, into and through the Notch; the distance is only yards, not to exceed twenty or twenty-five, as I now remember. At the northerly edge of the Notch, Estes Park was before me for the first time. I wondered at and admired the view but for an instant; the summit of that peak seemed very close, and that was what I was after. I started up on the Estes Park side, using hands and feet, and traveling along where it would seem utterly impossible to go when viewed from Long's Peak Inn. All was well until I paused and looked down to my right on Estes Park. There, not to exceed ten feet below and away from me, was what seemed to be the eaves of the world's roof. I looked to my left toward camp, but the still unascended Peak was now between me and that. A lonesome feeling came over me. I started back. As any one who has had experience in that kind of climbing will know, descent was far more difficult. I proceeded, keeping farther away from those eaves than when I went up, and where the way was more difficult.

Finally I got where I could let go without slipping over, and dropped a short distance onto an ice formation in the northwest corner of the floor of the Notch. I feel quite sure that the ice has not yet melted away. Of that occasion I will say this: never before and never since have I so completely lost all nerve. I was trembling from head to foot.

After congratulating myself upon the fact that I had not become a permanent occupant of Estes Park, the next thing was to get back to camp. To my dismay, I saw the sun was getting low and those two difficult places must be passed before it went down. This was accomplished, but darkness fell and camp was at quite a distance. The party had become alarmed, and Major Powell had sent Jack Sumner up the mountain carrying bundles of dry sticks to kindle beacon fires. To see his fires and hear him hallooing were pleasing incidents of the return trip. It was about ten o'clock when I reached camp. I well know that the reports of a "last survivor," who after the lapse of half a century tells of occurrences in which he participated, are ordinarily to be received with some allowances, but a full account of these incidents, including the part taken by me, was written at the time by Mr. Byers and appeared in the *Rocky Mountain News* within a week after the occurrence.... His article errs in one particular. He says I got within 1,000 feet of the top. Mr. Enos Mills, who has made the ascent hundreds of times and is an authority on such matters, says I was within 150 or 200 feet of the summit, and I am satisfied he is correct. If Mr. Byers meant the distance to be traveled rather than the direct-line distance, he may be about right.

That night we camped under a shelving slab of rock leaning to the south. It was quite cold. We spread our blankets under the incline and kept fires burning in front. There was not room for the entire party under the rock. When those on the outside got tired of being out in the cold they replenished the fires so as to make it too hot for those under the rock. In this way there was more or less alternating between those within and those without during the night.

Early the next morning seven of our members, including myself, started up. We followed the line of my ascent the day before, going along the downward continuation of the Notch until we got within a few hundred feet of the Notch proper. Then we obliqued to the left until we reached the line now followed by those who ascend by going through the Keyhole from Estes Park, and made the final ascent at the same place where it is now made. There were no indications of any prior ascents. In making this ascent Mr. Byers and I both carried barometers. He was so unfortunate as to break his in climbing. I took the necessary readings, from which, in connection with the complete series taken in the days following in the immediate vicinity, I determined the altitude of the Peak to within twenty-five feet of what has since been found to be correct. For some reason, as yet I believe unexplained, barometer readings go, as it were, in waves, with about eight days between crest and crest. For this reason the several readings I had taken on the summit did not furnish the data necessary for correct determination. Before leaving the summit we erected a monument, in which we placed our names in a baking-powder can.

One incident may be mentioned. Major Powell, though one-armed, insisted on doing his stint the same as the rest, even in "packing." At the camp where we left our horses he said, "This is my time to make the bread." I insisted on taking his place, but he would not consent. I carried with me always the picture of the major paddling with his one hand the sticky dough. But he made the biscuits, such as they were. When we put our names in the can, one of these biscuits was put in also, with the statement that this was placed in the can "as an everlasting memento of Major Powell's skill in bread making." As we were about to leave the major thought that was hardly up to the dignity of the occasion, and the biscuit was taken out. We insisted that his real reason was he did not want future generations to know how poor a bread maker so good a mountain climber was. The biscuit was of the kind which when cut with a sharp knife would show a fine-grained, smooth, dark-colored surface. Candor compels me to say that the biscuit would not have been different if he had let me take his place.

As we were about to leave the summit Major Powell took off his hat and made a little talk. He said, in substance, that we had now accomplished an undertaking in the material or physical field which had hitherto been deemed impossible, but that there were mountains more formidable in other fields of effort which were before us, and expressed the hope and predicted that what we had that day accomplished was but the augury of yet greater achievements in such other fields....

We then returned to where we had left our horses, at the foot of Mount McKinstry. The names of our party were found by those who next made the ascent several years later, and were published in the Denver papers....

Forty years later I again made the ascent of Long's Peak—this time from Estes Park and through the Keyhole. This route is quite easy as compared with the way we went. As I approached in plain view of the Peak there came over me a strange, vivid feeling, as if I were being greeted with shouts of recognition and glad welcome, as one of those who first brought the pressure of human footsteps for which there had been such long waiting and yearning.

# 7

## THE EARL COMES TO COLORADO

1872

*Earl of Dunraven*

*Windham Thomas Wyndham-Quin (1841–1926), the Fourth Earl of Dunraven, had two great passions in life: hunting and yachting. It was the former, as well as the search for investment opportunities, that brought him to America in the summer and fall of 1872, and in the days after Christmas to Estes Park—beginning a relationship that would last until 1908. After having spent better than a month hunting elk and buffalo out of Fort McPherson on the North Platte (in the company of a "pleasant young fellow" named William Cody), the Earl and his personal physician and traveling companion, Dr. George Henry Kingsley, came on to Denver. It was there, while socializing at the exclusive Corkscrew Club, that Dunraven first heard about Estes Park and its hunting opportunities. Leaving Kingsley behind, the Earl and his Scotch servant (or "gillie") Sandie took the train thirty miles north to Longmont. There they switched to horse and wagon for the trip to Estes Park where they headquartered at Griff Evans's small guest ranch. Eight years later, in the September 1880 issue of* Nineteenth Century, *a British monthly, Dunraven recalled the details of that first visit interspersed with recollections of those that followed. Dunraven would return in 1874 and again in 1876, when he brought with him German-born artist Albert Bierstadt to execute a commissioned painting and help locate the site for his Estes Park Hotel, which opened the following year. The Earl's last visit apparently took place in 1879, the year before he published this essay.*

Among all the states and territories that lie wholly or partially within the borders of this vast, upheaved region [the Rocky Mountains], there is none, so far as I am aware, more favoured by nature, and, at the same time, more accessible to man, than Colorado. It is easily reached from all the great cit-ies of the Eastern States; its scenery is varied, beautiful, grand, and even magnificent. Crystal streams of pure, wholesome water rush down the hill-sides, play at hide-and-seek in the woods, and wander deviously through the parks. The climate is health-giving—unsurpassed, as I believe, any-where—giving to the jaded spirit, the unstrung nerves, and weakened body a stimulant, a tone, and a vigour that can only be appreciated by those who have had the good fortune to travel or reside in that region....

It was sport—or, as it would be called in the States, hunting—that led me first to visit Estes Park. Some friends and I had visited Denver at Christ-mas to pay our proper devotions to the good things of this earth at that festive season, and, hearing rumours of much game at Estes Park, we deter-mined to go there. We spent a day or two laying in supplies, purchasing many of the necessaries and a few of the luxuries of life, and wound up our sojourn in Denver with a very pleasant dinner at an excellent restaurant, not inaptly styled the "Delmonico" of the West. During the dinner one of those sudden and violent storms peculiar to that region came on. When we sat down the stars were shining clear and hard with the brilliancy that is as beautiful in those high altitudes on a cold dry mid-winter night, and not a breath of wind disturbed the stillness of the air; but, before we had half satisfied the appetites engendered by the keen frosty atmosphere, the stars were all shrouded in cloud, the gale was howling through the streets, and snow was whirling in the air, piling up in drifts wherever it found a lodgment, and sifting in fine powder through every chink and cranny in the door. It did not last long. Before morning the sky was clear, cloud-less, steely, star-bespangled as before, and when we left by an early train for Longmont Station the sun was shining undimmed upon fields of freshly-fallen snow....

The next morning we loaded up a wagon with stores, and started out on our toilsome expedition to the Park. It is very easy work—it is not work at all, in fact, to get into the Park nowadays. It was a very different affair at that time. There are two good stage roads now; there was no road at all then—only a rough track going straight up hill and down dale, and over rocks and through trees and along nearly perpendicular slopes, with the glorious determination to go straight forward of an old Roman road, but without any of the engineering skill and labour expended upon the latter. It was a hard road to travel, covered with snow and slippery with ice; but by dint of literally putting our shoulders to the wheel uphill, by chaining the wheels downhill, and by holding up the wagon by ropes and main strength on precipitous hill-sides, we got to our destination very late at night with only one serious accident—the fracture of a bottle containing medical comforts.

The road from Longmont to the Park traverses the level plain for about fifteen miles, and then enters a canon flanked on either side by strange-shaped masses of bright red sandstone, outcropping from the surface, and in some places tilted nearly on end. It then follows along the bank of the St. Vrain River—teeming with trout—crosses that stream, and works its way with many curves and twists up through the foot-hills, along grassy slopes, through pine forests, past fantastic masses of rock, crosses a little creek hiding deep among aspens and poplars, and, after plunging down two violent descents and mounting up again, enters a long valley rejoicing in the euphonious title of "Muggins's Gulch." I do not know who Muggins was—no doubt an honest citizen; but he should have changed his name before bestowing it upon such a pretty spot. You ascend this valley at an easy gradient till you reach the summit, when suddenly a lovely view bursts upon you, and the Park lies spread out at your feet. On the left the hill-side rises steeply, crowned with a buttress of frowning rock. On the right a mountain of almost solid rock stands naked and savage. In front, beyond the Park, the main range of mountains rears itself, topped with snow, rent in great chasms, pierced by the gloomy heavily-timbered depths of Black Canon. On the extreme left and in the distance Long's Peak towers above its fellows; and beneath you, in strange contrast with the barren foot-hills through which you have passed, and the savage stern grandeur of the range, lies the Park—undulating, grass-covered, dotted with trees, peaceful and quiet, with a silver thread of water curving and twining through its midst.

A log-house is comfortable enough at any time; and on that particular night it appeared eminently so for us, as, cold and wearied, we passed the hospitable threshold. What a supper we devoured, and what logs we heaped upon the fire, till we made the flames leap and roar on the open hearth! and then lay down on mattresses on the floor, and listened to the howling of the wind, till the noise of the tempest, confusedly mingling with our dreams, was finally hushed in deep, unbroken sleep.

The winter in Northern Colorado is most enjoyable. At the high altitude of Estes Park, between 7,000 and 8,000 feet above sea level, it consists of alternate short storms and long spells of fine weather. You will have several days of bright clear weather, hard frost, the thermometer very low, but the sun so powerful that you can lie down and go fast asleep, as I have frequently done, on a warm, sunny, and sheltered bank in the very depth of winter. Then the clouds begin to accumulate, growing denser and denser, till they break and descend in a snowstorm of some hours duration. The cattle, which before dotted all the open ground, disappear as if by magic, seeking and finding shelter in little gulches and unnoticed valleys, and the land looks utterly desolate. The snowstorm is invariably succeeded by a violent tempest of wind, which speedily clears the ground of snow, heaping it up in drifts, and blowing the greater part of it into the air in such a thin powdery condition that it is taken up by the atmosphere and disappears completely....

In spring and summer the scene and climate are very different. Ice and snow and withered grass have passed away, and everything is basking and glowing under a blazing sun, hot but always tempered by a cool breeze. Cattle wander about the plain—or try to wander, for they are so fat they can scarcely move. Water-fowl frequent the lakes. The whole earth is green, and the margins of the streams are luxuriant with a profuse growth of wild flowers and rich herbage. The air is scented with the sweet-smelling sap of the pines, whose branches welcome many feathered visitors from southern climes; an occasional humming-bird whirrs among the shrubs, trout leap in the creeks, insects buzz in the air; all nature is active and exuberant with life.

I and a Scotch gillie, who had accompanied me from home, took up our abode in a little log-shanty close to the ranche house, and made ourselves very cosy. There was not much elegance or luxury in our domicile, but plenty of comfort. Two rough rooms—a huge fire-place in one of them—two beds, and no other furniture of any kind whatever, completed our establishment. But what on earth did we want with furniture? We were up before daylight, out hunting or fishing all day, had our food at the ranche, sat on the ground and smoked our pipes, and went to bed early. One's rest is a good deal broken in winter time, and it is necessary to go to bed early in order to get enough sleep, because in very cold weather it is highly advisable to keep a fire burning all night; and, as yet, hunters have not evolved the faculty of putting on logs in their sleep. It would be most useful if they could do so; and, according to the law of evolution, some of them by this time ought to have done it. However, I was not much troubled; for Sandie, who slept by the fire, was very wakeful. I would generally awake about two or three in the morning to find the logs blazing and cracking merrily, and Sandie sitting in the ingle smoking his pipe, plunged in deep thought.

"Well, Sandie," I would say, "what kind of a night is it, and what are you thinking of?"

"Oh, well, it's a fine night, just a wee bit cheely outside (thermometer about 25° below zero); and I'm thinking we did not make that stalk after the big stag just right yesterday; and I'm thinking where we'll go to-day to find him." Then we would smoke a little—*haver* a little, as Sandie would call it—and discuss the vexed questions of how we made the mistake with the big stag; and having come to a satisfactory conclusion, and agreed that the stag had the biggest antlers that ever were seen—which is always the case with the deer you don't get—we would put out our pipes, and sleep till daylight warned us to set about our appointed task, which was to find a deer somehow, for the larder wanted replenishing.

In those days you had not far to seek for game, and you could scarcely go wrong in any direction at any season of the year. In winter and spring the Park still swarms with game; but it is necessary in summer to know where to look for it, to understand its manners and customs, to go further and to work harder than formerly, for Estes Park is civilized. In summer time beautiful but dangerous creatures roam the Park. The tracks of tiny shoes are more frequent than the less interesting, but harmless, footprints of mountain sheep. You are more likely to catch a glimpse of the flicker of the hem of a white petticoat in the distance than of the glancing form of a deer. The marks of carriage wheels are more plentiful than elk signs, and you are not now so likely to be scared by the human-like track of a gigantic bear as by the appalling impress of a number eleven boot. That is as it should be. There is plenty of room elsewhere for wild beasts, and nature's beauties should be enjoyed by man. I well remember the commencement of civilization. I was sitting on the stoop of the log-shanty one fine hot summer's evening, when to me appeared the strange apparition of an aged gentleman on a diminutive donkey. He was the first stranger I had ever seen in the Park. After surveying me in silence for some moments he observed, "Say, is this a pretty good place to drink whiskey in?" I replied "Yes," naturally, for I have never heard of a spot that was not favourable for the consumption of whiskey, the State of Maine not excepted. "Well, have you any to sell?" he continued. "No," I answered, "got none." After gazing at me in melancholy silence for some moments, evidently puzzled at the idea of a man and a house but no whiskey, he went slowly and sadly on his way, and I saw him no more.

On the morning that Sandie and I went out, it was not necessary to go far from the house. We had not ridden long before we came to a likely-looking country, got off, unsaddled and tethered our horses, and started on foot, carefully scanning the ground for fresh sign. Soon we came upon it—quite recently—formed tracks of three or four deer. Then we had to decide upon the plan of operations in a long and whispered conversation; and finally, having settled where the deer were likely to be, and how to get at them, we made a long circuit, so as to be down wind of the game, and went to work. The ground to which I am referring is very rough. It slopes precipitously towards the river. Huge masses of rock lie littered about on a surface pierced by many perpendicular jagged crags, hundreds of feet high, and long ridges and spurs strike downward from the sheer scarp that crown the canon of the river, forming beautiful little glades—sheltered, sunny, clothed with sweet grass—on which the deer love to feed....

It must not be supposed that, because we were half asleep and wholly dreaming, we were not also keeping a sharp look-out; for in a man who is very much accustomed to take note of every unusual object, of every moving thing, and of the slightest sign of any living creature—more especially if he has roamed much on the prairies where hostile redskins lurk and creep—the faculty of observation is so constantly exercised that it becomes a habit unconsciously used, and he is all the time seeing sights, and hearing sounds, and smelling smells, and noting them down, and receiving all kinds of impressions from all external objects, without being the least aware of it himself. However, none of our senses were gratified by anything that betokened the presence of game, and, after resting a little while, we picked up our rifles and stole quietly on again. So we crept and hunted, and hunted and crept, and peered and whispered, and wondered we saw nothing, till the pine trees were casting long shadows to the east, when suddenly Sandie, who was a pace or two in front of me, became rigid, changed into a man of stone, and then, almost imperceptibly, a hair's-breadth at a time, stooped his head and sank down. If you come suddenly in sight of game, you should remain perfectly motionless for a time, and sink out of sight gradually; for if you drop down quickly, the movement will startle it. Deer seem to be short-sighted. They do not notice a man, even close by, unless he moves. I never saw a man so excited at the sight of game, and yet so quiet, as Sandie. It seemed as if he would fly to pieces; he seized my arm with a grip like a vice, and whispered, "Oh, a great stag within easy shot from the big rock yonder! He has not seen me." So, prone upon the earth, I crawled up the rock, cocked the rifle, drew a long breath, raised myself into a sitting position, got a good sight on the deer, pulled, and had the satisfaction of seeing him tumbling headlong down the gulch, till he stopped stone dead jammed between two trees.

Leaving Sandie to prepare the stag for transportation, I started off as fast I could, and brought one of the ponies down to the carcase. It was pretty bad going for a four-footed animal; but Colorado horses, if used to the mountains, will go almost anywhere. The way they will climb up places, and slither down places, and pick their way through "wind-falls," is marvelous. They seem to be possessed of any number of feet, and to put them down always exactly at the right moment in the right place. I do not suppose they like it, for they groan and grunt the while in a most piteous manner. My pony was sure-footed and willing, and moreover, was used to pack game; so we had little trouble with him, and before long had the deer firmly secured on the saddle and were well on our way home. It was well for us that we killed the deer in a comparatively accessible place, or we should not have got him in that night or the next day. It was almost dark when we topped the ridge, and could look down into the Park and see the range beyond, and there were plenty of signs there to show that a storm was at hand. Right overhead the stars were shining, but all the sky to the west was one huge wall of cloud. Black Canon, the canon of the river, and all the great rents in the range were filled with vapour, and all the mountains were wrapped in cloud.

When we left the ranche that night after a good supper, a game of euchre, and sundry pipes, it was pitch-dark, and light flakes of snow were noiselessly floating down to the earth; and, when we got up the next morning, behold! there was not a thing to be seen. Mountains, ranche-house, and everything else were blotted out by a densely-falling white, bewildering mass of snow. Towards noon it lightened up a little, and great grey shapes of mountains loomed out now and then a shade darker than the white wall that almost hid them; but the weather was not fit for hunting, and, as there was nothing else to be done out of doors, we made a fete of it, as a French Canadian would say, and devoted ourselves to gun-cleaning and spinning yarns....

A few years ago Estes Park was a hunter's paradise. Not only were all the wild beasts of the continent plentiful, but the streams also were alive with trout, as for the matter of that they are still; and we often devoted a day to fishing, by way of varying our sport and obtaining a little change of diet. In summer there was nothing peculiar about the method of fishing; we used artificial flies, or live grasshoppers, and caught multitudes of trout, for they generally took the fly so well that I never remember finding myself in the position of a gentleman who was heard complaining to a friend that he had been "slinging a five and twenty cent bug, with a twenty-foot pole, all day, and had not had nary bite"; and on the rare occasions on which they did not rise freely at the artificial insect, you were pretty sure to get them with a live "hopper." There is another advantage also in using the last-mentioned bait, namely, that it insures a double amount of sport and labour, for catching grasshoppers is a great deal harder work than hooking trout. But in winter we had to fish through holes in the ice, and that is a somewhat peculiar proceeding. The first time I ever fished trout through the ice was in the Park. Three of us started off one fine bright winter's morning, and rode about ten or twelve miles up the main creek, to a place near some beaver dams, where trout was said to be plentiful, carrying with us an axe, a sack, some twine and hooks, a bit of raw pork, and of course our rifles. Having dismounted, tied up my horse, and selected what I thought was a likely-looking spot, I set to work to cut through the ice, while my companions rode some way further up the stream....

I cannot say that fishing through the ice under ordinary circumstances is very exciting sport, but there is something comical about it, and it affords a certain amount of innocent enjoyment.... We caught, I should be ashamed to say how many dozen trout on that occasion. I know we had the best part of a sack full, but as to the exact size of the sack I propose to retain a strict reserve, lest I should be accused of taking a mean advantage of that noble little fish the trout.

On the way home we shot a mountain sheep. We came suddenly and unexpectedly upon three of them, started our host of the ranche Griff Evans' huge hound Plunk after them, jumped off our horses, and put out up the mountain on foot after the dog. What a pace those sheep went up that mountain, and what a pace old Plunk went up after them, and what a ludicrously long way behind we were left! It made one quite ashamed of being a man to see the manner in which the sheep and the dog got away up the mountain and out of sight before we had panted and perspired up a few hundred feet. We might have saved ourselves the trouble of climbing, for presently down came one of the sheep, followed closely by Plunk and preceded by a small avalanche of rattling gravel and bounding stones, in such a hurry that he as nearly as possible ran between the legs of one of the sportsmen. The animal passed literally within two yards of him with such startling effect that he had no time to do anything but fire his rifle off in the air in a kind of vague and general way. Plunk stuck to the sheep gallantly, and pressed him so hard that he went to bay in the bed of the river, at a place where the water rushes foaming down a steep descent among a mass of huge boulders, and there he met his fate.

# 8 AN ENGLISH LADY IN ESTES PARK
1873

## Isabella Lucy Bird

*She was a most unlikely candidate for mountain adventure. The daughter of a British clergyman, Isabella Bird (1831–1904), at age forty-two suffered from a host of physical infirmities. These included a chronically bad back that forced her to wear a brace and bouts of insomnia, headache, and depression. Once she arrived in Estes Park in the golden autumn of 1873, all this was forgotten. Despite the fact that her visit lasted only a little more than two months, and was interrupted by a six-hundred-mile, month-long trip on horseback to southern Colorado, Isabella Bird embraced the world she discovered at Griff Evans's ranch with a gusto. Not the least of it was her brief and uncertain relationship with hunter-rancher James Nugent, the man known locally as "Rocky Mountain Jim." Badly scarred from an encounter with a "monstrous" bear in Middle Park, Jim was paradoxical and unpredictable: a man of education, grace, and wit given by turns to self-promoting histrionics and dark moods of self-pity. Theirs was, in fact, a mutual attraction. Ever the Victorian lady, Isabella's public conclusion was that "he is a man any woman might love, but no sane woman would marry." Their enigmatic and tempestuous relationship is clearly one of the thematic centers of the book that grew out of Isabella's letters home to her beloved younger sister, Henrietta. That book,* A Lady's Life in the Rocky Mountains, *published in London in 1879, has long-since become a classic of nineteenth-century travel literature.*

*The relationship between Isabella Bird and James Nugent is highlighted in the chapter recounting her adventuresome ascent of Longs Peak. "I wonder how you will like the 'Long's Peak Letter,'" she wrote Henrietta on Sunday, November 30. "I like it almost better than any for it represents what I thoroughly liked."*

*They were, in fact, a party of four. Isabella and Jim were accompanied by Platt Rogers and Sylvester Downer, the two young men who, somewhat reluctantly, had agreed to accompany her from Longmont to Estes Park. Their ascent turned out to be a rather comical affair. Mountain Jim, for all his bravado, was far from a competent guide. Leaving and later returning to the Keyhole, Jim insisted on descending to the bottom of the Trough, the long, rock-filled gully leading to the summit, a roundabout and totally unnecessary route that added greatly to Isabella's fatigue. "When Jim got her to the top again," Platt Rogers wrote in 1905, "she was unable to mount her horse. She was therefore lifted on and practically held on until we got to camp, where she was lifted off, in fact, she was completely 'done.'" The plucky Miss Bird proved to be the consummate good sport. She modestly added the following footnote to* A Lady's Life: *"Let no practical mountaineer be allured by my description into the ascent of Long's Peak. Truly terrible as it was to me, to a member of the Alpine Club it would not be a feat worth performing."*

## ESTES PARK, COLORADO TERRITORY, OCTOBER 2

But still I have not answered the natural question, "What is Estes Park?" …Dismiss all thoughts of the Midland Counties. For park palings there are mountains, forest skirted, 9,000, 11,000, 14,000 feet high; for a lodge, two sentinel peaks of granite guarding the only feasible entrance; and for a Queen Anne mansion an unchinked log cabin with a vault of sunny blue overhead. The park is most irregularly shaped, and contains hardly any level grass. It is an aggregate of lawns, slopes, and glades, about eighteen miles in length, but never more than two miles in width. The Big Thompson, a bright, rapid trout-stream, snow-born on Long's Peak a few miles higher, takes all sorts of magical twists, vanishing and reappearing unexpectedly, glancing among lawns, rushing through romantic ravines, everywhere making music through the still, long nights. Here and there the lawns are smooth, the trees so artistically grouped, a lake makes such an artistic foreground, or a waterfall comes tumbling down with such an apparent feeling for the picturesque, that I am almost angry with Nature for her close imitation of art.…

The only settlers in the park are Griffith Evans, and a married man a mile higher up. "Mountain Jim's" cabin is in the entrance gulch, four miles off, and there is not another cabin for eighteen miles toward the Plains. The Park is unsurveyed, and the huge tract of mountainous country beyond is almost altogether unexplored. Elk-hunters occasionally come up and camp out here; but the two settlers, who, however, are only squatters, for various reasons are not disposed to encourage such visitors. When Evans, who is a very successful hunter, came here, he came on foot, and for some time after settling here he carried the flour and necessaries required by his family on his back over the mountains.

As I intend to make Estes Park my headquarters until the winter sets in, I must make you acquainted with my surroundings and mode of living. The "Queen Anne Mansion" is represented by a log cabin made of big hewn logs. The chinks should be filled with mud and lime, but these are wanting. The roof is formed of barked young spruce, then a layer of hay, and an outer coating of mud, all nearly flat. The floors are roughly boarded. The "living-room" is about sixteen feet square, and has a rough stone chimney in which pine-logs are always burning. At one end there is a door into a small bedroom, and at the other a door into a small eating-room, at the table of which we feed in relays. This opens into a very small kitchen with a great American cooking-stove, and there are two "bed closets" besides. Although rude, it is comfortable, except for the draughts. The fine snow drives in through the chinks and covers the floors, but sweeping it out at intervals is both fun and exercise. There are no heaps or rubbish-places outside. Near it, on the slope under the pines, is a pretty two-roomed cabin, and beyond that, near the lake, is my cabin, a very rough one. My door opens into a little room with a stone chimney, and that again into a small room with a hay bed, a chair with a tin basin on it, a shelf and some pegs. A small window looks on the lake, and the glories of the sunrises which I see from it are indescribable. Neither of my doors has a lock, and, to say the truth, neither will shut, as the wood has swelled. Below the house, on the stream which issues from the lake, there is a beautiful log dairy, with a water-wheel outside, used for churning. Besides this, there are a corral, a shed for the wagon, a room for the hired men, and shelters for horses and weakly calves. All these things are necessaries at this height.

The ranchmen are two Welshmen, Evans and Edwards, each with a wife and family. The men are as diverse as they can be. "Griff," as Evans is called, is short and small, and is hospitable, careless, reckless, jolly, social, convivial, peppery, good-natured, "nobody's enemy but his own." He had the wit and taste to find out Estes Park, where people have found him out, and have induced him to give them food and lodging, and add a cabin to take them in. He is a splendid shot, an expert and successful hunter, a bold mountaineer, a good rider, a capital cook, and a generally "jolly fellow." His cheery laugh rings through the cabin from the early morning, and is contagious, and when the rafters ring at night with such songs as "D'ye ken John Peel?" "Auld Lang Syne," and "John Brown," what would the chorus be without poor "Griff's" voice? What would Estes Park be without him, indeed? When he went to Denver lately we missed him as we should have missed the sunshine, and perhaps more. In the early morning, when Long's Peak is red, and the grass crackles with the hoarfrost, he arouses me with a cheery thump on my door. "We're going cattle-hunting, will you come?" or, "Will you help to drive in the cattle? You can take your pick of the horses. I want another hand." Free-hearted, lavish, popular, poor "Griff" loves liquor too well for his prosperity, and is always tormented by debt. He makes lots of money, but puts it into "a bag with holes." He has fifty horses and 1,000 head of cattle, many of which are his own, wintering up here, and makes no end of money by taking in people at eight dollars a week, yet it all goes somehow. He has a most industrious wife, a girl of seventeen, and four younger children, all musical, but the wife has to work like a slave; and though he is a kind husband, her lot, as compared with her lord's, is like that of a squaw. Edwards, his partner, is his exact opposite, tall, thin, and condemnatory-looking, keen, industrious, saving, grave, a teetotaller, grieved for all reasons at Evans's follies, and rather grudging; as naturally unpopular as Evans is popular; a "decent man," who, with his industrious wife, will certainly make money as fast as Evans loses it....

The regular household living and eating together at this time consists of a very intelligent and high-minded American couple, Mr. and Mrs. Dewy, people whose character, culture, and society I should value anywhere; a young Englishman, brother of a celebrated African traveller, who, because he rides on an English saddle, and clings to some other insular peculiarities, is called "The Earl;" a miner prospecting for silver; a young man, the type of intelligent, practical "Young America," whose health showed consumptive tendencies when he was in business, and who is living a hunter's life here; a grown-up niece of Evans; and a melancholy-looking hired man. A mile off there is an industrious married settler, and four miles off, in the gulch leading to the Park, "Mountain Jim," otherwise Mr. Nugent, is posted. His business as a trapper takes him daily up to the beaver dams in Black Canyon to look after his traps, and he generally spends some time in or about our cabin, not, I can see, to Evans's satisfaction. For, in truth, this blue hollow, lying solitary at the foot of Long's Peak, is a miniature world of great interest, in which love, jealousy, hatred, envy, pride, unselfishness, greed, selfishness, and self-sacrifice can be studied hourly, and there is always the unpleasantly exciting risk of an open quarrel with the neighboring desperado, whose "I'll shoot you!" has more than once been heard in the cabin.

The party, however, has often been increased by "campers," either elk hunters or "prospectors" for silver or locations, who feed with us and join us in the evening. They get little help from Evans, either as to elk or locations, and go away disgusted and unsuccessful. Two Englishmen of refinement and culture camped out here prospecting a few weeks ago, and then, contrary to advice, crossed the mountains into North Park, where gold is said to abound, and it is believed that they have fallen victims to the bloodthirsty Indians of that region. Of course, we never get letters or newspapers unless some one rides to Longmount for them. Two or three novels and a copy of *Our New West* are our literature. Our latest newspaper is seventeen days old. Somehow the park seems to become the natural limit of our interests so far as they appear in conversation at table. The last grand aurora, the prospect of a snow-storm, track and sign of elk and grizzly, rumors of a big-horn herd near the lake, the canyons in which the Texan cattle were last seen, the merits of different rifles, the progress of two obvious love affairs, the probability of some one coming up from the Plains with letters, "Mountain Jim's" latest mood or escapade, and the merits of his dog "Ring" as compared with those of Evans's dog "Plunk," are among the topics which are never abandoned as exhausted....

ESTES PARK, COLORADO, OCTOBER

As this account of the ascent of Long's Peak could not be written at the time, I am much disinclined to write it, especially as no sort of description within my powers could enable another to realize the glorious sublimity, the majestic solitude, and the unspeakable awfulness and fascination of the scenes in which I spent Monday, Tuesday, and Wednesday....

Long's Peak, "the American Matterhorn," as some call it, was ascended five years ago for the first time. I thought I should like to attempt it, but up to Monday, when Evans left for Denver, cold water was thrown upon the project. It was too late in the season, the winds were likely to be strong, etc.; but just before leaving Evans said that the weather was looking more settled, and if I did not get farther than the timber line it would be worth going. Soon after he left, "Mountain Jim" came in, and said he would go up as guide and from under the two youths who rode here with me from Longmount and I caught at the proposal. Mrs. Edwards at once baked bread for three days, steaks were cut from the steer which hangs up conveniently, and tea, sugar, and butter were benevolently added. Our picnic was not to be a luxurious or "well-found" one, for, in order to avoid the expense of a pack mule, we limited our luggage to what our saddle horses could carry. Behind my saddle I carried three pair of camping blankets and a quilt, which reached to my shoulders. My own boots were so much worn that it was painful to walk, even about the park, in them, so Evans had lent me a pair of his hunting boots, which hung to the horn of my saddle. The horses of the two young men were equally loaded, for we had to prepare for many degrees of frost. "Jim" was a shocking figure; he had on an old pair of high boots, with a baggy pair of old trousers made of deer hide, held on by an old scarf tucked into them; a leather shirt, with three or four ragged unbuttoned waistcoats over it; an old smashed wideawake,[1] from under which his tawny, neglected ringlets hung; and with his one eye, his one long spur, his knife in his belt, his revolver in his waistcoat pocket, his saddle covered with an old beaver skin, from which the paws hung down; his camping blankets behind him, his rifle laid across the saddle in front of him, and his axe, canteen, and other gear hanging to the horn, he was as awful-looking a ruffian as one could see. By way of contrast he rode a small Arab mare, of exquisite beauty, skittish, high spirited, gentle, but altogether too light for him, and he fretted her incessantly to make her display herself.

Heavily loaded as all our horses were, "Jim" started over the half-mile of level grass at a hard gallop, and then throwing his mare on her haunches, pulled up alongside of me, and with a grace of manner which soon made me forget his appearance, entered into a conversation which lasted for more than three hours, in spite of the manifold checks of fording streams, single file, abrupt ascents and descents, and other incidents of mountain travel. The ride was one series of glories and surprises, of "park" and glade, of lake and stream, of mountains on mountains, culminating in the rent pinnacles of Long's Peak, which looked yet grander and ghastlier as we crossed an attendant mountain 11,000 feet high.... From the dry, buff grass of Estes Park we turned off up a trail on the side of a pine-hung gorge, up a steep pine-clothed hill, down to a small valley, rich in fine, sun-cured hay about eighteen inches high, and enclosed by high mountains whose deepest hollow contains a lily-covered lake, fitly named "The Lake of the Lilies." Ah, how magical its beauty was, as it slept in silence, while there the dark pines were mirrored motionless in its pale gold, and here the great white lily cups and dark green leaves rested on amethyst-colored water!

From this we ascended into the purple gloom of great pine forests which clothe the skirts of the mountains up to a height of about 11,000 feet....

We rode upwards through the gloom on a steep trail blazed through the forest, all my intellect concentrated on avoiding being dragged off my horse by impending branches, or having the blankets badly torn, as those of my companions were, by sharp dead limbs, between which there was hardly room to pass—the horses breathless, and requiring to stop every few yards, though their riders, except myself, were afoot.... The timber line was passed, but yet a little higher a slope of mountain meadow dipped to the south-west towards a bright stream trickling under ice and icicles, and there a grove of the beautiful silver spruce marked our camping ground. The trees were in miniature, but so exquisitely arranged that one might well ask what artist's hand had planted them, scattering them here, clumping them there, and training their slim spires towards heaven. Hereafter, when I call up memories of the glorious, the view from this camping ground will come up.[2] Looking east, gorges opened to the distant Plains, then fading into purple grey. Mountains with pine-clothed skirts rose in ranges, or, solitary, uplifted their grey summits, while close behind, but nearly 3,000 feet above us, towered the bald white crest of Long's Peak, its huge precipices red with the light of a sun long lost to our eyes....

Unsaddling and picketing the horses securely, making the beds of pine shoots, and dragging up logs for fuel, warmed us all. "Jim" built up a great fire, and before long we were all sitting around it at supper. It didn't matter much that we had to drink our tea out of the battered meat tins in which it was boiled, and eat strips of beef reeking with pine smoke without plates or forks.

"Treat Jim as a gentleman and you'll find him one," I had been told; and though his manner was certainly bolder and freer than that of gentlemen generally, no imaginary fault could be found. He was very agreeable as a man of culture as well as a child of nature; the desperado was altogether out of sight. He was very courteous and even kind to me, which was fortunate, as the young men had little idea of showing even ordinary civilities. That night I made the acquaintance of his dog "Ring," said to be the best hunting dog in Colorado, with the body and legs of a collie, but a head approaching that of a mastiff, a noble face with a wistful human expression, and the most truthful eyes I ever saw in an animal. His master loves him if he loves anything, but in his savage moods ill-treats him. "Ring's" devotion never swerves, and his truthful eyes are rarely taken off his master's face. He is almost human in his intelligence, and unless he is told to do so, he never takes notice of any one but "Jim." In a tone as if speaking to a human being, his master, pointing to me, said, "Ring, go to that lady, and don't leave her again to-night." "Ring" at once came to me, looked into my face, laid his head on my shoulder, and then lay down beside me with his head on my lap, but never taking his eyes off "Jim's" face.

The long shadows of the pines lay upon the frosted grass, an aurora leaped fitfully, and the moonlight, though intensely bright, was pale beside the red, leaping flames of our pine logs and their red glow on our gear, ourselves, and "Ring's" truthful face. One of the young men sang a Latin student's song and two Negro melodies; the other "Sweet Spirit, hear my Prayer." "Jim" sang one of Moore's melodies in a singular falsetto, and all together sang, "The Star-spangled Banner" and "The Red, White, and Blue."

Then "Jim" recited a very clever poem of his own composition, and told some fearful Indian stories. A group of small silver spruces away from the fire was my sleeping place. The artist who had been up there had so woven and interlaced their lower branches as to form a bower, affording at once shelter from the wind and a most agreeable privacy. It was thickly strewn with young pine shoots, and these, when covered with a blanket, with an inverted saddle for a pillow, made a luxurious bed. The mercury at 9 p.m. was 12° below the freezing point. "Jim," after a last look at the horses, made a huge fire, and stretched himself out beside it, but "Ring" lay at my back to keep me warm. I could not sleep, but the night passed rapidly....

Day dawned long before the sun rose, pure and lemon colored. The rest were looking after the horses, when one of the students came running to tell me that I must come further down the slope, for "Jim" said he had never seen such a sunrise....

By seven we had finished breakfast, and passed into the ghastlier solitudes above, I riding as far as what, rightly or wrongly, are called the "Lava Beds," an expanse of large and small boulders, with snow in their crevices. It was very cold; some water which we crossed was frozen hard enough to bear the horse. "Jim" had advised me against taking any wraps, and my thin Hawaiian riding dress, only fit for the tropics, was penetrated by the keen air. The rarefied atmosphere soon began to oppress our breathing, and I found that Evans's boots were so large that I had no foothold. Fortunately, before the real difficulty of the ascent began, we found, under a rock, a pair of small overshoes, probably left by the Hayden exploring expedition, which just lasted for the day.[3] As we were leaping from rock to rock, "Jim" said, "I was thinking in the night about your traveling alone, and wondering where you carried your Derringer, for I could see no signs of it." On my telling him that I traveled unarmed, he could hardly believe it, and adjured me to get a revolver at once.

On arriving at the "Notch" (a literal gate of rock), we found ourselves absolutely on the knifelike ridge or backbone of Long's Peak, only a few feet wide, covered with colossal boulders and fragments, and on the other side shelving in one precipitous, snow-patched sweep of 3,000 feet to a picturesque hollow, containing a lake of pure green water. Other lakes, hidden among dense pine woods, were farther off, while close above us rose the

Peak, which, for about 500 feet, is a smooth, gaunt, inaccessible looking pile of granite. Passing through the "Notch," we looked along the nearly inaccessible side of the Peak, composed of boulders and debris of all shapes and sizes, through which appeared broad, smooth ribs of reddish-colored granite, looking as if they upheld the towering rock mass above....

You know I have no head and no ankles, and never ought to dream of mountaineering; and had I known that the ascent was a real mountaineering feat I should not have felt the slightest ambition to perform it. As it is, I am only humiliated by my success, for "Jim" dragged me up, like a bale of goods, by sheer force of muscle. At the "Notch" the real business of the ascent began. Two thousand feet of solid rock towered above us, four thousand feet of broken rock shelved precipitously below; smooth granite ribs, with barely foothold, stood out here and there, melted snow refrozen several times, presented a more serious obstacle; many of the rocks were loose, and tumbled down when touched. To me it was a time of extreme terror. I was roped to "Jim," but it was of no use; my feet were paralyzed and slipped on the bare rock, and he said it was useless to try to go that way, and we retraced our steps. I wanted to return to the "Notch," knowing that my incompetence would detain the party, and one of the young men said almost plainly that a woman was a dangerous encumbrance, but the trapper replied shortly that if it were not to take the lady up he would not go up at all. He went on the explore, and reported that further progress on the correct line of ascent was blocked by ice; and then for two hours we descended, lowering ourselves by our hands from rock to rock along a boulder-strewn sweep of 4,000 feet, patched with ice and snow, and perilous from rolling stones. My fatigue, giddiness, and pain from bruised ankles, and arms half pulled out of their sockets, were so great that I should never have gone half-way had not "Jim," nolens volens,[4] dragged me along with a patience and skill, and withal a determination that I should ascend the Peak, which never failed. After descending about 2,000 feet to avoid the ice, we got into a deep ravine with inaccessible sides, partly filled with ice and snow and partly with large and small fragments of rock, which were constantly giving away, rendering the footing very insecure. That part to me was two hours of painful and unwilling submission to the inevitable; of trembling, slipping, straining, of smooth ice appearing when it was least expected, and of weak entreaties to be left behind while the others went on. "Jim" always said that there was no danger, that there was only a short bad bit ahead, and that I should go up even if he carried me!

Slipping, faltering, gasping from the exhausting toil in the rarefied air, with throbbing hearts and panting lungs, we reached the top of the gorge and squeezed ourselves between two gigantic fragments of rock by a passage called the "Dog's Lift," when I climbed on the shoulders of one man and then was hauled up. This introduced us by an abrupt turn round the south-west angle of the Peak to a narrow shelf of considerable length, rugged, uneven, and so overhung by the cliff in some places that it is necessary to crouch to pass at all. Above, the Peak looks nearly vertical for 400 feet; and below, the most tremendous precipice I have ever seen descends in one unbroken fall. This is usually considered the most dangerous part of the ascent, but it does not seem so to me, for such foothold as there is is secure, and one fancies that it is possible to hold on with the hands. But there, and on the final, and, to my thinking, the worst part of the climb, one slip, and a breathing, thinking, human being would lie 3,000 feet below, a shapeless bloody heap! "Ring" refused to traverse the ledge and remained at the "Lift" howling piteously.

From thence the view is more magnificent even than that from the "Notch." At the foot of the precipice below us lay a lovely lake, wood embosomed, from or near which the bright St. Vrain and other streams take their rise. I thought how their clear cold waters, growing turbid in the affluent flats, would heat under the tropic sun, and eventually form part of that great ocean river which renders our far-off islands habitable by impinging on their shores. Snowy ranges, one behind the other, extended to the distant horizon, folding in their wintry embrace the beauties of Middle Park, Pike's Peak, more than one hundred miles off, lifted that vast but shapeless summit which is the landmark of southern Colorado. There were snow patches, snow slashes, snow abysses, snow forlorn and soiled looking, snow pure and dazzling, snow glistening above the purple robe of pine worn by all the mountains; while away to the east, in limitless breadth, stretched the green-grey of the endless Plains. Giants everywhere reared their splintered crests. From thence, with a single sweep, the eye takes in a distance of 300 miles—that distance to the west, north, and south being made up of

mountains ten, eleven, twelve, and thirteen thousand feet in height, dominated by Long's Peak, Gray's Peak, and Pike's Peak, all nearly the height of
Mont Blanc! On the Plains we traced the rivers by their fringe of cottonwoods to the distant Platte, and between us and them lay glories of mountain, canyon, and lake, sleeping in depths of blue and purple most ravishing
to the eye.

As we crept from the ledge round a horn of rock I beheld what made
me perfectly sick and dizzy to look at—the terminal Peak itself—a smooth,
cracked face or wall of pink granite, as nearly perpendicular as anything
could well be up which it was possible to climb, well deserving the name
of the "American Matterhorn."

*Scaling*, not climbing, is the correct term for this last ascent. It took one
hour to accomplish 500 feet, pausing for breath every minute or two. The
only foothold was in narrow cracks or on minute projections on the granite. To get a toe in these cracks, or here and there on a scarcely obvious pro-
jection, while crawling on hands and knees, all the while tortured with
thirst and gasping and struggling for breath, this was the climb; but at last
the Peak was won. A grand, well-defined mountain top it is, a nearly level
acre of boulders, with precipitous sides all round, the one we came up
being the only accessible one.

It was not possible to remain long. One of the young men was seriously
alarmed by bleeding from the lungs, and the intense dryness of the day
and the rarefication of the air, at a height of nearly 15,000 feet, made respi-
ration very painful. There is always water on the Peak, but it was frozen as
hard as a rock, and the sucking of ice and snow increases thirst. We all suffered severely from the want of water, and the gasping for breath made our
mouths and tongues so dry that articulation was difficult, and the speech
of all unnatural....

We placed our names, with the date of ascent, in a tin within a crevice, and descended to the ledge, sitting on the smooth granite, getting
our feet into cracks and against projections, and letting ourselves down
by our hands, "Jim" going before me, so that I might steady my feet
against his powerful shoulders. I was no longer giddy, and faced the
precipice of 3,500 feet without a shiver. Repassing the ledge and Lift,
we accomplished the descent through 1,500 feet of ice and snow, with

many falls and bruises, but no worse mishap, and there separated, the young men taking the steepest but most direct way to the "Notch," with the intention of getting ready for the march home, and "Jim" and I taking what he thought the safer route for me—a descent over boulders for 2,000 feet, and then a tremendous ascent to the "Notch." I had various falls, and once hung by my frock, which caught on a rock, and "Jim" severed it with his hunting knife, upon which I fell into a crevice full of soft snow. We were driven lower down the mountains than he had intended by impassable tracts of ice, and the ascent was tremendous. For the last 200 feet the boulders were of enormous size, and the steepness fearful. Sometimes I drew myself up on hands and knees, sometimes crawled; sometimes "Jim" pulled me up by my arms or a lariat, and sometimes I stood on his shoulders, or he made steps for me of his feet and hands, but at six we stood on the "Notch" in the splendor of the sinking sun, all color deepening, all peaks glorifying, all shadows purpling, all peril past.

"Jim" had parted with his *brusquerie* when we parted from the students, and he was gentle and considerate beyond anything, though I knew that he must be grievously disappointed, both in my courage and strength. Water was an object of earnest desire. My tongue rattled in my mouth, and I could hardly articulate.... Three times its apparent gleam deceived even the mountaineer's practised eye, but we found only a foot of "glare ice." At last, in a deep hole, he succeeded in breaking the ice, and by putting one's arm far down one could scoop up a little water in one's hand, but it was tormentingly insufficient. With great difficulty and much assistance I recrossed the "Lava Beds," was carried to the horse and lifted upon him, and when we reached the camping ground I was lifted off him, and laid on the ground wrapped up in blankets, a humiliating termination of a great exploit. The horses were saddled, and the young men were all ready to start, but "Jim" quietly said, "Now, gentlemen, I want a good night's rest, and we shan't stir from here to-night." I believe they were really glad to have it so, as one of them was quite "finished." I retired to my arbor, wrapped myself in a roll of blankets, and was soon asleep....

We reached Estes Park at noon of the following day. A more successful ascent of the Peak was never made, and I would not now exchange my memories of its perfect beauty and extraordinary sublimity for any other experience of mountaineering in any part of the world. Yesterday snow fell on the summit, and it will be inaccessible for eight months to come.

NOTES

1.  A soft felt hat with a wide brim.
2.  This grove of miniature trees has long-since been known as Jims Grove.
3.  These shoes, it is surmised, may well have belonged to celebrated lecturer Anna E. Dickinson (1842–1932), who as a member of the party led by Ferdinand V. Hayden, head of the United States Geological and Geographical Survey, had reached the summit just weeks before on September 13, 1873. The two women were about the same size.
4.  "Willy-nilly."

# 9

## A FISHING EXPEDITION

1875

*Lewis B. France*

*Horace Ferguson, one of Estes Park's pioneers, was an expert angler. In July of 1875, not long after he had moved his wife and family into their new sod-roofed log cabin above Marys Lake, he was visited by a family of three who, perhaps by prearrangement, made camp nearby. The trio would subsequently be identified in print only as "Bourgeois," "the Governor" (Bourgeois's precocious young son), and "the Governor's mother" (Bourgeois's wife). After an evening before the Ferguson fireplace and talk of fishing, Bourgeois engaged his host to guide him into Horseshoe Park and Willow (now Moraine) Park to try his luck fishing Fall River and the Big Thompson. The result was the charming account that follows.*

*Bourgeois, it turned out, was the pen name of Denver lawyer Lewis Brown France (1833–1907), who spent his leisure hours writing about Colorado and the out-of-doors in such books as* With Rod and Line in Colorado Waters *(1884),* Mountain Trails and Parks in Colorado *(1886),* Mr. Dide, His Vacation *(1890), and* Over the Old Trail *(1894). He was also a regular contributor to national outdoor magazines. His influence was substantial. According to one historian, France's first two books "did more to make readers aware of Colorado fishing than any publication to that time." The essay excerpted here was included in* Fishing with the Fly: Sketches by Lovers of the Art, *a beautifully illustrated collection put together in 1883 by Charles F. Orvis, founder of the famous fly-fishing company, and A. Nelson Cheney, the angling editor of a hunting and fishing magazine.*

Among the delightful summer resorts of Colorado Estes Park may be justly considered one of the most attractive. It is now easy of access. Seven years ago it began to be frequented, the trail having given way to the wagon road. Before the days of easy ingress, I had cast my lures upon the waters of the Thompson and Fall River, with gratifying success.

In the summer of 1875, the Governor, the Governor's mother, and myself, determined upon Estes Park for a six weeks' vacation. With this end in view, in the latter part of July, I sent off the team loaded with the camp outfit.

Two days after we took the morning train for Longmont, on the Colorado Central, and had an early lunch at the tail end of the wagon just outside the town. Before noon we were on the fifteen-mile drive into the canon of the St. Vrain, for camp.

By sunrise the following morning we had started, with twenty miles to make over a new road part of the way, and no road at all in places, and the places were many....

As the sun dropped behind the range, lighted up the high peaks with his golden rays, and the pines were beginning to take on tints of darker green, we reached the head of the Park, and within three miles of our camping ground. To the right of us, "Olympus," with the dying sunlight dancing on his granite head, to the left Long's Peak, with patches of snow here and there, towering godlike above the surrounding giants. Before us, Prospect Mountain with its rugged front far reaching above its robes of green, while around its base and toward us came leaping the beautiful mountain stream for two miles through the meadow-hued park, with scarce a willow upon its banks. What a place to cast a fly! Aye, indeed it is; and what a place it was to catch trout. But we must move on around Prospect Mountain to Ferguson's for camp, which we make on a little eminence near a great spring and close by the cabin where we know we shall be welcome.

A late supper disposed of, and the Governor stowed away in the blankets, Ferguson and I fall talking at his broad fire-place about Horse Shoe Park and Fall River; of course trout are plenty there; he had been up the day before and knew whereof he spoke; yes, there were quite a number of tourists in the park, but the streams were not "fished out." He rather thought that with "a pole" to every rod of the stream the fishing improved; at least for him.

Our genial friend who obeyed Joshua in the long ago, was out of bed next day sooner than I. Dick, the pony, gave me a cheerful good morning as I put in an appearance and changed his picket pin. I received his salutation as a good omen.

Breakfast over and Dick saddled, it was eight o'clock. We had five miles to go. I strapped my rod and creel to the pommel, and with a caution to the Governor's mother not to let him fall into the spring, Ferguson and I were off. There was no occasion to hurry; if we reached the beaver-dams in Horse Shoe Park by ten o'clock we would be just in time. Experience had taught me that the two hours before noon, and after five o'clock were the hours for success.

Our route was a "cut off" without any trail, but familiar; across the Thompson, up stream, westward for a mile, we turned up a "draw" to the right, for a swale in the ridge dividing the Thompson and its tributary, Fall River. By nine o'clock we had reached the summit of the divide. Before and below us lay a beautiful park, three miles in length, by a mile in width toward its upper end, where it rounded at the base of the mountain range, giving it the shape of a horse shoe, which no doubt suggested its name. To the north it is guarded by an immense mountain of rocks, where towering and impenetrable cliffs stand out against the background of blue sky, as though the Titans had some time builded there, and mother earth had turned their castles into ruins, and left them as monuments of her power. To the south a long low-lying, pine-covered hill, while from the range in the west with its snow covered summit and base of soft verdure, comes a limpid stream winding down through the grass-covered park, its course marked by the deeper green of the wild grass and the willows. A mile away a band of mountain sheep are feeding; they have evidently been down to water and are making their way back to their haunts in the cliffs, and whence we know they will quickly scud when they see or wind us. Ferguson longed for his rifle; it was just his luck; he had the "old girl" with him the last time, but "nary hoof" had he seen. To me they were precious hints of man's absence, and the wilderness.

Reaching the stream we picketed the ponies in the grass to their knees; the nutritious mountain grass, the mother of cream so thick that you have to dip it out of the jug with a spoon. The ponies were happy, and I became nervous; it seemed half an hour before I could get my tackle rigged. But after I sent my favorite gray hackle on its mission and had snatched a ten-inch trout from his native element, my nerves were braced. A second and third followed; I heard nothing from Ferguson except the "swish" of his old cane pole above the music of the waters. The trout struck and I landed them so fast that the sport began to be monotonous, and I followed up the sound of the cane. Going round a clump of willows I discovered the old gentleman upon the edge of the pool, and that old rod going up and down with the regularity of a trip hammer, the owner combining business and sport. I asked him what he was doing; he said he was fishing, and I thought he was.

Wandering up stream, taking it leisurely, I had by noon filled my creel, and was enjoying a sandwich under the shelter of some willows, when my companion came along with his sixteen pound lard-can filled, beside a dozen upon a stick. I asked him when he intended to quit. He said he had never seen fish "bite" so; he hated to stop, and yet had all he could carry, but concluded with me that enough was as good as a feast. Then he began to banter me about my ash and lancewood, and the excess of his catch over mine. I told him to wait till some other day. It came in the course of time, upon the same stream. The trout refused everything I had, grasshoppers included. Finally I fished up an old fly-book from the depths of my coat pocket, and in it were half a dozen nameless blue-bodied flies with a mouse-colored feather upon a number six Kirby. Upon sight, I remembered to have discarded them in disgust, but I thought I would try one for luck, and lo! the mystery was solved. I had been working industriously for two hours and had two trout. Ferguson had been no more successful, but was in sight when the trout began to rise to my cast-off fly. He came down my way, wanted to know what I was using, and I gave him one; he lost his leader in some half-sunken brush, and I gave him another. But his good genius had deserted him; I persuaded a trout right away from his lure, and he quit in disgust, while I said never a word. Though a little sensitive upon the score of success, he was and is a genial and companionable angler, and one who can make a good cast withal....

Willow Park, an adjunct to Estes Park, through which runs a branch of the Thompson, has afforded me many a day's sport, and is nearer to camp.

Upon a memorable occasion I had been fishing down stream, when, with a well-filled creel, I encountered a gigantic boulder on the bank. Just beyond it was a pool that was suggestive; to reach the base of the boulder it was necessary to get over a little bayou of about five feet in width and three in depth. To jump it were easy but for the willows, yet I must get to that pool. Selecting a place where I think the willows will give way to my weight, I essay the leap. My feet reach the opposite bank, my body presses back the brush, but I feel a rebound that assures me of my fate. I clutch frantically at the swaying brush; it breaks in my hand, and I sit down quite helpless, muttering a prayer till the cold water bids me shut my mouth. Emerging I hear a well defined laugh, but not being in the mind to fear the spirits that haunt these wilds, I make for the base of that boulder and the coveted pool. A moment after I discover a face bedecked with glasses upon the opposite side of the brook, and recognize the smiling countenance of a genial member of the guild looking at me through the willows....

I took my revenge by competing with my brother for the contents of that pool, and beat him by one. But to this day he greets me with a smile. When I got back to camp I learned that the Governor had been trying to follow in the footsteps of his father, and had tumbled into the spring. He had been fished out by the combined efforts of his mother and Mrs. Ferguson, and I discovered him swathed in a blanket by the kitchen stove, mad as a hornet; I shook hands with him.

Our camp is pitched in a pleasant spot, with two tall pines, a hundred feet away, for sentinels.... To the right is Prospect Mountain, with its west end a beetling cliff, perhaps two thousand feet high, where I once had the buck-ague[1] during an interview with a "big-horn." To the left and in front, the range, where the storm-king holds high carnival, while lower down and nearer is a mountain of towers and pinnacles of brown and gray, carved out by that whimsical sculptor, Old Time. With the sun for my artist, the range for both his easel and background, I have lounged away many an hour under one of the old pines. My gaze wandering down the green slope to the river half a mile away, and with the weird music of the tumbling waters coming and receding on the summer breeze to help my dreams, we have together wrought out fantastic ruins and ghostly shapes to people them....

So I have dreamed, and might go on dreaming, but this time I am brought back to the green slope and a little figure. The Governor is toiling up the trail with a quart bucket, his special chattel, from the spring, whence he volunteered to bring a drink for his mother. I can see no impediment in his path, yet he stumbles and falls. Would I had been there to warn him; but the water is spilled. He does not cry, but gathers himself and his property up, and goes back to begin his task over again. Just then there came to me pat, an aphorism, I think, of "Poor Goldsmith"[2] "True greatness consists not in never falling, but in rising every time we fall;" and I took it as an omen of good for the boy.

The time is approaching when we must break camp and go back to the brick and mortar and the realities of civilization. Duties to be performed will be undertaken with better zest when I get to them, but I cast lingering looks toward my mountain ruins as the day of departure draws nigh. I even have a thought that it would be pleasant to relapse into barbarism, if out of such as mine our civilization has grown—we might build up a better. As this may not be, I am encouraged by the thought that another season will come, and with hope in my heart I am better prepared for the work awaiting me. I know that I shall go back with a fresher feeling for my kind, and more charity. So when one September morning, after a day of gray mist hanging over the range, the wind comes down chill from the heights, and the morning sun lights up my castles and pinnacles in diadems of new-fallen snow, I say we must be off. We gather together our lares of nomadic life, and with a regretful farewell to those I cannot bring away, we make the journey home, a better man and woman, with a nut-brown, healthy boy, for much of which I give credit to the artificial fly, and the beautiful denizens of the mountain streams.

NOTES
1. Buck ague, or buck fever, is the nervous excitement that inexperienced hunters sometimes get.
2. Oliver Goldsmith (1730–1774), the Irish novelist, poet, and playwright.

# 10

## MY FIRST WINTER IN ESTES PARK

1850–1943

*Abner Sprague*

*The winter of 1875 to 1876 was an important test for the pioneer settlers of Estes Park, a number of whom had arrived the previous spring and summer intent upon putting down permanent roots. One of these was twenty-five-year-old Abner Sprague (1853–1943), who spent that winter with his younger brother, Fred Sprague (1858–1922), in a small claim cabin on the north side of what is now Moraine Park (then Willow Park), much of it in the company of Hank Farrar, a local hunter and guide. In his later years Sprague, who during his lifetime successfully operated two major guest resorts within what became Rocky Mountain National Park, wrote a great deal about life in early Estes Park. Much of what we know about the first decade of settlement is, in fact, the result of his efforts. In 1922 Sprague published an account of that first long and snowy winter in the* Estes Park Trail.

My first winter in Estes Park was that of 1875–1876. After spending the summer of 1875 with me in my peat-covered claim cabin in Willow Park, my mother returned to our valley home, not far from where the town of Loveland is now located. My brother Fred and I spent the most of our time that winter at the cabin, as we had stock to look after that we wished to keep on the place, if possible, during the winter.

As I remember that winter, it was as bad or worse than any of the many I have spent in the Park since that time. The snowy season began on the 20th of September, and came to an end on the 22nd day of May, 1876....

We had agreed to do a certain amount of work on the Bald Mountain, Pole Hill, and Estes Park road, then being built to give us a free wagon road. We finished this work and reached the cabin a day or two before the big storm of that winter began, which was in the first week of November.

One afternoon, dark clouds formed over the range, the wind changed to the east, and about dark it began to snow in large feathery flakes. It snowed for two nights and a day.

The second day the sun came out bright and shone on more than two feet of snow on a level. The boulders, both large and small, had disappeared; the trees were covered; and the mountain sides were one dazzling white sheet. We could not stir out to look after the stock. Early in the evening, after one day of quiet, it began to blow, increased into a gale and kept it up for thirty-six hours. Most of the time you could not see twenty-five feet. The snow drifted to the eaves of the house on the east side, where the only door was, and we had to shovel every time we wished to go outside.

The second morning after it began to blow, it quieted down; the sun came up clear and bright. After digging ourselves out, and a late breakfast, Fred and I started on a trip to see if we could find any of the stock alive. There was no snow left on anything like level ground; it was all packed on the east side of the rocks, in the aspen groves, and in the willows of the low ground. We found the cows and the livestock feeding on bare ground as if starved, but they were all right. Toward evening of this nice day, the clouds began to bank over the range as in the beginning of the storm.

Henry (Hank) Farrar, the hunter and guide, bringing the "Old Man," his hunting greyhound dog, came up in the afternoon in time to go out on the moraine north of the cabin and kill us some meat. It took him only a short time to do this—he killed two deer at one shot—and brought one to the cabin. This proved to be a good thing, as we were to be shut in for some time. At dark it began to snow again and was a repetition of the last one, over two feet of snow falling in two nights and a day, followed with wind that drove the snow into the corners and quiet places on the east side of the mountains and in the timber.

After that it would snow from six to eight inches every night and blow it away the following day. It kept it up for about two weeks, and we were practically confined to the house all the time.

"Hank" was quite a "sourdough" cook, and he and Fred spent much of their time looking through my mother's cook-books and recipes that she had cut from some domestic column of a newspaper for some kind of a change of food. They could find no recipe that did not require milk or eggs, neither of which they had. They did fix up some combination "messes" that I hardly think any cook tried. Some were fairly good, and others far from that.

Fred and "Hank" slept together, and I remember one night they could not go to sleep, having slept most of the day, and in their restlessness thought up something to eat that they had not tried; so up they got, made a fire, fixed up their new dish (I have forgotten what it was), together with a meal, and made me get up about midnight and eat with them. Whatever it was they cooked, I know it was not worth the sleep I lost.

We estimated the snowfall in that two weeks to be at least eight feet. Finally it cleared up about the 20th of November, and until Christmas we had nice warm weather; then it turned cold. The hunters could kill elk for the market, as the carcasses would freeze and so be marketed in Denver. The elk came down that year from their high feeding grounds during the big storm, or just after it. They came in droves of a hundred or more, so the hills in the west side of the Park were covered with them. It was only a matter of business.

Mr. Ferguson and "Hank" Farrar were expecting to hunt together, and Hunter Ferguson, a son, was to haul the game to Denver and market it. As the elk, after coming down, ranged in our part of the Park, "Hank" stayed with us most of the time until the hunt began, and much of the time during the winter.

A few days before Christmas, "Hank" and Mr. Ferguson located a large band of elk on the mountain at the head of Beaver Creek, and killed four large ones in Windy Gulch. Fred and I helped pack them out, being obliged to cut down timber to do so, and in this way we started Windy Gulch trail, which has since been used to cross to the other side by hunters first, then by prospectors, and now by tourists.

Fred and I did not have a good rifle, or money on hand to buy one, so we put in a few days fishing through the ice. We caught more than a hundred pounds of trout, which we kept frozen until I took them to Denver and sold them to the hotels for fifty cents per pound.

I bought a Remington rifle, paying fifty dollars for it. It was a killer. After that we did not have to depend on anyone for our meat.

It was a crime the way our big game was slaughtered in those days for market, and with only slight returns to the hunter for his trouble. In fact, the meat of our wild animals became so cheap in the valley markets, that it did not pay for the haul.

We had cold, windy weather during January and the most of February, but as I remember well, we had several big snow storms in March—one about the middle of the month. It came warm and remained warm with a fall of about eighteen inches. Just after this storm a big bear came out of his den somewhere in the Fern Lake region and plowed his way through the new and old snow in the canyon, and through the new snow in the open ground, going in a direct line to the carcass of a big steer that had died in the aspen grove east of our cabin. He moved about a hundred yards from a direct line to miss our cabin. We found his track early in the morning and decided we wanted his hide. The tracks were fresh, and the largest I ever saw. We followed them about a half mile to the grove of aspens, and there found that he had not touched the carcass to eat any of it, but had dragged it about twenty-five feet and covered it with leaves, sticks, and snow. The dead animal was a large bull that must have weighed more than a thousand pounds.

After fixing it in this way for further use, he returned, paralleling his tracks, keeping to the north of them until he reached the mouth of the canyon, then taking his down track for the return. The snow was four or five feet deep in this canyon at that time, and his tracks were so far apart that it was hard work to follow the trail, so after about a mile we gave it up, deciding to get his hide in the spring when he came back to his cache. As far as we know, he never came back. The bear must have scented that carcass during the storm, as the wind was in the east and would carry it directly up the canyon.

But why the bear would make that hard trip just to smell of, and to cover up that carcass, I will leave for some naturalist to guess at.

The last of March, that first winter, we had one of the worst storms of its kind I have ever seen in the Park. We had more than a foot of wet snow fall; then it turned very cold and froze a hard crust, over which stock could walk without breaking it....

Just after this snow, the three of us, "Hank," Fred and myself, decided to go to the valley for a few days. We had two saddle ponies for the three, so we made the down trip "ride and tie"—that is, two started out on the horses and one on foot. After riding about two miles, one would tie his horse. As the one on foot came to a tied horse he would ride, passing one on foot, a tied horse, and the other one walking; ride about two miles beyond the tied horse, hitch his mount and go on afoot. We made the trip this way almost as easily and as quickly as we would with a horse apiece.

We had a blizzard in the valley the fore part of April and a deep snow in the Park.

To wind up that long winter it began to thunder and snow the 20th day of May, and kept it up for about thirty-six hours, three feet or more of heavy snow falling. The weight of the snow stripped many of the limbs from the large yellow pine trees.

We lost only one cow that winter, and she broke through the ice into a spring and could not get out. Strange to say, the stock lived through without feed, only what they got on the range, as well as through many milder winters since then.

# 11

## SUMMERING AT MACGREGOR RANCH

### 1878

*Carrie Adell Strahorn*

*Like most early Estes Park residents, pioneers Alexander and Clara MacGregor, who settled the mouth of the Black Canyon, welcomed summer visitors to their ranch. Some stayed in the MacGregor home or in nearby rental cabins; others camped out along Black Canyon Creek. Two of their guests during the summer of 1878 were Carrie Adell Strahorn (1854–1925) and her husband. Born in Marengo, Illinois, and educated at the University of Michigan, she studied abroad before returning to Marengo where she met and in 1877 married Robert Strahorn (1852–1944), a native of Pennsylvania who had established himself as a journalist during the Great Sioux War of 1876 to 1877 by writing dispatches for the* Chicago Tribune, Rocky Mountain News, *and* Omaha Republican. *Those writings, together with the publication of* A Hand-Book of Wyoming and Guide to the Black Hills and Big Horn Regions for Citizen, Emigrant, and Tourist *brought Robert Strahorn to the attention of Jay Gould, who immediately sought to hire him to work for the Union Pacific Railway Company publicizing the West "to prospective home-seekers." Gould's offer came a week after the Strahorns' wedding, and was accepted with the stipulation that Carrie be allowed to accompany him. Gould begrudgingly consented, and the two began a six-year tour of exploration that would carry them some fifteen thousand miles. Their journey brought them to Estes Park from Omaha the following year. Carrie Strahorn subsequently recorded their experiences at MacGregor Ranch in a chapter of her sprightly narrative* Fifteen Thousand Miles by Stage, *published in 1911. Their adventures in Estes Park were climaxed by a memorable ride with legendary guide Hank Farrar up the Black Canyon to Emma Lake (today's Potts Puddle), a mile east of Lawn Lake, deep in the future national park.*

Estes Park is a veritable Eden nestling on the north side of Long's Peak, twenty-five miles from Loveland or Longmont. The stage ride was one of grandeur from the very first turn of the wheels, up, up, up, along the zigzag trail until the day was nearly spent; then just as the sun was slipping away for the night we emerged from a dense wood to the face of a precipice, and there, down a thousand feet below were the fifty thousand undulating acres of this grand mountain eyrie.

It was an entrancing sight with its green fields and meandering streams surrounded by rocky walls thousands of feet high, up into the very domain of the snow king. The hotel and little ranch homes dotted the park with life and old Long's Peak seemed to stand as sentinel and guard towering over all its grandeur and dignity.

The crack of the whip sent the tired horses galloping down the steep grade to the MacGregor ranch, where there were many people on pleasure bent, some in tents or small cottages, and some in the main home building. Mrs. MacGregor was an artist possessing rare merit, her decorative work around the house proved her ability with the brush, while our host was a retired man of the quill. The refined atmosphere of the home was most attractive. Among the guests was Sol Smith Russell's favorite brother, who was enjoying his honeymoon up among the crags.[1] There was also one Colonel Jones, a lawyer of much renown from Texas....

Mr. MacGregor had about twelve hundred acres in his ranch, from which the table was supplied with fresh vegetables, eggs, butter, cream, and other tempting viands. The cool breezes coming down from the snowy cliffs and ringing in sweet cadences through the pine trees were fairly hypnotic in their influence to hold travellers in that enchanting spot during the heated term of the lowlands.

There were days of exploring that kept up the excitement for the venturesome. Lily Lake was especially interesting. Midway up the side of Long's Peak, the lake contained hundreds of acres so thickly covered with lilies that the only water visible was along the shore line. Instead of being the more common white-lilies they were of a deep orange color, and the odor was also of that fruit....

An irrigating ditch taken from Lily Lake was dammed every night by the beavers and every morning a ranchman had to ride three miles to tear down the dam. It was a good illustration of the industry and persistency of that energetic water worker, who so zealously keeps up his work under most adverse conditions, and it is a good example for imitation by the human race.

Midway to Lily Lake there was another small body of brackish water called Mary's Lake, which was noted for a peculiar variety of fish which inhabited it. When grown they are about a foot long and have much the same color as a trout, but they have four legs and wallow about in the soft muddy pools. They also have a covering over the head like a hood, and when they are jerked out of the water with a hook they squeal like a pig.[2]

Mountain sheep are fond of this brackish water and in the days of 1878 they came every day in large numbers to drink. We saw several fall under the hunter's bullet and many mountain cabins were adorned with the horns of these wary cliff climbers....

In Willow Park we were invited into a spring-house for a drink of milk, or of water from a fine spring which was harnessed to do the churning by means of wheel and shaft.

On one side stood a freezer of ice-cream, most tempting to warm and tired scenic enthusiasts, and close by were saddles of two fine elks. There was scrupulous neatness in every pan and board. We noticed our young men making goo-goo eyes at several responsive orbs, and fearing that we might permanently lose several of friend MacGregor's boarders we hastily mounted our horses and led the way at a gallop down the mountainside.

Another day we were on our horses in the early morning to explore the mysterious depths of Black Canyon, with its thick growth of pines and black and gloomy shadows. None but an experienced woodsman would have known that we followed a trail, but the confidence in Hank Farrar, our guide, was absolute, and we plunged recklessly wherever he led. I rode a cross saddle which was not as popular as it is at this advanced age, and my costume was long trousers and short skirt, with close fitting bodice. Then with a long skirt strapped to my saddle I could quickly change my appearance when I dismounted. I always carried such an outfit throughout my frontier experiences and oftentimes it was the only suit I could carry. On some long trips when we had but one pack animal there was no way to carry anything but food and blankets except what I could have strapped to my own saddle.

We followed the Black Canyon Creek, and as we went stumbling up the mountainside the creek went tumbling down its headlong course as if trying to equal the gaiety of our cavalry brigade. Three miles up the canyon the Black Falls at eleven o'clock in summer time are crowned with rainbow colorings. There was one fall of twenty-five feet and then after many lesser falls the whole river seemed blocked by a huge boulder, perfectly smooth and gently inclined, but the waters struck the rock and leaped over it, falling a hundred and fifty feet in a great unbroken sheet shimmering in the sunlight. On either side of the river the ride through the canyon was in a dense white pine forest whose lofty tops are never cheered by the merry songsters, for no bird but the eagle lives at such an altitude. We climbed on up to Emma Lake, ten thousand five hundred feet above sea-level, and there we stopped for our noonday rest, and luncheon in the warm sunshine, which was most grateful on this July day. We gathered flowers close beside a snowbank, and in a little cove of a smaller lake still higher up some half dozen of the party paddled about on a huge cake of ice. Some of the most ambitious ones scaled heights from which they declared they could see all of this continent and part of Europe, but we smothered them in snow before they could further slay their reputations for veracity....

The return from Emma Lake was somewhat more eventful.... Night came on and we were still eight miles from home.

After pushing along vigorously for two or three miles, the guide held up a warning hand and faced about, but we were not prepared for his announcement that we were off the trail. Whoever heard of Hank Farrar, the guide, being off the trail? It seemed like some joke he was playing, until he dismounted and made several side trips into the woods to get his bearings. He led us at last over rocks and fallen trees and through "cutoffs," until hope seemed to vanish from every face and a night on the mountainside, without food, shelter, or blankets was momentarily growing to a certainty, when suddenly he called out "All right, I have found it," and we knew "it" was the trail, and we were merry in an instant, although it was too dark to see the glad light that beamed in every eye.

Mr. MacGregor had become anxious for our safety and we met him coming to us with lanterns and a basket of food. He said he knew we would get in all right, but some of our friends were decidedly uneasy. After a good supper every one was glad of the experience of being lost and rescued, and camp fire stories of the trials in the dark woods grew quite thrilling....

It required a day or two of quiet before one felt like making other explorations, but as the uncanny feeling fled, the plans were made again to follow our trusty guide through Horseshoe Park to the cascades of Fall River. Thus do we all forget strange and unseemly conditions when the skies clear and health bounds in the veins.

We had to leave our horses at the entrance to the Fall River Canyon and climb over rocks and fallen timber for miles on foot. There was a wild cataract of immense volume tumbling madly over grotesque rocks in a width of one hundred and fifty feet, at the head of which, some miles farther on, a perpendicular fall of one hundred feet gave an impetus to the motion that lent to these two miles of cascades a force uncontrollable....

Along the banks of the many streams throughout the park were numerous bright tents, betokening camp life. A Boston party were reminders of the Aztecs in their barbaric costumes. They looked as if they had spent a winter in reading yellow literature and then concluded that a camp trip to the Rockies necessitated costumes of outlandish design. One stripling wore a pair of schapps [*sic*], a six-shooter strapped around his waist, his blue flannel shirt decked with a white braid and brass buttons, and he crowned it all with a large sombrero trimmed with tinsel chord.

His sweetheart was attired in the same unconventional way, with the gayest of gypsy colors. Her feet in brogans, not ornamental, were swinging below her too short gown of navy blue. Her skirt and waist were profusely trimmed with scarlet flannel and brass buttons, and finished with a long fringe made of the same flaming flannel. A gay red sash girdled her waist, a bright red bow tied the braids of her long black hair and her shapeless hat had the same gaudy ribbons flowing to the breeze. Such were two of the party, not more conspicuous than their companions. It must have been a surprise to them to see people in civilized dress in the camps about them.

The wonderful scenery about the park is more seductive than the Garden of the Gods, and as we turned our backs upon its enchantments, the sun never shone more brilliantly, the flowers never blossomed more beautifully, and the waters never chanted more hypnotic music, all luring us to stay. But the high stone walls and pinnacled buttresses of the highway soon hid the charms and left us to the plain, practical, and unpoetic experience of chuck-holes and sidling roads in the ride down to Longmont and the iron horse in waiting. We longed for the trout supper, the crackling camp fire, the soughing of the pines, the mellowing lights of evening time, without the smoke of factories to dim their lustre, and we longed for the quiet hush of the night and the faces grown dear among the Bohemian experiences. But all were now engraven on the tablet of memory and new conditions with new faces were again around and about us. We had a long trip ahead of us into Montana, and we hastened on to Salt Lake City again and then to the northern border of Utah which ended the rail route.

NOTES
1.    Sol Smith Russell (1848–1902) was a well-known comic actor of the day.
2.    Undoubtedly a species of salamander.

# 12

## CAMPING IN MORAINE PARK

### c. 1878

## S. Anna Gordon

*S. Anna Gordon's* Camping in Colorado: With Suggestions to Gold Seekers, Tourists, and Invalids *(1879) is typical of the promotional literature of the 1870s and 1880s publicizing the increasingly accessible American West. Despite her subtitle, Gordon's major focus is on the vacationing summer tourist, for whom she sets out "to briefly portray" the "popular and more inviting resorts of the Rocky Mountains." One of those is Estes Park.*

*We know comparatively little about Sarah Anna Steele (1835–1896), other than she married a physician, William A. Gordon, had two children, and died in a mental institution at the age of sixty-one. Clearly reticent, her book tells us only that "it was a bright beautiful evening, about the middle of July, in the summer of 18–, when, after a day of wearisome excitement…a small party might have been seen to enter the depot in the city of H—…[to begin a] long anticipated tour of the Rocky Mountains." Forty-two hours later, a thousand miles from home, she arrived in Denver. From there, taking but a single trunk, "containing the necessary wardrobe of four persons, our tent, shot-gun, and edibles," Anna and her party (which included both children) set out for Boulder City, "a pretty town," and then continued on to Estes Park.*

*Gordon's detailed description of camp life in what is now Moraine Park provides perhaps the best we have of an experience that was typical for thousands of early vacationers—those hearty souls who preferred the rough amenities of the out-of-doors to what the nearby guest ranches and hotels had to offer. Her account begins as her party approaches the crest of Park Hill.*

Leaving the gulch, we climbed over a succession of hills or small mountains. I here use the word climbed in its fullest sense, for I believe that seven out of eight, the whole number of our party, took each a cane a la mode, and performed that part of the journey on foot. We had but few miles further to travel before reaching the end of a long journey. We were but a short distance from the entrance to the park, and to this we were gradually ascending. The morning sun shone warm, and the air was crisp and clear. Now and then we met a party of campers on their return trip to the country below. Upon reaching the gate to the park, the highest point over which our way led, range after range of peaks greeted us; some crowned with domes of solid granite; some bearing the appearance of vast and magnificent ruins; some resembling castles; some piercing the clouds with their uplifted spires; some presenting fantastic shapes which seemed real caricatures of birds, beasts, and human beings.

Upon one summit sit the famous two owls, so distinct in outline that no observing traveller passes them without recognition. Upon another is an immense rotunda, and still upon another the ruins of an old monastery....

Close by the gates of the park we discovered an open cabin. It was built of unhewn logs, and covered with earth. The door and window were gone, and the paths that once led to it were overgrown with bramble. We learned that this had once been the home of Mountain Jim, who, during his life, had been known as a trapper, hunter, fisherman, ranchman, and guide; as the man who once had a hand fight with a grizzly bear, and killed his ferocious enemy with a knife just in time to save his own life, with the providential care of friends, who found him bleeding to death from the wounds he had received. He was also known as the man who drank whiskey, and—finally fell in love. The latter was the most unfortunate circumstance of an eventful life, as it resulted in tragedy.[1]

The lady who had unconsciously won his affections rejected his suit. Her parents forbade him to visit their home. Enraged by the conflicting passions of love and of war, he taunted her friends, making use of vile epithets, until his conduct became unbearable. During an unguarded hour, when in a state of intoxication, he indulged in visiting the home of the lady of his choice. Unpleasant words occurred between him and the young lady's father, when, both becoming exasperated, the lover aimed his gun at the father, which he in turn thrust aside, at the same time taking fatal aim at the would-be murderer. The victim of the tragedy lived several months after receiving his death-wound, having ample time to repent his folly.

The desolate cabin still serves as a monument to his memory; and, as it is pointed out to strangers, the thrilling events of his strange life and tragic death are related; all of which have become historically associated with the park.

We saw the lady whose name circumstances had so unfortunately and unfavorably associated with his. She is young, pretty, gentle, and retiring. She will doubtless live to grace a sphere in life more congenial to her better qualities.

Two hours from the time we left our camp ground we had entered the beautiful fane of nature, whose walls were vast mountains and whose ceiling was a beautiful minaret of heaven, frescoed with systems of inhabited worlds....

Through this beautiful picture of nature flowed the clear, cool waters of the Big Thompson River, mirroring both earth and sky. The undulating meadow land was flecked with tents, and the smoke arose from the camp fires on all sides. Cattle were leisurely grazing or lazily reposing, in every direction. Tents were picketed on camp grounds, and white-covered land schooners almost invariably lay anchored nearby. In many instances the latter served every purpose of a tent. Campers were to be seen fishing along the stream, strolling at leisure, on duty about their tents, or sitting by their camp fires. These were the principal life figures in the scene, though the unpretentious home of the mountaineer was not left unobserved. Our eyes banqueted upon the beautiful prospect that greeted them. Could nature have spread a more inviting repast? In this park are several small lakes of crystal clearness; the principal ones are the St. Mary's and Lily Lakes. There are also crystal rivers whose sparkling waters are fraught with floating fortunes of speckled trout. Two gentlemen residing there (sons of our landlord) went out on a piscatorial expedition, during our stay in camp, and brought in specimens of these fish, said to weigh two and a half pounds each, and to measure eighteen inches. Some were caught by members of our party and brought into camp, measuring fifteen inches. They are said to be taken from the streams very easily in winter. The gentlemen to whom we have referred remarked that, in their experience, they together had taken from the water, by opening the ice, over a thousand pounds in a single day. These they took to Denver, and sold them at twenty-five cents a pound. The trip could be performed by private conveyance inside of four days, the proceeds of which would amount to over two hundred and fifty dollars....

The principal part of this park is the purchase of the Earl of Dunraven. By him it is being enclosed where nature has not already fenced it in by almost insurmountable walls. The earl has there erected a commodious hotel, with the available capacity of fifty rooms. This building is richly furnished, and is conducted in a manner to please its most fastidious patrons. It is managed by an efficient landlord, who looks well to the comfort of his guests. The site upon which it stands was selected with reference to the view of and distance from Long's Peak. Tourists "making the summit" can avail themselves of the use of a vehicle the first few miles, from the hotel, if desirable; after which they must consent to abandon it; for the only choice to within two miles of the peak is between going on horseback or on foot. The last two miles can only be accomplished on foot. The park is about ten miles in length and five miles in width....

Adjacent to and on the north-east side of Estes, lays Cascade [Horseshoe] Park. This miniature park or parquette is situated near the snowy range, and consists of grove and meadow, lakelets and streams. It is surrounded by some of the most delightful mountain scenery that it was our good fortune to observe. Roaring River comes from its snowy source above; its rapid current dashing over a rocky channel in its precipitous descent to the park. Leaping from the mountain side, just above, the waters come tumbling down, lashed into rainbows and foam, forming a beautiful cascade, from which the park takes its name.... A short distance below the cascade, Roaring River unites with Fall River, forming one of those large, cool, limpid streams peculiar to the mountains....

In this park is a boulder projecting on one side so that man or beast may find shelter and safety underneath. Mountain Jim, of whom we have previously spoken, chose this as his place of refuge, while hunting or fishing in its vicinity. The open side of this granite-roofed dwelling had been enclosed by the interwoven branches of trees, whose withered foliage still clung to their paternal source. The smoke of fires that had been kindled by this rock yet blackens and discolors its surface, and the temporary wall once built there now hangs from the ceiling in broken ruins.

A deserted habitation, with its surroundings of ruin and decay, serves to remind the older inhabitants of, probably, the first resident of the park; while the foundations of two other cabins showed that claims had since been made, though at the time of our visit there the place was without a human tenant.

Other claims have since been made, the land surveyed, and it is now, doubtless, the possession of some fortunate capitalist.

Here and there were hunters' ambuscades, built of logs in open field. These structures were about four feet high, four feet wide, and six feet long. In them hunters conceal themselves while watching for mountain sheep, as they come down from their homes above to graze upon the more accept-able pasturage of these uncultivated meadows.

When discovered, they become almost sure mark for the practised sportsman's aim, which is taken from the crevices between the logs, where the hand that levels the gun, under a well-directed eye, remains concealed.

In this delightful solitude our party spent one day. We cooked our coffee and spread our edibles by "Mountain Jim's rock," and dined in its umbrage. We visited the cascade, and drank of the waters transformed from its rain-bows. We plucked wild flowers in the native grove of this shaded retreat, and traced the embankments of the streams and lakelets, while we breathed the sweet incense of nature's offering upon God's holy altars.

When the day began to fade we took a reluctant leave of that garden of the mountains, the associations of which afford a bright gleam of sunshine to a grateful memory, making our way back to camp....

Fall River Canyon, laying between Cascade and Estes Parks, affords one of the most delightful places in the mountains for a drive during the silent evening hours. Its scenery, always delightful, is then doubly compensating.

On a beautiful eminence of ground in Willow Park, an arm of Estes Park, on the west side, at an altitude of about eight thousand feet, our party pitched their tents, where we remained just one month. At the foot of the hill the Big Thompson swept by, its song current blending its strains with the soughs of the pines, as they came echoing down from the heights around us. Our uncultivated lawn was picturesquely decorated with shade trees, of native growth, huge boulders, and elk horns. Cacti, wild everlasting, mountain lily, mountain daisy, and sage brush, embellished the rich carpet of buffalo grass spread out upon our grounds. On all sides, save that by which the park is entered, were mountains, alternating with ravines, constituting a most romantic prospect. At the foot of the hill on the east was a group of cottages, ever suggestive of the pleasures of home life;[2] and, promiscuously scattered, were the tents and canvas-wagons, dotting the camp grounds of transients. The former were often pitched at night and taken down in the morning, while their tenants moved to visit other points of interest.

The place selected for our kitchen was furnished with boulders, promiscuously arranged, without seeming reference to the uses to which they were, in the events of time, to be appropriated. There was one about four feet high, against which our fire was built whenever there was cooking to be done. The particular side of the rock upon which the fire was kindled depended upon the direction of the wind at the time it was built.

Near this boulder was a tree, into which nails were driven, where our cooking utensils were hung. Close by was another boulder which answered the purpose of a kitchen table. Availing ourselves of these natural conveniences, together with the use of a trunk containing our canned goods, we prepared the food for our little camp.

Our dining room consisted of a small arbor of pine trees, on one side of which was stretched a tent fly. Our table was constructed after the fashion of a kitchen table, supported by a frame-work of cross pieces. On either side was a bench measuring the entire length of the table, which not only served to furnish us with seats during our meals, but also at our camp fires.

The cabinet work was done by the gentlemen of our party, whose professional labors would, doubtless, have prohibited so fair a development of their mechanical skill but for the urgent demand of this, or a similar occasion, to exercise it.

Our side-board, washstand, ottomans, tetes [settees], etc., were of solid mountain granite, hewn out by nature's artistic hand; though, from an occasional want of adaptability, we sometimes feared we had perverted their uses.

Our indoor life was limited to two tents, each occupied by four tenants. Living in this limited capacity but for a short time only, taught us how few were man's real necessities when compared with his desires.

"How was your time spent while in camp?" is a question often asked; so I will anticipate and answer it. We had our hours of restful leisure, our hours for recreation, our hours for reading, and our hours for social enjoyment. We had also our days for excursions.

The principal pleasure of a purely recreative character in which all could participate was that of trout fishing. We had ample opportunity to indulge in this sport, though one circumstance made it objectionable.

No sooner was our descent made to the stream than we were attacked by an innumerable and irresistible army of buffalo gnats, that were en bivouac upon a bog which lay between the two arms that united below, forming the main body of the river.

These gnats are about twice as large as a mosquito. They have shorter limbs and more murderous bills, the latter of which they dip deep into the flesh of their prey. They draw blood without pain to their victim, and never give warning of their approach. The wound they produce is of a dark purple color, deeply underlying the skin, and is of a very poisonous nature, bleeding profusely at first, and afterwards swelling, and itching with painful intensity. I have seen the gentlemen of our party return to camp from one of their piscatorial excursions, their visages so covered with patches of blood as to elicit the sympathy of any (unhardened) observer. A few hours later their faces would become so swollen as to almost close their eyes.

(I might with propriety add, that it was only a lack of perseverance on our part that saved us from the same dilemma.) These wounds are several days in healing; and when one is badly bitten the poison absorbed from them into the blood results in sickness of a somewhat serious character. These insects sometimes visited our camp in swarms, and were a source of great annoyance. Not all locations were infested with these obnoxious pests; only such as were within the vicinity of damp or wet places....

To better facilitate our opportunities for viewing the prospects of the mountains, we were tendered the free use of a saddle horse, and a span of carriage horses, carriage, and every appurtenance to constitute a luxurious outfit for a drive. We were also kindly tendered conveyance to some of the most desirable parts of the park by private parties.

For reading matter we could depend upon whatever the mails might bring us three times a week; aside from which we availed ourselves of whatever books we had taken with us. But our leisure was devoted more to observation than to reading, as we were never without objects of interest to contemplate.

Social customs in camp life are purely oriental. The stranger pauses before your tent, and you go out to greet him. A friend is announced, and welcomed at the open door of your pavilion. The latter is always invited to eat bread with you; and, if near your meal time, the stranger too has claims upon your hospitality.

It is a place where one cannot judge of whom he meets by external appearances. In this respect camp life admits of unconventional freedom. I heard a celebrated divine say that he was compelled to go from camp in a suit of clothes that had been patched with a portion of his gum blanket [rubberized blanket]; and, coming nearer home, I am compelled to acknowledge the acquaintance of a lady who went from camp into Denver wearing shoes that had been mended with shoe tongues, the work having been done with her own hands....

Residents are usually very socially inclined. They lose no time in making the acquaintance of those who camp near by, and seem ready to do all in their power to make the temporary stay of the stranger pleasant. They avail themselves of the talent of some speaker who may chance to be near by, and in turn open their homes for sacred worship and invite all within their reach to join with them in their devotions....

Among those with whom we met, as transients, were persons emaciated with care and close indoor confinement, in quest of health and recreation. The adventurer was also there, satiating himself with new incident, and in quest of new fields of enjoyment. The explorer was there, urging his way into the mountains beyond, in quest of some unvisited nook or some pinnacle which the footsteps of man had not pressed.

In these beautiful retreats the poet finds sentiment for verse and the minstrel finds joy for song. The artist finds the broadest range of the most sublime subjects for his canvas; and the student finds volumes for scientific research that are nowhere reproduced. The chemist there finds the crucible in which every mineral constituent has been dissolved. The geologist finds nature's cabinet filled with gems of unknown value and untold variety and number. The divine finds inspiration in mountains and sermons in stone. The statesman finds the statutes of universal law written by the great Law-giver....

In whatever direction one turns, or upon whatever one fixes his attention, his observation is repaid by the enjoyments of new interests and their consequent pleasures....

NOTES

1.  The reference is to James Nugent, better known as "Rocky Mountain Jim," see chapter 8 of this volume. Jim was mortally wounded by Griff Evans in April 1874. One of the reasons later cited for the shooting was that Jim was paying too close attention to the older Evans daughter, Jennie.
2.  The reference is to Spragues Ranch, operated by Abner Sprague and his family.

# 13

## THE DEATH OF CARRIE WELTON

1884

James H. Pickering

*Shortly before midnight on Tuesday, September 23, 1884, Carrie Welton, a forty-two-year-old woman from Waterbury, Connecticut, became the first recorded death on Longs Peak. She died alone, huddled against the rocks of the Boulder Field as a demonic gale flailed at her garments. Welton was a victim not only of exhaustion and exposure, but also of her own willfulness, recklessness, and love of adventure. In the immediate aftermath, her death was also the subject of controversy. In the years that followed, many other climbers would perish on Longs Peak, but their spirits—as far as we are told—did not return to the places where they lived, and died. Carrie Welton's did.*

Caroline Josephine Welton's family traced its origins in Waterbury back to at least 1679. Her father, Joseph Chauncey Welton, a highly successful businessman, began his career as a quintessential Yankee peddler, selling clocks and other merchandise throughout the antebellum South as a traveling agent. Returning north in 1839, he became partner in the firm of William R. Hitchcock and took charge of the company's store in New York City. That same year Welton married Jane E. Porter, the youngest daughter of Deacon Thomas Porter, the original owner of the Waterbury Brass Company. Their daughter and only child, Caroline Josephine, or Carrie, as they called her, was born three years later, June 7, 1842.

By the time Carrie was eleven, the Weltons were back in Waterbury, where Joseph, a tireless worker who prided himself on never taking a vacation, purchased interests in both the Waterbury Brass and the Oakville Pin companies. Success and prosperity quickly followed, culminating a decade later, in 1863, with the purchase of Rose Hill Cottage, a handsome stone mansion on Prospect Street.

The Weltons spared little expense in securing their daughter's education, sending her off to Miss Edwards' School in New Haven and the Mears-Burkhardt School in New York, following which she studied drawing and oil painting in New York with several well-known artists of the day. None of this, including attentions paid by Waterbury society and its eligible bachelors, seems to have mattered much to Carrie Welton.

From the age of twenty, the center of her life was her beloved horse Knight, a gift from her father. Carrie Welton loved animals, keeping dogs, cats, and rabbits, but Knight was her favorite. She installed him in a velvet-draped stall in the Rose Hill stables, equipped him with special shoes and tack trimmed with silver, and fed him oats from a bone china bowl, hand painted with pansies and lettering bearing his name in gold. Carrie and her spirited black horse became familiar figures around town as they rode the woods, fields, and streets of Waterbury even in the most inclement weather.

Blue-eyed and brown-haired, Carrie Welton became a striking woman. A life-sized portrait now in Waterbury's Mattatuck Museum reveals her as tall and dark-complexioned with a bearing that is self-confident and almost regal. Long before she left home for Colorado, Carrie Welton had become known among her contemporaries as a woman of social graces "with a propensity to do uncommon things" and with a "reputation for courage and physical endurance." She also was impulsive and headstrong, accustomed to having her own way, and confronting life on her own terms.

On March 26, 1874, Joseph Welton, by then president of Waterbury Brass, was killed by a kick from Carrie's horse, Knight. For his two survivors, money was not a problem, for Welton had seen to it that wife and daughter were well taken care of. The distribution of his estate was odd in at least one respect, however, for Rose Hill was divided: Jane Welton was given the house; Carrie was given the grounds.

Both women initially sought consolation through travel, and in 1875–1876 mother and daughter visited California. By 1880, however, their relationship had significantly changed. There was a deep and lasting estrangement, and for reasons never entirely clear. From that point on, Jane and Carrie were content to go their separate ways. After 1880, Carrie Welton never returned to Rose Hill, and in 1883 she removed her mother as executor of her will.

By 1884 Carrie Welton had become what was then regarded as a spinster, whose life was plainly in transition. Again she turned to travel and physical activity, coming West that spring, first to Yellowstone Park, where she spent several weeks exploring, and then to Colorado Springs. For Carrie, this was a second visit to Colorado. Though it would later be intimated that she suffered from a heart condition, Carrie Welton had been in Colorado Springs the previous year, presumably staying with Augusta A. Warren who then ran two popular boarding houses. The highlight of that visit was a climb of 14,110-foot Pikes Peak, which Welton completed despite encountering a severe storm.

Welton now took up residence at the splendid new seventy-five-room Antlers Hotel on Cascade Avenue, which had opened only that June. Carrie and the hotel's manager, fellow New Englander Augusta Warren, were apparently friends of long-standing. The two women shared a love of nature and the out-of-doors, and during the weeks following her arrival, Augusta took Welton to Bear Creek Canyon where she had a homestead log cabin, and to other attractions including Manitou Springs.

Welton was determined not only to repeat her Pikes Peak success but also to accomplish the mountain's first ascent of the season. The winter of 1883–1884 had been an exceptionally cold one, and well into summer the trail, clogged by deep snows, remained almost impassable. An augur of things to come, Welton was warned that the undertaking was a foolish and dangerous one. Somehow obtaining the service of two guides, she departed Manitou at midnight and reached the summit after a tedious and cold trip.

From Colorado Springs, Welton went north by rail to Denver, where she stayed with friends at the Brown Palace Hotel. The lure of the mountains (reinforced, perhaps, by encouragement from Augusta Warren) next brought her to Estes Park, apparently during the week of September 14, 1884. She took up residence at the Estes Park Hotel on lower Fish Creek Road, which since its opening seven years earlier had served as the centerpiece of the Earl of Dunraven's Estes Park holdings. Welton's first days in that valley were spent largely sightseeing by horseback. On Monday the

22nd she announced her intention to ascend Longs Peak, which at 14,259 feet was about the elevation of Pikes Peak but a more difficult climb.

Mountain climbing had clearly become a passion for Welton. In fact, she had informed an acquaintance prior to her arrival at Estes Park that she intended "to have a gold band put around the handle of her pretty riding whip for every peak she had climbed." Theodore Whyte, Dunraven's resident manager, tried to dissuade her. Whyte doubtless told her that the remaining snow of the preceding winter had left the peak unclimbable until late August, particularly on its north and west sides, and that September weather in Colorado, however warm and golden, was unpredictable.

Buoyed by her successful climb of Pikes Peak, Welton was adamant. On Monday afternoon, leaving behind a small package at the hotel but taking her jewelry, she engaged Henry S. Gilbert, a local livery operator, to take her to Lamb's Ranch. By 1884 the Reverend Elkanah Lamb (1832–1915), the first professional guide to the Longs Peak region and who for many years ran a small hotel, Longs Peak House, at its base, had turned the guide business over to his son Carlyle (1862–1958). It was with the younger Lamb that Welton made arrangements to guide her on the eight-mile ascent of Longs Peak the following day, Tuesday. Gilbert departed, stating that one of his drivers would return to the ranch and take her back to Estes Park at 8 a.m. on Wednesday.

After Monday night at the ranch and a hasty breakfast, Welton and Carlyle Lamb left Lamb's Ranch at 5 a.m. on horseback. She was warmly (if somberly) clad. Over a pair of black broadcloth riding pants she wore a black alpaca dress and a heavy black saque in addition to an elegant black dolman coat trimmed with fur. Around her neck was a heavy cashmere shawl, on her hands a pair of heavy kid gloves. She carried a gossamer raincoat, which she would later put on against the weather. Wisely, she covered her face with a silk mask as protection against the sun.

Though the day broke warm and pleasant, it took some five hours to make the first six miles. As on Pikes Peak, the snows of the preceding winter were still very much in evidence, at times obscuring the trail itself. The horses, usually surefooted, kept breaking through snowbanks warmed by the sun. At length it proved so difficult for the horses that Carlyle and Carrie decided to leave them well below the usual tethering place at Boulder Field, the famous tumbled mass of rocks at the east edge of the peak's formidable face. That decision, made in sunshine while the two climbers were still fresh, probably cost Carrie Welton her life.

Lamb and Welton made their way on foot across Boulder Field and then toward the Key Hole, the jagged opening with its rocky overhang on the northeastern side of the peak and through which they must pass to proceed to the summit. At the Key Hole the weather began to turn against them. They encountered a strong, chilling wind and dark clouds, a sign of worse weather still to come. Young Lamb, who had been climbing Longs Peak since age seventeen, wisely advised retreat, telling Welton that even if they did succeed in gaining the summit there would be no view. Welton would have none of it. She had heard such objections as this before from her guides on Pikes Peak. Her response, Carlyle Lamb later told his father, was that "she had never undertaken anything and given it up." They proceeded.

It was known even then that it is best to be off of Longs Peak by noon to avoid the generally inevitable afternoon storms, some of which can be fierce. By the time Carrie and her guide reached the summit it was cold and quite late—3 p.m. by the elder Lamb's later account. Welton was weary and their stay was brief. As Lamb had feared, dark clouds had intensified, a sign that a storm had already set in below. Leaving the summit, the clouds briefly lifted. But now, as they recrossed the Narrows and headed down the Trough, they found themselves caught in a fearsome snowstorm—the worst, Lamb would later report, that he ever had seen in any part of the mountains. Their descent became increasingly slow. Carrie began to complain of weariness, and by the time they reached the bottom of the Trough, she displayed signs of exhaustion. During the next two hours, they covered no more than two-thirds of a mile, Lamb alternately leading and carrying Welton. Fully dressed, she weighed about 130 pounds, and Lamb too began to tire. They struggled to the Key Hole, but by then Welton, growing increasingly numb from the cold, had become, as Lamb recalled, "so utterly exhausted and chilled that she could not stand alone." The moment of crisis and decision had come. It was now 10 o'clock at night.

Descending a short distance below the Key Hole, over terrain so rough and steep that it is almost impossible for one person to help—let alone carry—another, Carlyle Lamb called a halt. Sitting down, he confided to

Welton that he too was exhausted and so cold that he could scarcely walk. The only chance that either of them had for survival, he told her, was for him to leave her and go ahead for help. At first Carrie objected to being left. Finally she agreed to remain where she was until he could return. Lamb removed his vest and tied it around her feet, arranged her waterproof and shawl as best he could against the cold and wind, and then plunged into the darkness.

The storm had lifted momentarily, and Lamb was aided in his descent by the light of the moon. Reaching the horses, he rode one and led the other five miles through the timber to his father's ranch. He made good time. Awakening his father and fortified by a quick cup of tea, the two began the return trip. Elkanah Lamb, strong at fifty-two and as experienced as any man in the ways of Longs Peak, took the lead. Son Carlyle, "almost completely exhausted" and plainly suffering from his ordeal, fell behind. It was now nearly 1 o'clock Wednesday morning. As they reached timberline, the wind was blowing a gale, making progress difficult as they continued up the moraine toward Boulder Field. Just before daybreak, the elder Lamb reached the edge of the uplift. Elkanah Lamb would never for the rest of his life forget the sight awaiting him. "Almost a mile across the Boulderfield," he wrote years later,

> I came in sight of the tragic spot, where Carrie J. Welton lay at rest, having died alone amid the wind's mad revelry and dismal dirge, and which was yet holding high carnival over her body by blowing every section of her garments in its unrelenting fury, seemingly sporting with its victim in demonical triumph. I remember, with clear distinctness, my involuntary expression as I approached the body: "I fear, my young lady, that you are past saving."

Welton had struggled about ten feet from the spot where young Lamb had left her, and fallen over a rock, bruising head and wrist. She lay in a snowbank, still wearing the silk mask of the day before, covering a face now rigid yet placid. Beside her was the ivory-handled riding whip upon which she hoped to record her mountaineering achievements. In her belt was a five-cylinder Smith & Wesson revolver. A gold watch was fastened to her dress with a black silk cord, and in her bosom, it was later discovered, she carried a small chamois bag containing three elegant rings, one with a large solitaire diamond.

The Lambs placed Welton's body in a double blanket, tied together by a small rope cut in sections. It took two hours to reach the horses. By 10:30 a.m. Wednesday they were back at Lamb Ranch, where they found Gilbert's driver waiting as instructed two days earlier. Elkanah Lamb summoned Justice of the Peace Peter J. Pauly, Jr., who had the remains placed in a box. At 6:30 p.m. he left by wagon on the seven-hour trip to Longmont where the body could be embalmed and from where the Welton family was notified for further instructions. Almost a half-century later, Margaret Ross, who helped to lay out Welton's body, would recall that "her hair was so beautiful and all her clothing so wonderfully neat and handsome; and her complexion was like velvet."

On October 17, a small, invitation-only service took place at Rose Hill Cottage. Following the hymn "Abide With Me," Carrie Welton's remains were interred in the family plot. Two thousand miles to the west, among the rocks of the Boulder Field on Longs Peak near the spot where Welton laid down to die, Elkanah Lamb erected a small rude wooden slab: "Here Carrie J. Welton lay at Rest…Died Alone…Sept. 23, 1884."

By Friday, September 26, the story of Welton's death circulated nationally, including an article in the *New York Times*. The *Longmont Ledger* and the *Denver Times* had the story first, the *Ledger* having talked with Carlyle Lamb. "Under the circumstances," the paper reported, "Mr. Lamb could see no other way out of the difficulty but to leave Miss Welton and proceed with all practicable haste to his father's house for help." The press pushed ahead with inquiries, and the next day follow-up stories appeared in the Denver *Tribune-Republican* and the *Colorado Springs Gazette*. The *Tribune-Republican*'s account was particularly detailed, and quoted I. N. Rogers, the Denver undertaker who was summoned to Longmont to embalm the body, as saying that young Lamb ("a rough, good-hearted country boy")

> is not censured by the people living in the park, for he undoubtedly did what he considered the best thing to do when he abandoned Miss Welton and hurried on for assistance. Fault is found

by some who think that Lamb could have kept the lady from freezing by gathering some dry wood when he had reached timber line and kindled a fire where he left her.

Rogers also squelched any rumor of foul play when he reported that Carrie Welton's money, mostly in the form of three large drafts against banks in New York, had been given by her to the proprietor of the Estes Park Hotel for safekeeping.

This story appeared on Saturday, September 27. The next day the *Tribune-Republican* focused on Carlyle Lamb. The thrust of the accusations, euphemistically described as "new developments," was carried under front page headlines: "THE DEATH ON LONG'S PEAK. Additional Facts in Regard to the Sad Fate of Miss Welton. SOME EVIDENCE OF GROSS NEGLECT. A Suspicion that She Was Deserted by the Guide When Most in Need of His Assistance." The source of this new "evidence" was liveryman Henry Gilbert.

The driver, Gilbert said, had proceeded that morning past the Lamb ranch and "up to timberline, five miles above the house." There at 10 a.m., Gilbert continued, the driver had met the Lambs carrying Welton's body. To be sure, the prospect of driving a team and wagon to timberline on Longs Peak under any conditions in 1884 is difficult to imagine. Nonetheless, the *Tribune-Republican* story yielded to conclusion "that it does not seem reasonable that it would take two men six hours to carry the body but one mile" and the accusation that the Lambs thus had not returned promptly to the death scene to retrieve the body, as they claimed. The newspaper's special correspondent in Longmont added:

> Those who are best acquainted with the location and guide do not hesitate to charge young Lamb with cowardice in the matter. They think when he saw Miss Welton was first taken with a fainting fit in the dark, that he became frightened at the prospect of a night on the peak, and that he abandoned her to her fate, and that he and his father did not ascend the peak in search of her until after daylight the next morning.

The story was repeated in the *Colorado Springs Daily Gazette* the next day, September 28.

Elkanah Lamb was of course upset by the charges against his son Carlyle. Not only did he have faith in Carlyle's veracity and courage, but as a seasoned mountaineer the elder Lamb knew all too well about mountain dangers. On October 1, four days after Gilbert's comments first surfaced, Elkanah told the *Fort Collins Express* that

> his son did everything possible under the circumstances, and that the roughness of the path made it impossible to carry the now-helpless lady any farther, and that it even would have been difficult for a person unencumbered to pass over the route. He added that the day upon which Welton lost her life was the coldest in four weeks. Miss Welton, he continued, made the ascent of the peak despite warnings which seemed only to make her more anxious to undertake the climb.

The Elder Lamb continued to press his side of the story, furnishing the following week's issue of the *Courier* with his own accounts of the events of September 23. It began,

> In view of the many reports and some of them very exaggerated, that have been published, we think justice to ourselves and to the community at large demands an intelligent statement concerning the tragic fate of Miss Carrie J. Welton...

By the time of Elkanah Lamb's letter, Carlyle had already received public support from an unexpected quarter. It was a front-page letter to the editor of the *Denver Tribune-Republican* "in defense of young Lamb, the guide who has been censured, to some extent, for leaving Miss Carrie Welton on Long's Peak." The writer, E. S. Darrow, said: "I believe this to be entirely untrue, and unjust to a brave and faithful guide." Darrow continued that he and his two daughters had made the ascent of Longs Peak the preceding year, guided by Carlyle Lamb. Having lost their way, and being late in returning, they were forced to spend the night on the mountain, a mile or two below the spot where Miss Welton perished and about a mile above timber line. We were overtaken by darkness before reaching the timber; a terrible thunder storm of hail and sleet coming on; it was impossible to regain the trail. Young Lamb was thoughtful and considerate and most faithful to his charge, building a fire from the gnarled roots and underbrush. He spent the night in watching the camp and looking for the trail, and was constant in his efforts to minister to our comfort and safety, and at the dawn of day, resuming our descent, he brought us to the hotel...a quiet and manly fellow and fearless of danger.

This journalistic exchange of later September and early October essentially brought to an end the public discussion of Carlyle Lamb's conduct on the night Carrie Welton died. To the extent that a verdict was rendered, it was that Carrie Welton was a headstrong and adventurous young woman who perished because of her own recklessness.

## EPILOGUE
Even before Carrie Welton's remains reached Waterbury, newspapers reported that she had been seen on dark nights, riding her beloved horse Knight about the grounds of Rose Hill Cottage. But that was not all. In his 1913 memoirs, Elkanah Lamb wrote that only forty-eight hours following Welton's death he was alone in his ranch house late at night, and his thoughts turned to her:

I tried, by imagination, to conjecture her state of mind as she lay there alone, exhausted, and not able to travel, with the wild wind howling its dismal requiem as it swept over the Boulderfield; and knowing that in nature's realm of darkness and chilling night, there was no pity nor tears to shed over suffering humanity. While musing thus...I lay down upon my couch to rest and sleep, incidentally casting my gaze towards the window in my chamber; and there, under my startled gaze, and seemingly as natural as life, stood Carrie J. Welton, looking directly toward the bed where I lay, the yellow silken mask over her features adding intensity to the uncanny presentation. Now I am not superstitious, and I do not believe in ghosts, spooks, or hobgoblins, but this ghostly appearance in the solitude of my lonely situation was the severest test of my equilibrium and courage ever before experienced in my life. Even while I was denouncing my superstitions, fears and feelings, a strange inexplicable fascination drew my eyes toward the window again, and there she stood gazing steadily towards me on the couch. Well, I leave the witchery of this peculiar mental phenomenon and experience to the expert psychologists to explain.

# 14

## THE PEAKS ABOUT ESTES PARK

1887–1888

*Frederick H. Chapin*

*Frederick Hasting Chapin (1852–1900), a wholesale druggist from Connecticut, was an experienced mountaineer. By the time he made his first visit to Estes Park in 1886, he not only had climbed in the Adirondacks of New York and the White Mountains of New Hampshire, but had successfully taken on the challenges of Mont Blanc and other major peaks in Switzerland. When he returned to Colorado in 1887, and again in 1888, he brought with him his wife, Alice, and several fellow members of the Appalachian Mountain Club. Chapin and his friends established their summer headquarters at Horace Ferguson's guest ranch below Marys Lake. There they made the acquaintance of rancher William Hallett, who willingly became their companion and guide. Chapin published several articles on their mountaineering adventures in* Appalachia, *the official AMC journal, and then in 1889 collected them in a volume he titled* Mountaineering in Colorado: The Peaks About Estes Park, *wonderfully illustrated with his own glass-plate photography. The accounts of their climbs of Hallett Peak, Mummy Mountain, and Mount Ypsilon, reprinted here, remain classics of early-day mountaineering.*

### HALLETT PEAK

After having made the ascent of Long's Peak and a number of lower elevations, I was bent on investigating the rock walls of the range that extend around to the northwest from Long's Peak to Hague's Peak, the eastern face of which in many places rivals the mural cliff of Long's Peak itself. As observed from high points in the centre of Estes Park, it is evident that there is but one pass in the chain, and that is over Table

[Flattop] Mountain. The rest of the range is one solid rampart,—at least as far as Willow [Forest] Canon,—and impassable for pack mules....

The first difficulty which presents itself to the mountaineer in Colorado is a lack of guides; there is much trouble about securing them to accompany one even as far as trails go and as far as a horse can carry. The hunters object to climbing or walking; and although very familiar with the country, hunting as they do all around the peaks, it is rarely that they climb to the mountain tops....

But our little company at Ferguson's was well provided with a leader in the person of a gentleman who has a cottage near this range, who spends all the summer months in the mountains and knows thoroughly every trail and stream for many miles around. To him I am indebted for all that I saw of the Front Range, excepting in my ascent of Long's Peak and some of the lower elevations.

The sharpest peak in the Front Range, as seen from the valley of the Big Thompson Creek, which runs through Estes Park, is a mountain near the centre of the range, to the left of Table Mountain. It rises from the large snow-field which hangs like a true glacier to a steep ridge connecting the peak with Table Mountain. For several weeks I had looked with longing eyes at this peak and its snow surroundings, wishing to climb it in a single day from Ferguson's ranch, and to do this in connection with a ride over Table Mountain toward Middle Park. When our acknowledged leader proposed taking our little company, consisting of a member of the Appalachian Mountain Club, the surgeon,[1] and myself, over the mill trail to the Continental Divide, I had no doubt that my plans would succeed.

The day fixed upon was late in August. We were to have been off at six o'clock, but it was half past six before we left the ranch. We intended to take a barometer, but our leader dropped it on the porch as we were packing, and it fell three thousand feet. We rode off, however, in good spirits, thinking ourselves fortunate in getting started even so early, for the horses had to be "rounded up" for us; and Tom, the mule, galloped all over the hillside before he was captured.

We rode down the hill and crossed the Big Thompson Creek, recrossed it to the Wind River Valley, then over the Wind River and south branch of the Thompson, and followed the latter by a road leading through sage-brush until we came to a flat meadow and ranch at the base of the mountain.

We reached this ranch at about eight o'clock, then followed the rapid stream up through tall aspens to an old saw-mill. The timber is very heavy on this mountain, but the mill did not pay financially, as the lumber had to be hauled so far to market; so everything has been abandoned and has gone to ruin. We were now by the side of Timber [Mill] Creek, and in twenty minutes struck the trail leading through tall spruce, and left all sound of tinkling cow-bells and lowing cattle far below us. The wood was dark, the ground damp, and wonderful flowers and moss grew on the trail. Deep-colored Painted Cups, and the tiny fragrant bells of the *Linnaea borealis*, the white *Pyrola chlorantha*, the curious Lousewort (*Pedicularis racemosa*), and the *Arnica alpina* gleamed out of this green darkness. These flowers were carefully transferred to boxes, for the inspection of botanists down at Ferguson's, to whom also we carried several genuine alpine plants, found far up toward the mountain tops.

We found a deep snow-bank in among the trees a little below timber-line, which is at about eleven thousand feet above sea-level on this, the northeastern side of the range. Here we turned off from the trail to a ledge a few steps away, from which we had a wonderful view, through a deep gorge, of the rocks belonging to the peak which we intended to scale. A thousand feet below us was a large lake, which appeared dark as night and is evidently very deep, as the sides run down steep from the edges; we called it "Black Lake." A little higher up was another, from which the eye followed up the ravine, over bowlder waste and white snow coverings, to the large snow-field, which looked still more like a glacier than it did from the valley below. It is evident from the succession of moraines that a mighty ice-stream once filled the entire length of the canon.

This scene, which has been looked upon by very few persons, is certainly alpine. Taken in conjunction with the view of the tower of Long's Peak rising in the southeast three thousand feet above the observer and exposing a grand slope with a lake nestling at its feet, few sublimer sights can be met within the chain of the Rockies. From the opposite side of the gorge, a vertical wall rises to a height of not less than one thousand feet; the face of it nearly perpendicular—a marvellous exhibition on a stupendous scale of the geological phenomenon of cleavage. The surface of the ridge that we stood upon is broken in masses, bowlders, and blocks,—a wilderness of debris unevenly distributed, while upon the precipice there are no signs of uneven demolition or aqueous erosion. The rocks cleave off evenly in straight up and down planes along the whole extent of the face.

After leaving the timber the trail is very indistinct,—indeed there can hardly be said to be any trail at all, a possible way for horses being marked merely by stones placed one upon another at long intervals. These were set there by our leader or some hunter, on a previous trip....

A little farther on in the ascent we had a great surprise. We were keeping very quiet and were on the lookout for ptarmigan, when we came upon three Rocky Mountain sheep, quietly browsing only a few hundred feet distant on our right. Our leader told us to duck, and said in an undertone to me, "Follow me with your camera." I did so, and all of us dismounted and almost crawling along soon saw the big-horn again, though they had not observed us. The wind was blowing a gale in our faces, so they had no scent of us. Luckily my instrument was focussed. I pointed the lens at the animals and exposed one plate, although they were not so near us as when we first saw them. They now discovered us, and after a glance in our direction trotted off over the slope to the brow of the hill. It was remarkable how easily they moved over rocks and bowlders among which we could hardly find a way for our horses and mule. Imagine our surprise when they turned and walked a little way towards us again. I asked my friends to return to the packs for more plates, and while they were gone I focussed more carefully on the still distant animals, as they stared at me, their curiosity overcoming their fear. My companions now brought up the relay of fresh plates, and retired behind some ledges farther off. At this moment, as I remained there alone by the camera, the ram stood on his hind legs and struck out with his forefeet as if inviting combat; then the three stood looking at me. We were in one of the wildest spots on the mountains; a seemingly endless field of ledge and bowlder all around, snow mountains and rocky peaks only in the panorama; all signs of valley or glen, tree or river, far below. I had a moment to reflect on what I was beholding, and carefully adjusting the glass again on these rare creatures, closely watched them.

Our leader crawled up towards me, and as the quarry showed signs of alarm I attempted to take another picture; but I was now so excited that I took a slide out of one plate-holder before putting the cap on, and that ruined piece of glass now lies among the rocks to amuse the conies and ptarmigan, while the slide which I had placed on the camera was whirled far away by the strong wind....

Very soon after the adventure with the big-horn we reached the top of Table Mountain. The out-look was grand on all sides. We were out of the bowlder field, and could almost gallop our horses in any direction on the pebbly surface. We rode to the west end of the mountain, which we reached at one o'clock and looked right down upon the glacier-furrowed Middle Park, and upon Grand Lake, the large sheet of water in it. This side of the mountain was broken up into ledges, not very abrupt however. The distant lines of snowy ranges were very sharp and clear in the west, and the mountains of the Front Range around us somehow seemed higher above us than they did from the valley below. We rode back towards the peak to some water, where there was feed for the horses, and ate our lunch; but the surgeon and I made quick work of that, and left at quarter before two for our new peak, the real goal of my eyes. We rode up the western slope, which was a very gradual ascent, to the highest patch of grass, and were surprised to find how far up we had been able to ride. We then tethered the animals, and at quarter past two attacked the rocks. We could have found a more gradual but longer ascent by bearing around to the right and keeping more to the southern side; but for the interest of the ridge, and that we might have the snow and deep gorge in view, we bore to the left, up the edge, and after a short and rather easy climb reached the summit. The peak looks quite steep, but is deceptive. It is made up of a heap of rocks, and no ledges or precipices are upon any side but the north and northeast. We found a cairn on the summit, which was probably piled up years ago by some indefatigable member of the Survey party....

We stayed on the summit for half an hour, and studied the landscape. The view is not as extended as from Long's Peak, though nearly as fine. The great mass of Mummy Mountain, higher than our peak, hid North Park and much of the Medicine Bow Range in the northwest; but the view of Middle Park was much finer than from Long's Peak, as we were right over it. Grand Lake lay just below us. We could trace the course of the river which it feeds, winding through the deep valley on its way towards the great Colorado River and the Pacific Ocean, while on the northeast we could follow the mountain torrents that run into the Platte, and find their way to the Gulf of Mexico to be tossed about at last in the Atlantic....

We ran down the peak faster than we went up, keeping yet nearer to the precipice; and when we came to the head of the snow bank, we walked out upon it, kicking in steps with our heels, until it ran off so steep that it would have been dangerous to have ventured farther without ice-axes and ropes....

Time pressed, for we had crowded much work into one day; so we hurried on, and mounting our horses gained our friends near the opposite side of the snow. We had more trouble in finding a way down through the bowlders than in going up, but we finally sighted the trail at timber-line, emerged from the woods into the flat country at eight o'clock, and, with some "throwing in of steel," reached Ferguson's at nine o'clock.

## MUMMY MOUNTAIN

The Mummy is an immense mountain in northern Colorado, lying directly north of Long's Peak and in line with the centre of Estes Park. It is a spur range running out to the eastward from a point where the Front Range, Rabbit Ear, and Medicine Bow Mountains nearly meet. It has its name from the fancied resemblance to an Egyptian mummy reclining at full length, and the range has been so called for some years. The highest point, Hague's Peak (13,832 feet)[2], forms the head, and a height about two miles farther to the west marks the knees of the seeming prostrate figure.

On the north side of this west peak of Mummy Mountain is a large snow-field, of unusual interest on account of recent developments regarding its true character. It was discovered only a few years ago by a hunter named Israel Rowe, and in the following manner: It was in the time of the great grasshopper raid, when these insects flew over the range from Utah to Colorado; myriads of them fell on the snow fields in their passage, and many bears went up from the rocks to feed upon them. Hunters learning of this went up also to shoot the bears; and in such an expedition Rowe discovered what he called "the largest snow-field in the Rockies." Later he took two other hunters to see it. He afterward died while on a long hunt, but before his death mentioned this interesting discovery to the leader of our numerous expeditions in and about Estes Park. Four years ago Mr. Hallett visited it entirely alone, and nearly lost his life under circumstances which led him to wonder whether this snow-field might not be a glacier.

I had seen many snow fields in the Rocky Mountains, but none where the body and weight of the snow were sufficient to form a true glacier; therefore, hearing Mr. Hallett's story, I was very anxious to have an opportunity to ascend the Mummy, and, relying on my knowledge gained in Alpine climbs, determine the nature of this one—, a desire which happily I was able to realize. At the time of my visit the great snow-field had probably never been seen by other than the persons above referred to, not only because so little had been said about it, but also on account of the distance and the difficulty of reaching it. The expedition requires parts of three days, and few travellers have the facilities for carrying provisions and blankets so far. Our leader, however, seeing that our ambition was unflagging, offered to show the possible glacier to another member of the Appalachian Mountain Club and myself; and so, on Monday, August 1, a folding mattress, blankets, provisions, axe, and coffee-pot—in short, a complete camping-outfit—were packed on Tom, the mule, and mounting our horses at 1 p.m., and leading Tom behind us, we rode away from Ferguson's Ranch toward the Black Canon. I carried, strapped to the back of my saddle, a camera and tripod, and a package of sensitized dry plates. It had been my intention to take some stakes also, and to run a line of them across the snow-field for future observation, but I found that it was all that I could possibly do to carry my photographic apparatus to that altitude.

Our trail led up through the canon, under enormous cliffs on the right, than which there are few finer, though on the left or south side the steep walls are lacking. Above the canon the trail winds to the left, high above the brook, and runs between two mountains thickly clad with spruce. It is identical with the one leading to Lawn Lake. From there on, however, there is no trail, and even to this point there was no sign of the path's having been traversed for a year. Our leader showed great skill in guiding us among bowlders and through tangled dwarf spruce over the ridge of Mummy Mountain to a good camping-place....

We turned in early, slept well, and were up before the sun, that we might see it rise out of the plains. And such a sunrise as we beheld! The flat country of Larimer County is covered with artificial lakes; and as the sun came up we counted thirty-five small sheets of water glistening in its bright rays. The sky was clear, except high in the east where a mass of clouds was gorgeously colored. First picketing our animals in a new place, we then had our own breakfast. We had aimed to make an early start, but with all our expeditiousness we did not get our animals saddled and under us until seven o'clock.

We had considerable difficulty in getting through the dwarf spruce, which was very thick. The heavy snows of winter bow down the tops, leaving them one mass of tangled branches and twigs, while under the trees the footing for the horses is very rough. However, in a half an hour we were out of the small timber, and riding over a smooth grassy surface by the side of a deep gorge on our right, which was surmounted by steep cliffs and a large snow-field. The gorge was a wild, desolate scene, it being the former pathway of a glacier; down through it rocks were piled upon rocks for miles.

We reached the limits of the grass patches at nine o'clock, and could ride no farther. Leaving the horses, we walked up the rather steep ascent, arriving at the foot of the snow-field in an hour. We had seen the upper snows for two hours, but had no view of the whole mass until we were right upon it; for an immense rocky ridge heaped high around the base hides three quarters of the snow-field until it is surmounted. All at once this scene burst upon us. A steep snow-bank extended about a thousand feet above to the top of the mountain. The water which had collected at its base had been frozen again,—not solidly, but with occasional open spaces in which large blocks of ice were floating around. As the force of the wind moved them, they were lifted up by rocks of firmer ice from beneath, creaking and groaning; then broken up into fragments, but only to form new floes. The long line of the lower edge of the ice and snow curled over in beautiful combings as it hung over the open water.

The snow expanse is about a quarter of a mile in width, and entirely fills a kind of amphitheatre made by the main range of the Mummy and a spur which extends around to the northeast.... Our leader said that when he visited the place four years before there were larger icebergs in the water.... He was all alone, and ascending on the north side, trying to reach the curious shafts which stand as sentinels over that part of the ice. He was getting along all right, when, suddenly, he broke through the bridge of a hidden crevasse. Luckily the ice was firm at the rim on both sides, so that he held up by his elbows and managed to extricate himself. Safely out, he ran down the mountain, determined never to venture on the snow again without help.

We had no ice-axe. The snow was in the condition of neve, and very firm. I used my camera tripod for a feeler, and often could send it down deep in treacherous places; but we kept to a sort of arete, and by stamping foot-holes made some progress. It was very slow, however, as every step must be made, and the incline grew steeper as we advanced. If the snow had been in a more icy condition, we could never have reached the ledges without an axe, and as it was we had to make detours to avoid glare ice. From the summit of the arete we jumped over a suspicious bit of ice to the rocks, and congratulated ourselves that we were the first to tread these upper snows. The ledges we found very narrow and broken up into towers and spires. The west side of the peak was an indescribably wild scene, such as I had never beheld; there were precipices and gorges, masses of rock and bowlders, smooth cliffs, rough-hewn towers, and below us several thousand feet was a gem of a mountain park with a silver stream winding through it for miles down to the Poudre. Encircling the whole were the snow-clad mountains of the Rabbit Ear and Medicine Bow Ranges, and beyond was the

Park Range, filling the western horizon with its mountains piled upon mountains. Part of the wonder and delight of the scene was caused by the fact that we were looking upon an almost unknown land as we gazed into the west. The meadows at our feet, walled in by high mountains, are very difficult to get into with pack animals; hence over and among the mountains there is not a settlement until Utah is reached.

Unlike some of the difficult Swiss peaks, there is always some easy way of access to the high crests of the Rocky Mountains; but there is hard climbing to be found, if that is sought. To any mountaineer in search of such work, I would suggest that he ascend the Mummy glacier by an arete on the north side to the point where the shafts of rock are standing, then descend the mountain to the deep glen below, being careful to take provisions for two days from camp. After exploring the valley at its upper limit, let him ascend the west peak of the Mummy from that side directly to the summit, and I fancy he will have need of steadiness of head and strength of limb.

We began to make the remainder of the climb of the peak by the broken ledges, and found our way difficult. The rocks, broken and shattered, afforded poor hold, and if once they gave way, went spinning to the lake below with a whir and a crash that made us realize what would be the result should we fall from these heights. We had to help each other with boosts and pulls; for sometimes there were no firm rocks within reach, as we felt for them over the edges of platforms above us. It was not easy to get the gun and camera up; so finally, after passing the edge of the ice, which was too treacherous to venture upon at this point, we were forced to take the face of the mountain, by which we had an easy route to the summit.... The day is far distant when throngs of tourists will stream up the gorge to see the largest ice-field of Colorado, and by that time perhaps the granite rocks will have crumbled away, worn by rain and cracked by frost, and the profile which we saw will have vanished. Meanwhile many will doubtless be glad that we succeeded in securing a photograph of the strange and beautiful scene.

It was now five o'clock. We reluctantly turned away from the glacier, and scrambling over the moraine to the large snow-field where the bear had crossed, we glissaded down for several hundred feet, then took to the rocks, and soon reached our horses and mule. On the way down, we shot seven ptarmigans. We reached camp at dark in a very tired condition, but a cup of strong coffee so revived us that in an hour we were contentedly lying before the blaze, the thick hedge of spruce timber at our backs keeping off the strong blasts of wind. Then we told stories of bear, and stories of elk, and stories of "big-horn" and smoked the pipe of peace....

## YPSILON PEAK

Though making many climbs among the higher peaks and giving much study and investigation to the upper snows, not all of the time of two joyous summers in Estes Park was spent on the mountain-tops, but many days were whiled away in rides, drives, and strolls among the quiet scenes of this beautiful vale. Encircling the shores of Mary's Lake and tracing from afar routes which we had followed into the range, was a delight. We climbed the ledges of little Prospect Mountain, and studied the topography of the valleys at our feet or of the rugged mountains in the west. We galloped over pastures; we forded river and creek.... Still more interesting and novel are the scenes to be met with, or perhaps rather to be ferreted out, along the banks of the little torrents that flow into the Big Thompson from the north and from the south. One of these streams is Wind River, beautiful to me from many associations. It was on one of those happy days upon its borders that my great interest began in the mountain that I am about to describe.

That day I was in this pretty valley with my wife. We had spent the time lazily near a deserted cabin by the stream. I had been fishing a little. Later we were looking at the mountains, which from here are so beautiful in the west. One great peak with a steep wall facing the east, and a long reclining ridge leading toward the southwest, especially interested us. A large snow-field lay on the eastern face; two glittering bands of ice extended skyward to the ridge of the mountain, forming a perfect Y. My wife said to me, "Its name shall be Ypsilon Peak." So it went forth, and the name was accepted by the dwellers in the valley and by the visitors at the ranches....

Never anxious to send me away from her side into the mountains, the sponsor of Ypsilon was always desirous that I should ascend this peak; but the summer vacation of 1887 passed away, and it still remained unclimbed. During this last summer, however, the not difficult but very interesting feat was accomplished.

Thursday, August 9, a camping outfit was packed in Ferguson's stage; and our party, consisting of Mr. Hallett, Mr. Gilman, Mr. George Thacher, Mr. J. R. Edmands, Prof. C. E. Fay, and the writer, started for Horseshoe Park to attempt Ypsilon Peak.[3] Mr. Gilman and myself rode horses, which were to be used as pack animals on our arrival in Horseshoe Park. We left Ferguson's ranch at 9.30 a.m., and reached the end of the road at 11.30. There we unloaded the wagon and sent it home, packed the two horses with the necessary outfit, and turning to the right followed an old trail by the side of a creek which flows from Lawn Lake. We lunched in a park where there was feed for the horses, and higher up at four o'clock forded the creek under some difficulties, the operation consuming half an hour. After leaving the ford, there was no trail; so Mr. Hallett led the procession with axe in hand, and was obliged to cut and hew right and left.

With our faces now turned directly toward Ypsilon Peak, and several hundred feet above a brook which flows from its snows, we worked our way over the side of a great ancient moraine for three hours, and on the banks of the stream found a suitable camping-spot at dark. I acted as commissary and cook, but fear that my comrades were not over and above pleased with the very plain fare. We passed the night under cover of canvas, rubber, and blankets; we did not carry a tent. With the exception of one of our number, we all slept well.

In the morning we left camp at 7.20,—at first in a body, but, as is generally the case with such a large party, we were soon scattered all over the flanks of Mount Fairchild, over the top of which we intended to go. Mr. Hallett carried my sensitized plates,—a heavy load. I lugged the camera, and in addition to this burden was troubled with a very lame foot, and had little hope of standing on the summit of Ypsilon that day. Mr. Edmands soon made direct for the summit of Fairchild, which he reached at 10.55; while the rest of us bore to the right in order to gain a ridge, by following which we thought we should obtain good views the whole morning long. We kept nearly together, Messrs. Fay and Hallett arriving first on the ridge at 8.15. At that point I took pictures of Ypsilon, and higher up obtained fine views of Hague's Peak and the west peak of the Mummy Range. The deeply furrowed precipitous sides of the former peak, rising nearly three thousand feet above the timber, were marvellous to behold.

Messrs. Fay, Hallett, and Thacher now went ahead for Fairchild; and Mr. Gilman and I, not being in good condition, determined to skirt that mountain a few hundred feet below the summit. We were soon joined by Mr. Thacher, who was also out of sorts and had given up Fairchild. Luckily we had one canteen of milk and a flask of brandy with us, and constituted ourselves an invalid corps for a short time, when, strange to relate, my lame foot with exercise had become entirely well. Mr. Gilman also had quite recovered from his indisposition; so, leaving our friend to continue a direct high-level route to the notch between Fairchild and Ypsilon, we made straight for the top of the former, over the steepest part of the peak....

We reached the notch at 12.50 p.m., and there joining Mr. Edmands we began on the lunch. Mr. Thacher soon came in, and reported having seen two young cinnamon bears playing on ledges below him. The bear question was getting serious.

At 1.30 p.m. Messrs. Edmands, Hallett, and Fay started for Ypsilon's crest, which they reached at 2.25....

Ypsilon from above is even finer than from below. The snow gullies which form the long lines converging together at the base, which gave the peak its name, cut deep into the mountain's flanks, and have formed miniature canons. Weird shapes of snow cling to nooks which are sheltered from the sun. One cornice had a big hole in it, as if a cannon-ball had passed through. But the great point of interest is the steep character of the whole northeastern face. Numerous lakes were visible below, between us and our camp; some were perched on high moraines far away from the base of the peak; while straight down and over two thousand feet below, immediately at the base of the cliffs, we saw two large ones which were walled in by dikes. All the great peaks in the neighborhood have these characteristic glacial lakelets. The debris seems to have been swept away from the exit end, though great blocks lie on the side....

The three who first arrived on the summit soon left us, and following the ridge descended the next peak south on their way to camp. After parting with these companions we returned to the summit of Ypsilon and commenced to erect a cairn, but the rocks being too heavy to handle easily, we gave it up. As the wind had died down a little, we spread a map on the rocks, and with the aid of compass identified many points of interest; but soon abandoned that simply to take in the glorious view. Long's Peak with its grand tower never looked nobler....

All these things were seen in a few moments, and we began a rapid descent....

As we descended lower we came upon other beautiful lakes and extensive greenswards.... We got to camp at 7.45 o'clock, and were the last in. Camp-fire that night was an interesting one, as each had a story to tell....

Our camp was also a merry one; we knew no sadness. We had been upon a beautiful mountain, had met with adventures and no mishaps, and were now safe around a blazing fire within the circle of whose rays neither bear nor mountain lion would dare to venture.

## NOTES

1. Dr. James Osgood Otis of Boston, a noted specialist in pulmonary diseases. Otis Peak is named in his honor.
2. The reference is to Clarence King's 40th Parallel Survey, which came through Estes Park in 1871.
3. The references are to Benjamin Ives Gilman, an ethnomusicologist, soon to become secretary of the Boston Museum of Fine Arts; George Thacher of Boston (he and his wife were guests at Ferguson's ranch in both 1887 and 1888); John Rayner Edmands, an assistant at the Harvard College Observatory; and Charles Ernest Fay, a professor of modern languages at Tufts College near Boston. Fay Lakes, below Mount Ypsilon, are named in his honor.

# 15

## WILLIAM ALLEN WHITE AND THE BOYS OF '89 IN MORAINE PARK

James H. Pickering and Nancy Pickering Thomas

*In his 1946 Pulitzer Prize-winning autobiography, William Allen White (1868–1944), the much-admired editor-owner of the* Emporia Gazette *and a respected voice in Progressive and Republican politics for more than three decades, briefly recalls the summer of 1889, during which he and a group of Kansas University companions camped in Moraine Park beside the Big Thompson River. That summer's adventure would turn out to be the first of many. White and his wife, Sallie, would return to Moraine Park to honeymoon in 1893, and again as a family in 1911. A year later they purchased the cottage that would become a summer refuge for the rest of their lives.*

*For White, that first summer was a defining moment. "If I ever grew up and became a man," White would later write, "it was in the summer of 1889, in Colorado, in a little log cabin filled with a dozen boys on the Big Thompson River." It turned out to be only the beginning. The story of that summer among a group of boys who would become remarkable men is excerpted and slightly adapted from James H. Pickering and Nancy P. Thomas,* If I Ever Grew Up and Became a Man…: The Boys of '89: A New Glimpse at William Allen White's First Summer in Estes Park" *(2009).*

We do not know just how that first outing was planned, though it was clearly pre-meditated. White, a portly young man, who by his own admission shunned athletics and neither fished nor hunted—(strange credentials indeed for someone bound for the mountains)—had spent the previous spring with lifelong friend Vernon Lyman Kellogg (1867–1937) earning money for the trip by working for Colonel Oscar E. Learnard, owner of Lawrence's two daily newspapers, the *Journal* and *Tribune*—in White's case by soliciting printing jobs and subscriptions. Wages in hand, White and Kellogg purchased round-trip railroad passes to Loveland, a gateway to Estes Park.

Giving the summer expedition a legitimatizing purpose (handy, no doubt, in allaying the concerns of skeptical parents) was KU professor of natural science and mathematics, Francis Huntington Snow (1840–1908), Kellogg's "guide and friend," and with whom White had also taken courses. An 1862 graduate of Williams College, where he earned a masters degree and, later, a Ph.D., and Andover Theological Seminary, Snow had come to the University of Kansas in 1866 to teach mathematics following service in the Civil War. His association with KU would last forty-two years. In 1868, only two years into that career, a clear promise of things to come, Snow became one of the seventeen men who organized the Kansas Academy of Science, to whose *Transactions* he would subsequently contribute more than a hundred scientific articles. It was Snow who inspired Vernon Kellogg to embark on the distinguished academic career that took him to Cornell, Leipzig, and Paris, and then back to Kansas, where he briefly served as professor of entomology, before being chosen, in 1884, to fill the Chair of Entomology at Leland Stanford's new university in California.

A popular, if demanding, teacher, Professor Snow was responsible for much of the early biological exploration of the West. Between 1876 and 1907, he conducted summer scientific expeditions to various destinations in Kansas, Texas, New Mexico, Arizona, and Colorado collecting large quantities of plants, insects, mammals, birds, fossils, and meteorites for the university's museums. For these excursions, Snow regularly recruited students from the university (including women, unusual at the time) as well as young scientists and members of his own family. Thanks to their help, Snow's entomological collection, the largest, it was said, in the United States, came to contain over 21,000 species and 275,000 specimens of insects.

William Allen White found the university at Lawrence a small and welcoming place: some five hundred students in all departments, taking courses from thirty-six professors in five buildings. Here it was possible for students not only to build strong relationships with one another, but to interact with their professors in ways that would be unusual today. Even in such an intimate atmosphere, Professor Snow stood out. He was at once approachable and friendly, enthusiastic and serious about his subject, yet able to laugh at student horse-play without losing either control or respect. "In after-years," one of his students noted, "we loved to recall, not so much that we had studied botany and zoology at the University, as that we had studied them under Professor Snow."

One way that Snow reached out to students was through the Science Club, of which Kellogg, who later served Snow as an assistant secretary, was a member. The Club met informally on Friday evenings to discuss general scientific subjects. Because of his friendship with Kellogg, Will White, though an indifferent student (who would fail to graduate because he could not pass the required courses in mathematics), no doubt attended as well, at least upon occasion. "Professor Snow," he later recalled, "certainly gave me a great respect for the sciences and made it possible for Vernon in later years to keep me reading along the lines which otherwise I should have abandoned." During the 1888–1889 academic year Snow was elected president of the faculty; in the spring of 1890 he became chancellor of the university. Three of Francis Snow's twenty-six summer expeditions, in 1889, and again in 1892 and 1897, took him to Estes Park.

The first of these excursions provided William Allen White and his KU friends the adventure of a lifetime. They were, it now appears, twelve in number—mostly members of Phi Delta Theta, White's and Kellogg's own fraternity, together with three members of Phi Kappa Psi. And what a group they were! Though White recalled that his fraternity was "known for its scholarship," and that its members "all rose to decent careers, leaders in their line of work," this statement hardly does justice to the talented young men who were that summer's companions, most of them then in their late teens or early to mid-twenties. White and Kellogg were virtually inseparable, though they became a trio with the admission of Frederick N. Funston (1865–1917), or "Timmy," as he was called, a "pudgy, apple-cheeked young fellow, just under five feet five," who weighed less than one hundred and twenty pounds. Like Will White, Timmy Funston "indulged in no athletic sports whatever," but was both "fearless" and "a good rifle shot," and compensated for "his runty size by laughing at himself, clowning in short." According to one widely-circulated campus story, Funston once broke four of the Phi Delts' chairs while using them as waltzing partners. However unprepossessing and unpromising as a youth, for he was anything but a good student, the "clumsy but nimble" Funston, already the son of a U.S. Congressman, would go on to win fame as Major General "Fighting Fred" Funston, a national hero for his role in capturing Filipino President Emilio Aguinaldo during the Philippine-American War (1899–1902).

Their other companions included two brothers, Edward Curtis Franklin (1862–1937) and William Suddards Franklin (1863–1930), both of whom would later enjoy distinguished scientific careers. Ed, the older of the two, showed so much promise as an undergraduate chemist that he stayed on at Kansas to teach until 1893, when he joined classmate Vernon Kellogg at Stanford to conduct important experimental research. His younger brother, W. S. Franklin, also taught at Kansas after graduation, though after three years he left for the University of Berlin and a career in physics and electrical engineering that would eventually take him to Iowa State College, Lehigh University, and, finally, to M.I.T. As a tribute to the friends of their KU years, Ed Franklin would name one of his sons Vernon Lyman Kellogg Franklin, while his younger brother would title his 1913 collection of essays on education, *Bill's School and Mine*, whose title "and some of the material were borrowed from my friend William Allen White."

In addition to the brothers Franklin, there was Henry Earle "Harry" Riggs (1865–1949), who became a professor and head of the department of civil engineering at the University of Michigan; Frank Craig (1870–1926), who, like White, worked for the *Lawrence Daily Journal* as an undergraduate, before earning a law degree, practicing law, and founding and serving as president of a bank in Oklahoma; and Herbert Spencer Hadley (1872–1927), who also became a lawyer, and then, as attorney general of Missouri, prosecuted the Standard Oil Company for violating that state's antitrust laws. Elected governor of Missouri in 1909 on a reform-minded platform, Hadley, as White notes in his autobiography, "came within a pin scratch of being nominated by the Republicans in 1912 for President."

Hadley, one of the three Phi Psis, finished his career as Chancellor of Washington University in St. Louis.

That is eight. Thanks to a photograph of the group taken at their cabin in Moraine Park and labeled by William Allen White, and to an interview with General Frederick Funston published in *The Denver Times* in May 1902, we now know that the party also included Schuyler C. Brewster (1868–1930) of Iola, Kansas and his younger brother, Frederick William "Petit" Brewster (1872–1950), Alvin Lee Wilmoth (1857–1924), at thirty-two, the oldest of the group and a second year law student at the University of Kansas who would later serve as county attorney, KU regent, state legislator, and probate judge; and Amos H. Plumb (1869–1939) from Emporia, the son of Kansas' senior Senator Preston H. Plumb, who had helped to found the town in 1857. Unaccountably absent was William Appleton "Will" Snow (1870–1899), the professor's son, a close friend at KU with White, Kellogg, and Funston, who often accompanied his father on his summer adventures. The younger Snow, like White, embraced a journalism career, his with the *San Francisco Chronicle*. Ironically, he drowned in San Francisco Bay, washed overboard while sailing out to meet General Funston and his 20th Kansas Volunteers, triumphantly returning home from the Philippines. Will Snow wanted to be the first on the scene to chronicle the event for a Kansas City newspaper.

The acknowledged leader of this group of young men, White would recall four decades later in an article expressly written to honor him, was Edward Curtis Franklin, who at twenty-four was well into his collegiate years when White himself arrived in Lawrence. As White soon discovered, Ed Franklin occupied a special place both among the Phi Delts and in the campus classrooms. At the fraternity (it was Franklin who "spiked" White and invited him to join), Franklin served as "a sort of patriarchal sponsor," who took it upon himself "to go about the freshman prodding them up, making them study, keeping them straight." An elder statesman, Franklin led by example—by exercising a force of character that White somewhat elliptically attributed to "the wisdom of an understanding heart."... When it came to the Colorado outing with the Boys of '89, Franklin apparently (and, no doubt, inevitably) found himself once again cast in something of the role of chaperone, as well as "guide, philosopher, and friend."...

## TO THE HIGH COUNTRY

Although most visitors to Estes Park in the 1880s would have made the thirty-five mile journey from the railroad station at Loveland by stage over the hard hills of the old Bald Mountain–Pole Hill Road, the boys from Kansas were not "flush with money." So, sending their heavy outfits on by express, they set out on foot, each man carrying his blanket and a few provisions, cooking "a little 'grub' over a pine fire," and sleeping under the trees. Even by stage it was not an easy trip, for the grade, in places, ran as high as twenty percent, leading one traveler, four years later, to proclaim his trip "the worst climb you have experienced in a public road."…

## CAMPING IN MORAINE PARK

The location chosen for "Camp Phi Delt," as Kellogg and Funston would name their base of operations when they returned the following summer, was in Moraine Park (or Willow Park as it was originally called), a glacier-carved valley shaped by ice rivers flowing out of Forest, Spruce, and Fern Canyons to the west. Here, close by Eagle Cliff Mountain and the meandering banks of the Big Thompson River, the boys, "willing to rustle and economize," secured a rental. This small, but serviceable, chinked log cabin, heated by a stove, would become their home for the months of June, July, and August.

The cabin's rusticity ultimately proved too much for Amos Plumb, who at age twenty suffered from back problems. Funston, looking back on the episode a dozen years later in his interview with the *Times*, told the story this way:

> At the cabin, they took turns at cooking. One morning a few days after their arrival, the boys made humorous remarks about the bowlder quality of the biscuits that young Plumb had cooked for breakfast, at which the amateur chef took offense. He left the party and went to the ranch to board, and his comrades, at that time, said he escaped because they "guyed" [ridiculed] him. As a matter of fact, Plumb was an invalid—the only one of the party—, and found that his health would not endure roughing it.

Though White and his friends roughed it that summer, they were hardly without the resources of civilization. Beginning in 1880, Moraine Park maintained its own government post office. There was also a small general store run by the widowed Mary Sprague, who together with her two sons, Abner and Fred, operated the small, nearby cabin resort known as Sprague's Ranch, one of the region's pioneer tourist resorts. As...[period] photographs show, the area along the Big Thompson in the center of the valley was then being actively cultivated for its hay, both by the Spragues and their neighbors, the Fergusons (who maintained sizable herds of cattle in the area).

Professor Snow, as planned, joined the boys in August, turning for Kellogg, and some of the others, what had been mainly a summer's lark into something of a scientific expedition. Unlike his young companions, with whom he slept and "messed" during his first days in the park, Snow arrived aboard the regular stage. "After a stage ride of 32 miles (Loveland to Moraine), from 11:30 a.m. to 8 p.m.," he wrote,

> I was put down at the cabin of the "Kansas boys", as they are now quite widely known in this region. I found them just returned from a ten days trip to "Specimen Mountain", and came in upon them with a Rock Chalk, Jay Hawk[1] just as they had seated themselves to the supper table. Kellogg & Ed. Franklin did not return from their trip with the rest but they will be here tonight. The boys, having lived 10 days on oatmeal and corn-cake, were ravenously hungry. Supper consisted of toast mountain sheep (two of which were killed by Funston and Hadley) fried trout, biscuit & coffee. There is no butter in camp, but milk in abundance. The cake was much enjoyed and I had to unpack my trunk to get it out to round up the supper in becoming style. The boys are strictly enforcing the rule of "no razors in camp" and you would be amused to see the different stages in the evolution of beard illustrated by the various members of the party. Will Franklin & Harry Riggs have a patriarchal aspect, Funston, Wilmoth and Brewster have a less advanced development, while Hadley, Craig & the younger Brewster exhibit the incipient stages of hirsute

adolescence.... I slept last night on the cabin floor with W. S. Franklin for a bedfellow, and found him a very quiet non-calcitrant partner. When Kellogg gets back I will put up the fine new tent I bought in Denver. This is a nice lot of boys. The two Brewsters, Hadley & Wilmoth occupy a tent by themselves and have a separate mess, and I am with the 7 boys in the cabin, messing with them. They take turns as cooks, each of the 7 holding office for one day each week and they will not allow me to share the work, which is good of them. So I can collect at my pleasure. This is a fine locality for botanizing, and I hope to make a large collection of plants as well as insects.

Though neither White's autobiography nor Funston's 1902 newspaper account makes reference to the presence of women, much less to summer romances, a number of...photographs [that survive in the William Allen White Collection at the University of Kansas] show that the young men from Kansas did not lack female company on their mountain adventuring, including their trips to Longs Peak. One party, remarkably enough, was from Lawrence and KU, and, like the professor himself was in Moraine Park by pre-arrangement. It included Will Franklin's twin sister, Nellie, as well as Helen Sutliff (the Pi Beta Phi to whom White paid substantial attention during his KU years, including the summer of '89), Helen's younger sister Jennie and another KU schoolmate Eva Fleming, who together had established housekeeping of their own in a nearby cabin which Helen and Jennie's mother, Mrs. Jennie Sweet Sutliff, had rented for the season. Though Mrs. Sutliff was no doubt there to play the role of chaperone, her presence among the young seems to have had no more dampening effect than did Professor Snow, who would accompany a coed party to the top of Longs Peak and be photographed with the group....

The intrusion of these females into the bachelor world of White, Kellogg and the others clearly occasioned moments of merriment, one of which, thanks to another of Professor Snow's letters, we know about in some detail. In Snow's retelling, the sewing skills in mending their britches were hilariously called into question when the ladies appeared one afternoon unannounced....

Young Herb Hadley also celebrated the summer, sharing some of its details with his family at home. The trip was described in a letter to his father written at the end of June. "Our crowd is an especially jolly one. Will Franklin and Henry Riggs are both in for fun and Funston keeps the whole crowd laughing most of the time." Two months later, in August, as the summer wound to its conclusion, he succinctly summarized it all without, like White, mentioning female distractions. "This has been," he wrote, "the pleasantest summer I have ever spent."

Funston was the only member of the Boys of '89 to leave his name associated with the mountain nomenclature of Estes Park. On one excursion that summer, during which one may surmise, given his reputation, that he was clowning to impress one or more young ladies, Funston fell (or jumped—the stories differ) into the swirling pool just below where Spruce Creek and the Big Thompson come together. In later years, his male companions would claim that Timmy was being chased by a bear. Whatever the truth of the story, until at least 1919, the raging torrent on the Big Thompson, a favorite stopping place for those bound for Fern Lake and above, would be known as "Funston's Pool."

For the larger outlines of those three summer months of 1889 we have only White's autobiography, written at a distance of more than half a century, to call upon, as well as scattered references in White's letters and other writings. Like all such recounting, his memories...are clearly reshaped by time and are selective. In addition to the absence of any mention of women, there is no mention of Professor Snow nor of his summer collecting activities. One of the photographs [referenced] above, however, clearly shows the presence of a butterfly net, a necessity for capturing insects, and we know that a large part of Vernon Kellogg's time (part of which White must have shared) was spent in bird watching. The following year, when he returned to Lawrence, Kellogg wrote up a short article titled "Notes on Some Summer Birds of Estes Park, Colorado," listing 76 different types of "avian fauna." It was published in 1890....

Given its lasting personal importance, White's account of that summer is surprisingly brief. In fact, it comprises something less than three pages in what is a very long and often detailed work. "We were not a serious crowd," he writes.

We lived simply, gayly [*sic*]. We had two rules, only two, as the laws of our republic: every man must clean his own fish, and no razor would be allowed in camp. So we grew whiskers. Mine were red and upturned from under the chin—an Irish mustache. We cooked when the Franklins told us to cook, for they were our elders, and washed dishes without rancor or friction. Every man made his own bed, which was on the floor, of the one-room log cabin, for we all slept in a row over spruce boughs and under our own blankets. And every man looked after his own kit—a change of underwear, his store clothes which he never wore in the park, a book or two or three or half a dozen which he brought, and his gun if he had one, which I did not, and his fishing tackle—ditto with me.

It appears that the trout-cleaning rule was the outgrowth of a heated argument that William Allen White had early on with Frank Craig over just who should clean the trout caught that day. The discussion, Funston recalled, at length got so "warm" that Craig picked up a butcher knife and White, in retaliation, lifted a chair in the air. "Before the combatants came together, their companions rushed in and hostilities ceased, without any casualties resulting."

White, Kellogg, and Funston were a constant threesome. And whatever his stated reluctance, White accompanied Timmy Funston on his hunting forays, and after one of them was willing enough to cut up and cook the "contraband" mountain sheep that Funston bagged and then displayed as a trophy for the camera....

Funston put his rifle to decidedly better use on another occasion. Spotting some enterprising sign painters defacing a huge boulder not far from camp with an advertisement "admonishing the use of somebody's sarsaparilla," the pugnacious Funston pursued them down the road, scaring them off "largely by his unique and convincing profanity, supported somewhat by his cocked rifle." What inspired and provoked the fun-loving Funston on this occasion, White does not say. Perhaps it was because...the same boulder had been previously used as a place on which to pose some of the KU boys and their female companions. At any rate, Funston's act of bravery proved a Pyrrhic victory, for the painters had already done their work. To this day—some hundred and twenty-five years later—their hand-iwork, "Drink Denver Soda," splashed across the rock with lead-based paint, remains visible below the modern concrete bridge spanning the Big Thompson.

In White's retelling, their sojourn in Moraine Park was a magical, idyllic time, lived completely in the present with little or no concern about home, family, nor events in the world beyond the mountains. Days, weeks, and months easily collapse into one another in White's few pages, as he talks of gathering wild red raspberries and strawberries for "delectable shortcakes," making "passable" flapjacks, frying fish, and doing more than his share of "hauling down wood from the mountain for our cabin." He also read—passing many an afternoon with books while lying in a hammock hung in a wooded grove.

And for the first—and perhaps the last—time in his life the unabashedly unathletic Will White actually hiked and climbed. On two occasions he made the summit of 14,259-foot Longs Peak, once in the company of Vernon Kellogg, the other as a member of a party that included Timmy Funston, Herb Hadley, and Ed and Nellie Franklin, and the Sutcliff sisters. A "hard, long climb," to be sure, but one accomplished, apparently, without complaint or regret. "When I got to the summit for the first time," White recalls, "we could see across the plains the smoke of Pueblo two hundred miles away. We could see over into Wyoming. It was a beautiful sight. But when I started down that precipice I was frightened, literally scared numb and stiff, and Kellogg had to coax me down." What White does not mention was that while on the summit he and comrades posed for an obligatory photograph.

## TRIP TO LULU CITY

White also reports an even longer excursion, "forty miles from our camp"—though in truth probably a bit less—to the deserted mining camp of Lulu City on the banks of the Grand (now the Colorado) River. Organized and laid out in ambitious fashion in 1879 with nineteen streets and one hundred city blocks, Lulu soon boasted four lumber mills, a hotel, stores, saloons, and a post office, together with any number of private log dwellings. But the boom proved to be short-lived—the gold, silver, and lead mined there were of low grade and costly to extract—and by 1884 the fledgling town, as White and friends discovered, was empty—closed down, it would seem, almost overnight. "There was the post office," White remembers,

> with letters in the boxes; the saloons with the empty bottles on the shelves; the billiard tables with their green baize, moth-eaten and rat-gnawed; the stores with their shelves like grinning skulls empty of their fleshly furnishings; in the cabins the cookstoves stood in the kitchens, and iron safes standing open, too heavy to be moved. It was a dramatic picture—that little town of Lulu down on the Grand.

Other contemporary visitors have left similar descriptions, though none convey better the sense of eerie unreality that lingered over the hastily abandoned mining camp than William Allen White. What White does not tell us is that, having arrived, the boys took possession of the deserted town in the name of Kansas, hoisted over it their broad pennant, and for several days indulged themselves by living in one empty house after another.

## DEPARTURE

Having tramped into the mountains, the boys of '89 determined to tramp out as well. Setting off about the first of September, their route would take them west across the Divide, down along the Grand River past Grand Lake, and from there, by way of Berthoud Pass, to the Clear Creek mining camp of Lawson. Again we have Funston to thank for the anecdote which tells us that, though the boys had crossed the Divide before to get to Lulu City, this time they became lost and actually wandered about for days. "Late one night," Funston recalled for the *Times* reporter, who then retold it all in the third person,

> they went into camp worn out and discouraged. The only provisions left were coffee and condensed milk. In the morning they packed up their outfit and started on. They had proceeded only

300 yards when they reached the top of a hill and there, just below them, lay Grand Lake, a spot they had supposed was miles distant.

Reaching Lawson, the boys decided that the ascent of one more four-teener must cap the summer. They chose Grays Peak, the highest point on the Continental Divide even though it took them west rather than east. That summit gained, they at once turned east to Golden where they took the train, having walked some 145 miles from Sprague's ranch.

MOUNTAIN MEMORIES

"I should define that summer as hilarious," White recalls, filled with jokes, high-jinx and laughter. Nowhere is this more apparent than in the post-Fourth of July photograph the boys had taken of the assembled group, which evidently included several guests. "We were not a drinking crowd," White tells us. But there they are, mugging it up for the camera, posing with the empty bottles of the beer consumed during their all-day cele-bration of two or three days before. That photograph…White notes, later "printed in many a newspaper and magazine…when we were grown into man's estate and somewhat celebrated, has frozen us there as the young devils we were not."

And so that long-remembered summer of boyhood companionship and camaraderie ended. For White, the future moved ahead, and by the fol-lowing summer he was fully occupied with the beginnings of his journal-ism career. Not so with Vernon Kellogg and Fred Funston, the other two members of the "inseparable" trio. The very next summer they returned to Moraine Park, perhaps to the very same log cabin, a place which Kellogg, in a letter of June 1890, refers to as "Camp Phi Delt," a name which Herbert Hadley and his two Phi Psi brothers were obviously not there to contest….

Will Franklin also returned to Estes Park, which he had apparently first visited in 1886. He touches briefly on his experiences in the delightful col-lection of letters and poems that he printed privately (and anonymously) in 1903 as *A Tramp Trip in the Rockies of Colorado and Wyoming*, an account of a month-long pack trip through the mountains, presumably taken in the early 1890s before he left to study in Europe. The first three nights of the trip, he writes, were spent at Sprague's Ranch in Moraine Park, where they were warmly greeted by Fred Sprague. "Having seen our tracks (hob-nails)...he remarked...that 'God's people had come,' meaning the Kansas boys with whom he became acquainted in '86 and '89."

Though William Allen White missed the trip up Flattop Mountain in 1890 with Kellogg and Funston, it was White, alone...who returned to Moraine Park as an adult and made it his own. In later summers, the day's writing done, William Allen White would sit in his favorite chair, a cane rocker, on the front porch of the cabin he later bought above Moraine Park, looking down on the Big Thompson and the spot where he and his KU comrades spent the memorable summer of '89. One by one, those boys had slipped away, after having been translated, like White himself, into distinguished men. Timmy Funston, was the first to go, incredibly enough dead of heart failure at a border post in Texas in 1917, at the age of 51. The other boys of summer followed: Frank Craig in 1926, special friend Herb Hadley in 1927, Will Franklin in 1930, and both Ed Franklin and Vernon Kellogg in 1937, the latter, the most heart-felt loss of all. Only Frank Riggs, the civil engineer, outlived White, dying in 1949 at the age of 84.

On how many occasions, one must ask, as he sat on that porch, did William Allen White's thoughts turn to the boys of that first summer and their shared experiences in the cabin by the river. What White remembered most, it is clear, was the laughter, loud to the point of hilarity, born of the carefree days of youth when each day was full enough and the future would take care of itself. We can only imagine that White sitting there, grown old like his friends, shared the sentiments of another writer, an even earlier visitor to Estes Park, whose simple prayer upon departing spoke of treasured moments past, "Lord, keep my memory green."

NOTE
1.    The famous University of Kansas chant, "chalk" referring to the limestone outcroppings on Mount Oread, the hill on which the campus is located.

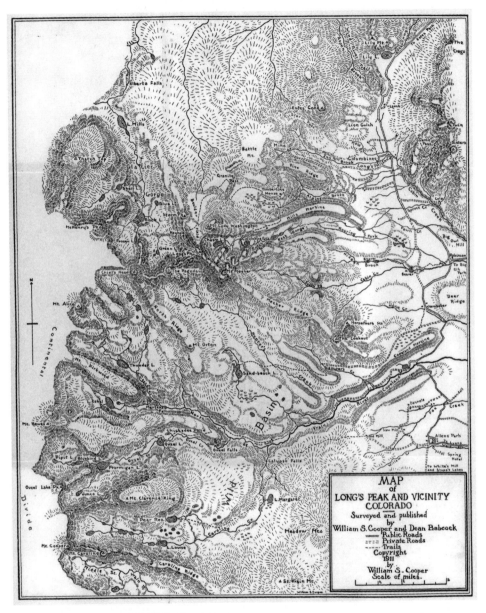

Cooper-Babcock Map of Wild Basin, 1911.

"Here Carrie J. Welton Lay to Rest." Wooden marker that Elkanah Lamb placed on the Boulderfield.

Early-day campers in Rocky Mountain National Park.

Stead's Ranch and Hotel in Moraine Park.

1914 Arapaho Pack Trip. From left: Shep Husted, Sherman Sage, Gun Griswold, Tom Crispen, and Oliver Toll; seated: Princeton student David Hawkins.

Dedication: Rocky Mountain National Park, September 4, 1915.

"Enos, I'm Proud of You!" The goddess Colorado congratulates Enos Mills on the signing of the park bill. *Denver Post*, January 20, 1915.

Park dedication. From left: Enos Mills, F. O. Stanley, Colorado congressman Edward Taylor, and Mary K. Sherman.

Tourists on the trail.

Original park headquarters building, located on Elkhorn Avenue in Estes Park.

Enos Mills and
Superintendent
L. Claude Way
sending off the
Eve of Estes.

Fall River Road.

Thornton Rogers Sampson.

Park Naturalist Dorr Yeager.

Colorado Mountain Club at the Boulderfield Shelter Cabin, July 31, 1927.

CCC Camp NP-1-C in Little Horseshoe Park, 1936.

Chasm Lake.

# 16

## A TRIP TO STONES PEAK

1890

Frederick Funston

*When Fred Funston and Vernon Kellogg, two of the "Boys of '89," returned to Estes Park the following summer to climb mountains, they brought with them a copy of Frederick Chapin's* Mountaineering in Colorado, *published the preceding year. Apparently inspired by the final chapter of Chapin's "charming book," the two set off from the summit of Flattop Mountain to attempt the ascent of 12,922-foot Stones Peak. The route chosen was an extremely rugged one. It took them down past the head of Spruce Canyon to the foot of Sprague Glacier, which they were in the process of ascending when overtaken by a ferocious storm. Funston published an account of their adventure as "Storm Bound above the Clouds" in the July 1891 issue of* St. Nicholas, *the popular juvenile magazine of the day.*

Extending north from Long's Peak, in Colorado, the Front Range or Continental Divide comprises a chain of stupendous peaks reaching into the clouds, and covered even in summer with great fields of snow and ice. This range, cut up by gorges and chasms thousands of feet in depth, which reach into it from the valleys on both sides, presents views of rugged grandeur excelled by none in the entire Rocky Mountain region. Many have compared them favorably with the world-famed glories of the Alps and Caucasus.

Below "timber-line," which in this region is at about eleven thousand feet elevation, the sides of the mountains are covered with a dense growth of spruce, which gives way in the lower valleys to the yellow-pine and quaking-ash. These grand forests have never been ravaged by fires nor marred by the woodman's ax; and in their gloomy depths the mule-deer, mountain-lion, and cinnamon-bear roam undisturbed by fear of man.

Above timber-line the mountains rise from two to three thousand feet more—in some places gentle slopes covered with huge granite boulders, and in others cliffs and crags rising almost sheer for hundreds of feet. Here and there are masses of hard packed snow, while in a sheltered spot on the south side of some cliffs grow tiny alpine flowers and dwarf grasses—the food of the wary big-horn sheep, which still frequent this range in considerable numbers.

Comparatively few persons have explored these, the grandest of all the Rockies. Distance from railroads and the total absence of the precious metals have left the range uninhabited, the nearest settlers being the scattered ranchmen in Estes Park.

But few tourists have had the hardihood to scale the great peaks of this chain and risk life by exposure to the storms which almost constantly sweep them; though notably one, Mr. Frederick H. Chapin of Hartford, Conn., spent several summers in this region, and has given us his experiences in a charming book.

Great peaks thirteen thousand feet in height have never been scaled, dark chasms and gorges are yet unexplored, and mountains higher than Mount Katahdin piled upon Mount Washington have never been deemed worthy of a name.

It was only a few years ago that the writer and a single companion, Mr. V. L. Kellogg, now an associate professor in the University of Kansas, stood on the summit of Table Mountain, a great elevation about six miles north of Long's Peak. Gazing down into the awful gorge which separates the mountain we were on from Stone's Peak, we marveled at its awful depths and precipitous sides, and resolved some day to explore it together, and to follow to its source the turbulent little stream that flowed at the bottom.

The wished-for opportunity came sooner than we had dared to hope, and May 1890, found us again in Estes Park prepared to attack the Front Range.

The winter of 1889–90 will be long remembered by the inhabitants of the Rocky Mountain region for its great severity and unusual snowfall. The mild spring sunshine had made little impression on the great drifts which covered the mountains and filled the upper forests; and gazing on them from the valley on a bright May morning, it seemed to us that mountains had never looked grander. Long's Peak, rearing his great cap fourteen thousand three hundred feet in air, was a mass of immaculate glittering white, broken only by the black cliff on the northeast front; the perfect cone of Mount Hallett was as white as the drifting cloud through which it peered; while Stone's Peak, a beautiful mountain thirteen thousand eight hundred feet in height, showed not a speck of brown through its wintry covering.

Despite the arctic surroundings, Kellogg and I determined to explore the great chasm without delay, though the old stage-driver to whom we broached our project shook his head ominously and said: "Boys, wait until the sun has hammered that snow for six weeks longer; even then it won't be any picnic."

But we were not to be scared out by a little snow. We had roamed over those mountains before, and more than once had been brought face to face with death by exposure or starvation but had always come out with little harm.

We soon procured the obstinate, mouse-colored little mule that had carried our packs on previous occasions; put "on board" blankets, cooking utensils, and three days' provisions, and immediately after dinner set out on an expedition, the recollection of which, as I look back on it, seems more a horrible nightmare than a reality.

It is needless to tell the story of the first afternoon's tramp—of the fruitless efforts of "Billy," the burro, to throw off his pack, and his almost human shamming of lameness when the steep ascent began.

Suffice it to say that for six long hours we plodded up the lonely trail and, just before the daylight began to fade, found a suitable camping place among the dense spruces near the entrance to the great chasm which was to be the scene of the next day's trials and sufferings.

The night was passed in a state of mild terror, caused by the presence of a mountain-lion, which prowled about camp for several hours, and was kept at a safe distance only by a blazing fire.

The next morning, at five o'clock, we crawled out of our blankets, and an hour later resumed the journey, leaving Billy to watch the camp and meditate upon the follies of his past life. With no encumbrance but our guns, we made good progress, and soon reached the entrance of the gorge, and for two hours followed up the little rivulet at the bottom. It was a weird, uncanny place. The growth of spruce was so dense that it seemed the damp, mossy ground could never have had a good look at the sunlight.

Here and there we passed little banks of last winter's snow, and soon crossed the base of a great field which we could see extended up the sloping sides of Table Mountain almost to the summit. Of this snow-field more anon.

Onward and upward we pushed, crossing and recrossing the noisy little stream, now and then walking over the crust of a big snow-drift, and occasionally falling in waist-deep when we came to a soft place.

As we ascended, the gorge narrowed to about three hundred yards and the sides became much steeper. The spruce-trees here were dwarfed and gnarled old fellows that had battled bravely for years against the snow and ice of their storm-beaten home, and had not yet given up the struggle. We were now only a short distance below timber-line, and a few hundred feet above us not a green sprig showed above the glittering white of the snow or the somber brown of the granite.

A little higher we followed the bottom of the gorge; but there were now no rocks to walk on, nothing but snow from ten to twenty feet deep—acres and acres of it. The direct rays of the sun, which was now high in the heavens, had softened the crust, and we broke through at nearly every step.

The fatigue of floundering through the snow, together with the rarity of the atmosphere, for we were now eleven thousand feet up, was beginning to tell on our strength. We determined to leave the gorge and push up to the left on the sides of Table Mountain, where we judged, and, as it proved, correctly, that the crust of the snow would be stronger.

A sharp, hard struggle of ten minutes brought us above the stunted growth at timber-line, where we sat down to recover wind and strength, and eat our noon lunch.

Up to this time not a cloud had crossed the sky; but now, as we looked toward Stone's Peak, Kellogg called my attention to a feathery, foamy mass which had rolled up over the range and, dropping almost to a level with us, scudded down the chasm before the rising wind. It was an ominous sign, and we finished our meal in nervous haste. Presently another and larger cloud came boiling over the pass at the head of the chasm, and followed closely in its leader's wake. For only a moment we watched the dark shadows they cast moving over the spruce forest, and rose to our feet just as two more clouds came over into the gorge.

The wind, which had been rising for an hour, moaned and whistled among the crags; and the mutterings of distant thunder could be heard from the west side of the range.

By this time, though little had been said, both realized full well the meaning of this turmoil: we were to be caught among the clouds in a mountain storm.

There was no further thought of exploring the gorge. All our strength and time must now be used in reaching camp.

Should we go down into the gorge and get out the way we had come in, or should we go farther up and avoid the tangle of fallen trees and the treacherous drifts below? Higher up on the mountain the snow was packed harder and would afford better footing; and that way we started without delay, our object being to work around the north side of the mountain and reach the old trail on the east side. Up and up we scrambled over the snow and rocks.

The wind was now blowing a terrific gale, and above us, below us, and around us, the clouds were being driven before it.

The storm was gathering over the whole range. Mummy Mountain and Hague's Peak, fifteen miles away, were enveloped in a mass of gray mist; while the thunder boomed and rolled over Estes Park from a black cloud which was deluging the lower valleys with rain. Stone's Peak, looming up through an occasional rift in the clouds, was a sight of awe-inspiring grandeur.

Despite the difficulties of the way and the surrounding storm, we made good progress upward, and in half an hour turned to the left and began working along the side of the mountain.

Here our trials began in earnest. The storm was upon us in all its fury. The wind blew almost a hurricane, and the air was so filled with sleet and fine snow that it was impossible to see more than twenty yards in any direction. There would be an occasional lull in the tumult, when we could take in our surroundings for a moment, but another cloud would envelop us and fill the air with driving torrents of frozen mist.

Hour after hour we struggled on with the nervous frantic energy born of desperation.

The rocks and snow were covered with ice thin as tissue paper, which caused many a hard fall, and made every step a source of peril. The force of the wind, too, threw us down continually, and we were bruised from head to foot. If we had carried steel-pointed poles instead of guns, they would have been of great service; the latter were now as much hindrance as help, though we were soon to find them useful.

Our hands and faces suffered terribly from the bitter cold, and the former were so numb that we dropped our guns repeatedly. Hair and clothing were matted with ice like a coat of mail. We realized that our progress was very slow, as we had not yet reached the great snow-field extending from timber-line to the summit, the base of which we had crossed in ascending the gorge. On and on we staggered, feeling our way over the slippery surface, and becoming weaker every moment from the hard struggle in the rarefied air of the mountain tops.

While stumbling over a mass of ice-covered boulders, I heard an excited exclamation and, looking up, saw Kellogg sink down behind a rock which afforded a slight shelter from the icy blast.

When I reached him he looked up and said, "Old boy, this is the worst box we were ever in. I guess we're at the end of our rope!" Both realized that the situation was desperate, almost hopeless. There was no sign of abatement of the storm, and weakened and enfeebled as we were by the long struggle, if we should not be able to cross the steep snow-field when we reached it, death from exhaustion and exposure would be a matter of only a few hours.

We dreaded to think of that snow-field, remembering how steep it had looked as we gazed upward from the bottom that morning, and knowing the condition it must be in now with the newly formed ice on the surface. However, it was thought best to rest a short time, and I lay down by Kellogg.

After a rest of about fifteen minutes we resumed the struggle, weak as before and much colder; but we had recovered our wind, a hard thing to keep at this altitude.

It was now four o'clock—ten hours since we left camp, and four since the struggle with the storm began. The battle for life could not last much longer.

Slowly and painfully we pushed forward, crawling on all-fours most of the time. I chewed savagely on a piece of tough grouse, the only remains of our dinner.

Would we ever reach the snow-field? A horrible thought crossed my mind. What if we had lost the direction and were going the wrong way? I did not mention my fears to Kellogg. What was the use?

Every few moments we sank down on our faces to recover our breath. At such times I found my mind wandering and could not think clearly. Kellogg made several remarks without any particular meaning, and his face had a vacant, sullen look. Almost the last ray of hope was gone. There was no complaining, no whining, only a sort of mad desperation which made us resolve to keep moving to the last.

Finally, through a rift in the clouds not fifty yards ahead, we saw the spotless white of the long-looked-for snow-field.

With a feeble shout we pushed forward, but when we reached its edge our worst fears were realized. It was terribly steep, being at an angle of about forty degrees, and the crust was a coating of hard, slippery ice, the thickness of pasteboard. Through a break in the clouds we saw that it extended downward to timber-line, fully 1,500 feet, as steep as the roof of a house and smoother than the smoothest glass. How broad it was we could only conjecture.

As we came up, Kellogg struck the crust with the butt of his gun, and I threw a rock upon the surface, which went sliding and bounding down the steep face with terrific velocity.

We looked at each other in despair. "It's no use," I said.

"Not a bit," was the answer.

We sat down and talked it over. To retrace our steps was out of the question, and we could not climb to the top of the field, probably a thousand feet, in our weakened condition.

Suddenly Kellogg leaped to his feet and rushed toward the slippery mass, crying out, "Come on, we've got to do it. I'll take mine this way." Without a second thought, in my hopeless desperation I followed. By using his gun as a brace Kellogg kept his feet; but I slipped and fell on all-fours and began sliding down. In a wild frenzy I tried to drive my bare fingers through the crust, but only succeeded in tearing the skin off them.

Luckily, I had retained my rifle, and by a frantic effort drove it muzzle first through the hard crust and came to a stop, having gone about twenty feet. Had it not been for this fortunate move my body would have been hurled to the bottom of the gorge more than a thousand feet below, and mangled beyond all semblance of human form.

Looking up at my companion I saw that he had turned away his head, unwilling to be a witness of my horrible fate; but as I called out to him he looked around, and I saw a face so white and horror-stricken that I can never forget it. Cold beads of sweat stood on my forehead, and I felt that my courage was all gone. The experience of that awful moment almost unnerved me, and I was weak and helpless as a little child.

Lying on my face I held on tightly to the rifle driven deep through the crust. How to regain my footing was a puzzle. Kellogg started to come down to me, and it was with difficulty that I persuaded him to desist.

At last I hit on a plan. Holding on to the rifle with one hand, with the other I drew my pocket-knife, and, opening it with my teeth, cut two holes in the crust for my feet, and after much effort stood upright. But we were still in a bad fix. Kellogg called out to me to break holes through the crust for my feet with the butt of the gun. Although not more than twenty feet distant he could hardly make himself heard above the roar of the storm.

But the suggestion was a good one and proved our salvation. We moved slowly forward, breaking a hole in the ice for each step. It was severe treatment to give valuable guns, but they had to suffer in the best interests of their owners.

Slowly and carefully we moved forward, occasionally stopping to rest and speak words of encouragement to each other, for now we had the first gleam of hope for five long, terrible hours.

Although very weak physically, our minds were much clearer than an hour before, and we even went so far as to chaff each other a little. But we had plenty of fears yet. Once my heart leaped as Kellogg slipped and came down on both knees, clawing frantically at the air; but he regained his feet without difficultly, and we pushed on. Would we ever get across? Every minute seemed an hour.

Kellogg said that, as nearly as he could calculate, we had been floundering about on that man-trap for a week!

But we kept going; the end must come some time, and sure enough it did; and at six o'clock we stepped on the granite boulders again, having been just one hour and ten minutes on that terrible, inclined snow-field. Neither of us was much given to demonstration, but there was a hearty hand-shake and a few things said which sounded all right up there, but might look a little foolish in print.

The wind had moderated, and the clouds had now settled far below us, while the sun nearly down, lighted up the surrounding mountains and snowfields with a sort of radiant glory. But the grandest picture was in the east: Below us, over the spruce forest, over Willow Park, and far away Estes Park, was a tossing, rolling ocean of foamy clouds, their upper sides glistening in creamy and golden light from the rays of the setting sun. To the right the great mass of Long's Peak and the shattered crags of Lily Mountain towered above the burnished sea.

It was a grand picture—such as only those who have the hardihood to climb the highest mountains can hope to look upon. Any attempt of art to imitate them can be but mere mockery.

But it was not to last long. The clouds drifted off over the foot-hills, and there were none to take their places; and then we saw, far below, the world that we had almost given up forever; and as we stood there it looked to us grander than any picture of sun-burnished clouds and snow-covered peaks. We were glad to have another chance at it. But we were not there yet. After a good rest we started again just as the sun was sinking below the horizon.

Compared with what we had been in before, the walking was good, though a discriminating person would not have preferred it to asphalt pavement.

Just as darkness was setting over the range we reached the head of the trail at timber-line. Here, there was some more hard floundering through snow-drifts and plenty of falling over prostrate tree-trunks. But we soon left behind the last snow-drift and ice-covered boulder, and hurried through the forest down the trail—easy to keep even in the darkness. Once we heard the long-drawn scream of a mountain-lion, but only slipped cartridges in our guns and kept on. We were in no mood now to be frightened by such small fry as a mountain-lion.

Finally, at nine o'clock, weary, hungry, and bruised, we staggered into the camp that we had left fifteen hours before—a terrible day in which we had more real experience than many people get in a lifetime.

Our great equine freak, Billy, was on the alert, and greeted us with such a series of whinnies that we feared he was trying something new in solos.

We built a fire and prepared supper with the usual accessory of strong coffee, and at eleven o'clock were asleep under wet blankets. But it was a glorious sleep, and when the sunshine woke us the next morning we felt greatly refreshed, though still very weak and stiff.

After breakfast we repacked the burro, and started for camp in Estes Park. Billy did not need any urging now and showed great enthusiasm in jumping over fallen trees; so much, in fact, that he threw himself down continually.

At eleven o'clock we reached camp, and spent the next few days in resting and eating with commendable energy.

We determined hereafter to heed the advice of the old stage-driver and "let the sun hammer that snow six weeks longer" before we tried any more mountain climbing.

For my own part, I am willing to let him hammer it six centuries longer before repeating that experience.

# 17

# EXPLORING AND MAPPING
# WILD BASIN
1908

William S. Cooper

*Well into the first decade of the twentieth century the rugged Wild Basin region south of Longs Peak remained remote and seldom visited. Enos Mills had explored the area and named a number of its prominent features, including Ouzel Lake. He also encouraged guests at Longs Peak Inn to visit, and furnished them a map of sorts. When possible, he accompanied them. William Skinner Cooper (1874–1978), a recent graduate of Michigan's Alma College, who spent the summer of 1906 at the inn, needed little encouragement.*

*"Enos Mills had often spoken of Wild Basin...as having more natural beauty and greater variety than any other nearby area," Cooper later recalled. That September, with his vacation drawing to a close, he persuaded Mills to accompany him as far as Ouzel Lake, from where he set out alone for two days of exploration. Cooper decided as a future project to revisit and map the entire region.*

*The opportunity came two years later in the company of Charles Edwin Hewes, an aspiring writer who had homesteaded near the inn. Cooper and Hewes spent eight days on an extensive exploring and mapping expedition, resulting in the first authentic topographical map of the region. It was published in 1911 with the help of Dean Babcock, another aspiring artist and a mutual friend of both Cooper and Hewes. William Cooper, who would go on to have a distinguished career as a plant ecologist at the University of Minnesota, kept a journal of that trip, which he made good use of in 1971 when he completed the unpublished manuscript titled "Mountains," a section of which is reprinted here.*

I arrived at Long's Peak Inn May 6. This time I traveled by way of Lyons and up the North St. Vrain, where the road had been changed to a route close to that of today. My conveyance was the mail stage; its motive power was a gasoline engine instead of four horses. I was the only passenger. Enos was absent on a lecture tour. Naturally the Inn was not in formal operation; there were present two or three workmen and a cook. In a day or two Joe Mills [Enos's younger brother] arrived and took charge of preparations for the summer season, bringing with him a beautiful Texas bride, Ethel. Being very busy, he turned her over to me for practice in mountain hiking. Thus began a friendship that lasted as long as Joe and Ethel lived....

My first job was laying out of a base line for my map, a half mile carefully measured on the levelest ground I could find in the immediate vicinity. Plane table work began with sightings on Estes Cone, Longs, Meeker, and the Lookout. When I later climbed the Cone I found it useless as a secondary station on account of compass aberration. The Lookout proved to be the most useful of all my stations. Upon its topmost, almost inaccessible rock I spent a day sighting on everything in view, including Wild Basin....

June 16. No back packs this time, but a real live pack animal—Pat, the burro. He is solemn and innocent—appearing like all of his kind, but possesses most of the peculiarities for which his tribe is noted. Joe tied him to my front porch. The pack saddle was brought, a makeshift affair, which tempted me to use bad language time after time.... Charley led off with the burro's rope, while I followed with the ax. For half a mile nothing happened. We stopped to look at the pack and discovered to our surprise that the cinch, placed too far forward, had already scraped the burro's skin badly. Off came every package and a readjustment was attempted while the burro contentedly fed upon yesterday's *Denver Republican*. We began our march once more and continued it for six miles without any serious trials other than a readjustment of the cinch every few minutes. At Copeland Lake we made our first real stop. Pat assumed that it was the end of the day's march and lay down, pack and all.

It was going to be a hard push to reach Ouzel Lake, where was to be our base camp, before dark—and we didn't make it. The road was a level one for two miles but was fearfully muddy from three days of almost continuous rain, and it took a diligent application of the butt end of the ax to persuade the beast to plunge through. Two bad washouts gave us some trouble, as the trail was obliterated in these places for some distance. Then an easy stretch, past the finest grove of aspens hereabouts; an open lodgepole forest thickly carpeted with mountain blueberries; a short, steep climb; and a nasty stretch through burned timber, with log after log lying across the trail. These had to be jumped, always unwillingly by the donkey, or we had to find a way around, often using the ax in cutting through. I had gone over this trail two years before, but with Enos as guide; it is not surprising that at a place where the trail branched, I took the wrong direction. By the time we had gone a few hundred feet we were hopelessly surrounded by fallen timber.

It seemed best to call a halt while I explored. It did not take long to discover my mistake and we retraced our steps and took the other trail, which led us straight to the river—considerably smaller than below but still a raging torrent. We looked at the river and then at our burro, then back at the swiftly rushing water with its tangles of brush and fallen logs. But the trial had to be made and it wouldn't do to risk our valuable supplies. We unpacked Pat and carried across the sleeping bag, blankets and everything else, using a nearby fallen tree for a bridge. Then we concocted a plan for getting the animal over. We decided to use our long pack rope to steady him and then drive him into the water and let him wade or swim, whichever he preferred.... A steep slope with the timber burned was our next trial, then a sharp climb through lodgepole and a long level stretch through open forest along the summit of the ridge. Here the trail was distinct and well blazed and we made excellent time. The smooth blaze marks on the trees were easy to distinguish even after the light was nearly gone.

Darkness came at last and still we were at an unknown distance from our destination. We lighted matches for a time and searched for blazes in this way. It was inevitable that we should finally lose the trail entirely. Even then we did not give up, but struggled on in the direction that we knew must be the right one, making wide detours around fallen trees, plunging into miry spots and tripping over stones and roots—all by starlight. At last we came to a dead stop, finding ourselves completely hemmed in by fallen timber. There was nothing to do but give up and camp for the night where we were....

June 17. In camp at last! A good dry one, with smooth ground and all the wood we want. We did well to stop, however, for we could never have done that last half mile in the dark. As it was, in broad daylight, we had a whole load of troubles crammed into it. I was comfortable last night and slept well, but Charley did not. We got up early, ate breakfast, extinguished our fire, washed the dishes (after a fashion) and packed the burro. In the meantime I easily located the trail less than a hundred feet away. Again we took up our travels, with the usual frequent adjustments of the old saddle. The trail is not well blazed here and we had difficulty in keeping it. At one place it led up a steep ascent and was completely buried under the remains of a winter's snowbank. No way around appeared possible and we drove the beast into the snow.... It seemed best to explore ahead, so I took a few of the light articles and went on toward the lake. I discovered that it was less than a quarter mile away, but the trail was thoroughly bad with snow and fallen timber. We therefore lightened the burro's pack, carrying some of the packages ourselves and came to our destination at Ouzel Lake without further incident....

After dinner (we indulged in three meals today) we started on a short expedition across the ridge to the North Fork country.... We descended into Mertensia Basin from about timber line, named Lake Ethel [after Joe Mills's new wife; today's Eagle Lake], and followed the stream down to Mertensia Falls, which I named in 1906. I found it more beautiful than ever, with wonderful snow bridges above and below and the falls set in a perfect frame of ice and snow.... Back to camp just before dark....

June 18. Mid-afternoon (probably; I can't be sure since our only watch stopped sometime during our first night out). An ideal June day! Snowing like sixty, and has been at it most of the day. We have fixed a shelter out of the tent fly. One half makes the carpet, the other half the roof. One end of the latter rests on a rock, being held there by a smaller stone; the other is supported by the plane table tripod. In the center we have placed a pole supported by a crotch. This arrangement makes two very noticeable sags in our roof, in which the snow accumulates, and melting, leaks through the canvas upon the carpet. Our camp is exceedingly picturesque but as to comfort it is not successful....

We got off very late this morning—at what time I don't know exactly for reasons already stated. We were both so delightfully comfortable, Charley wrapped up in his blanket and the tent fly, and I in my sleeping bag, that we dozed and dozed, although we had planned to climb Mt. Copeland today and should have made an early start. The only bad thing about a sheep-skin sleeping bag is that it is a hardship to have to crawl out in the morning....

To continue: Breakfast: grape nuts with condensed milk and sugar from Charley's stock, bread, jam, and coffee. We washed the dishes. Then off for Mt. Copeland. The weather was unpromising—low swiftly moving clouds which would have persuaded us to stay at home, had we not been unwilling to lose a day. Up through the woods over firm winter snow. When we reached the region of timberline the clouds fulfilled their promise and began to give forth quantities of snow. The ground was whitened in a very few minutes and the dirty winter drifts came to possess a clean surface once more. Still we pushed on, hoping for a change, which did not come. Some steep rocks afforded an unsatisfactory shelter and here we stayed for an hour. I removed much frozen snow from Charley's sweater and hair. We stood back to back and shivered, and still the snow drove by in clouds. Once the whole cloud curtain rolled away toward the south but soon closed in again, leaving us hopeless of anything better. Taking advantage of a lull in the storm we began our retreat. Here and there an early primrose or buttercup or alpine forget-me-not appeared above the fresh snow, their colors wonderfully vivid in contrast with the whiteness in which they were nearly buried. For an hour the weather favored us and we made excellent time by sitting down on the steep snow fields and shooting to the bottom in a few seconds. This is always excellent sport and somewhat consoled us for being defeated by the elements. Back to camp about 2 p.m. judging by the sun....

June 19. Brief conversation, 6 a.m.:

Billy: Let's wash—tomorrow morning.

Charley: All right—or next day....

It was a magnificent morning, without a cloud and the mountains freshly whitened with yesterday's snow. As far as timber line we followed our ill-fated route of the day before, and then struck off over the interminable snow and debris of Mt. Copeland. We walked on and on until we got there. I had been up before so the several apparent summits did not fool me. It was cold and windy on the summit and our feet were soaked. This did not prevent Charley from utilizing the next hour in making up for lost sleep in a sheltered, sunny spot. I photographed him with his mouth open. After I finished my plane table work we sat down and looked at our next door neighbor, Mt. Caroline [Cooper had named today's Elk Tooth after his mother]. It didn't look encouraging from our direction. Reluctantly we gave it up for the day. A narrow arete a mile or more long offered us a route to the Continental Divide. It proved interesting, and required more than two hours of careful work on rock and snow to traverse it. At the end of the ridge we faced a short abrupt ascent of 200 feet to the summit of the divide. This required an hour additional on account of the rottenness of the rock. In many places it seemed almost impossible to find a foot or hand-hold sufficiently firm to be trusted. Treacherous places were frequently covered with a thin layer of snow. In addition, the plane table tripod was an awkward encumbrance in such a place. After changing our route several times we reached the summit in safety. The Continental Divide in this region is a level or rolling plateau, extending in general north and south, bounded in most places by steep slopes or precipitous cliffs. For a way of descent the one by which we ascended did not attract us. We finally decided on a steep thousand-foot snow slope which ended in a disk of blue ice marking the position of a glacial lake in the bottom of the canyon. After a preliminary rock scramble I sat upon the snow and slid 800 feet before I reached the ice. Charley followed; having a path prepared for him he came much faster.

For the next two hours we traveled down the canyon over the snow-buried floor of the upper portion, then into the forest, beside a snow-bridged stream, which was beginning to burst its winter bounds, occasionally rushing out from beneath its roof in a cascade as white as the snow itself, soon disappearing again into an icy tunnel. Occasionally we could hear its faint rumble beneath us as we walked over the hard surface; sometimes it was impossible to know where it flowed and as we went on it would suddenly appear again in the most unexpected place. We passed three beautiful lakes, the last one especially fine [probably Bluebird Lake]. Charley has been puzzling ever since endeavoring to find a name worthy of it. He has a list of suggestions—Lake Solitude, Lake Serenity, Lake Chastity, but he can't decide and I expect more suggestions at any moment....

June 20.... Ouzel Lake is well named. It is an ideal place in which to study the graceful movements of that charming little bird. One has just been amusing himself in the water near by, floating a while upon the surface, then diving and turning water somersaults in a way no human swimmer could hope to imitate. The ouzel's song is a cheery one, resembling slightly that of our eastern brown thrasher, especially in its wonderful variety. Altogether he is a most agreeable companion to us as we lazily loaf in our camp. Charley just relapsed into poetry. Here is a sample: "Amid the silence of the tomb/ I ate my last and only prune." If he had not fed so many of his prunes to Pat he might have chosen a more cheerful subject for his verse....

June 21. It has been a strange day—decidedly a strenuous one. We moved our camp three miles down the canyon and are now settled in a spot of quiet beauty. The St. Vrain roars over its stones not far away. Two enormous glacial boulders lean against each other; the space between them provides shelter enough for half a dozen campers. There are rare flowers nearby. The exquisite orchid Calypso is abundant; the handsome purple clematis trails over the bushes. Supper tonight was an unusually good one: brown bread (part of our last loaf), chocolate, cheese, canned pineapple. Before dark we climbed the slope behind our camp and sat for a time enjoying the white top of Mt. Copeland rising above the dark spruce forest through which we came today.

Our trip from Ouzel Lake: we rose late; washed hands and faces in spite of having done it the day before. Charley in a sudden burst of cleanliness, took off shoes and stockings and put his feet in the lake. Upon his earnest recommendation I did the same rash deed. The water was cold—barely above 32 degrees, but so refreshing. Extinguishing our four days' fire was by no means the work of a few minutes. In spite of the original wetness of the ground the fire had burned down some distance into the humus and much digging and water carrying were required.

Pat allowed himself to be packed without protest and started off quite willingly on the homeward trail, evidently taking for granted that he was going all the way. The usual adjustments had to be made at frequent intervals. The trail was almost continuously down hill and we soon discovered that the back strap (in this case a plain rope) took all the weight of the pack and was cutting the beast badly. Off came everything and Charley fished a flour sack out of his pack and wound it around the rope. This relieved the trouble to some extent. Cutting through the timber, we found a way around that snowbank that was so nearly our Waterloo on the way up. The steep descent to the North Fork came next. Pat was eager to make fast time.... A few hundred feet before reaching the formidable ford of the North Fork the pack slipped forward and turned over. Rather than repack for so short a distance, we carried everything to the ford and across it.... We met a party of three Longmont farmers, prospecting for water sites. They looked suspiciously at our surveying instruments, as if they thought we had stolen all the water east of the Divide....

June 22. I laid out my bag under the rock last night and couldn't for the life of me go to sleep. After an hour I moved into the open; sleep came at once. We got up at daylight and were on our way by five o'clock. We ascended beside the South Fork (Cony Creek), here a series of roaring, foaming cascades. Its background is dark, mossy spruce forest—brown and gray trunks, fresh tips to the branches, bright crimson spruce flowers, gray lichens on the dead boughs, and on the ground, here and there, Calypso, singly and in groups. In honor of this flower, remembering also with respect the nymph who bore that name, I christen this stretch of white water Calypso Cascades. Quiet water and graceful curves finally replaced the roaring waterfall and we knew that we must be very near Lake Margaret.[1] Mile after mile, more cascades succeeded quiet water, and no lake. The course of the stream bore more and more to the west; it was evidently not upon the main stream but to one side upon a small tributary. Another lake just below timberline consoled us somewhat.

Mt. Caroline rose just before us; though not so lofty as some of its companions, it is an imposing mass of unusually striking form. After a debate as to the best way of ascent we decided to continue up the canyon and make use of a talus slope that led to within a few hundred feet of the summit. The climb was long and tiresome; the fragments were of small size and lay at a steep angle. They slipped under our feet in a provoking manner; often a single footfall would start yards of debris sliding. Above this were broken cliffs with safe and easy climbing. Quite suddenly we came out on the crest of the ridge; before us to the southward were the great peaks of the Front Range—Audubon, Arapahoe, Gray's, and that great hill called Pike's Peak. A few hundred feet to our right was the tusk-like summit of Mt. Caroline. An easy traverse along the north side of the ridge brought us to it, a short scramble placed us upon the top. The sun told us that it was exactly noon, seven hours from the start. A welcome rest ensued, then topographical work and photography. Charley, as is his custom on high mountains, took a nap....A graceful (?) cairn surmounts the peak to commemorate our ascent.

For our descent, a new route suggested itself—to follow Caroline ridge toward the east, thus keeping above timberline for a long distance. Our plan was next to drop down to Lake Margaret, upon reaching which we would be nearly home. For some distance the ridge was easy, but soon the edge became sharp and broken and we lost much time in searching out practicable routes. At one or two places the descent was quite spectacular, though safe in every case. Ultimately we reached good traveling ground again and made excellent time for several miles. By this time we were pretty tired, but Baldy Mountain (St. Vrain Mountain) just a mile ahead and a thousand feet higher, proved so attractive that we plodded on until we reached its summit.... The Alpine forget-me-not was in its glory—solid little cushions of dazzling azure. Alpine clover afforded a rich feast for a few early bees. Third in abundance was the dwarf primrose, deep red-purple—the list might be continued indefinitely. But I must mention the Alpine buttercup—the first flower to appear on spots left bare by retreating snow—a single blossom surmounting a low stem, the purest and richest gold, like the aspen leaves of autumn. Lake Margaret lay just below us. Setting a straight course for it, we plunged into the forest, which is here of fine proportions. After a long descent we came out upon a meadow just below the lake and in a few moments were standing upon its shore. In shape it is a beautiful oval and around it is a narrow band of meadow just now light pink with dwarf laurel. The forest surrounds the lake without a single break, untouched by fire or ax. Its background is a noble line of peaks, from Caroline to Longs. Near the lower end we found a single sign of humanity—a tin pail hung upon a tree and a sign claiming the lake as a reservoir site. A descent past Calypso Cascades brought us to the ford of the St. Vrain, and a few minutes later we were in camp, a little before dark; estimated time, fifteen hours. Supper—chocolate, sardines, apricots—very satisfying.

June 23. Our last day was not welcome—but we had only sugar and bitter chocolate left and very little of these. I spent the forenoon in collecting specimens and taking geological notes. About two o'clock we brought Pat in from his aspen grove and saddled and packed him. For a while we had more than our usual share of troubles. Pat was uneasy and eager to reach home and wouldn't stand still to be adjusted. In crossing the washouts we took the wrong trail and had to cut our way through rather than go around. After reaching the level road we had little trouble—no saddle difficulties at all. Our trip is ended, and we are satisfied with what we have accomplished: exploration of the south half of Wild Basin, ascent of Mt. Caroline, naming of several points of interest, mapping, ecological materials. Best of all, we both feel better than ever before in our lives....

End of the Summer. The exact chronology of those last few days is confused, for reasons that will be apparent. Field work on the map was almost finished; only the northeast corner of Wild Basin remained. About three days after I returned from Mt. Richthofen [August 26th] I started for that area, with Sandbeach Lake as intended headquarters. Dean Babcock went with me, and of course Tip and an equine friend of his. We established ourselves near the lake, enjoyed a good dinner, and settled ourselves for a pleasant conversation before retiring. A shot sounded in the direction of the trail by which we had come. Shortly out of the darkness rode Enos Mills; he had spotted our fire and had fired to warn us of his approach. A telegram had come stating that my father was dangerously ill and that I must come home at once. Mills had information as to trains out of Denver, and it appeared that nothing would be gained by my return that night. Enos left, promising to telephone home and make reservations. I discussed plans for the map with Dean, and it was decided that he should remain and finish the field work; thereby becoming co-author.

NOTE

1. Named after Cooper's girlfriend of the season; today's Finch Lake.

# 18

## THE BEAVER'S ENGINEERING

1913

*Enos A. Mills*

*From the time he arrived in Longs Peak Valley in 1884, watching beavers in nearby ponds was one of Enos Mills's favorite pastimes. No naturalist ever lavished more attention on a single species. On one occasion, he tells us, he quietly watched a local beaver colony for sixty-four straight days. He also introduced others. Visitors to Longs Peak Inn were regularly taken on personally guided walks to the local colonies. Mills wrote extensively about his many encounters and in 1913 gathered thirteen of his essays together in the miscellany he titled* In Beaver World.

*With beavers, as with all the animals he studied and wrote about, Mills was self-taught. He read widely in the available scientific literature of the day and combined what he read with his own personal observations and fieldwork. The results, most modern naturalists agree, were impressive, though Mills is clearly guilty of overrelying on unique and unsynthesized events in drawing his conclusions. There is also the problem of anthropomorphism—of his willingness to grant the beaver the ability to reason. Despite such flaws, Mills's essays on the beaver were some of his best and most popular.*

*In the essay excerpted here, he reports his observations on the Moraine Colony, located on Roaring Fork on the flanks of Longs Peak, some two miles from the inn.*

Realizing that the supply of aspens near the waters of the Moraine Colony close to my home was almost exhausted, I wondered whether it would be possible for the beavers to procure a sufficient supply downstream, or whether they would deem it best to abandon this old colony and migrate.

Out on the plains, where cottonwoods were scarce, the beavers first cut those close to the colony, then harvested those upstream, sometimes going a mile for them, then those downstream; but rarely were the latter brought more than a quarter of a mile. If enemies did not keep down the population of a colony so situated, it was only a question of time until the scarcity of the food-supply compelled the colonists to move either up or down stream and start anew in a place where food trees could be obtained. But not a move until necessity drove them!

Not far from my home in the mountains the inhabitants of two old beaver colonies endured hardships in order to remain in the old place. One colony, in order to reach a grove of aspens, dug a canal three hundred and thirty-four feet long, which had an average depth of fifteen inches and a width of twenty-six inches. It ended in a grove of aspens, which were in due time cut down and floated through this canal into the pond, alongside the beaver house. The other colony endured dangers and greater hardships.

During the summer of 1900 an extensive forest fire on the northerly slope of Long's Peak wrought great hardship among beaver colonies along the streams in the fire district. This fire destroyed all the aspens and some of the willows. In order to have food while a new growth of aspens was developing, the beavers at a colony on the Bierstadt Moraine were compelled to bring their winter supply of aspens the distance of a quarter of a mile from an isolated grove that had escaped the fire. This stood on a bench of the moraine at an altitude about fifty feet greater than that of the beaver pond. Aspens from the grove were dragged about two hundred feet, then floated across a small water-hole, and from this taken up the steep slope of a ridge, then down to a point about one hundred feet from the pond. Between this place and the pond was a deep wreckage of fire-killed and fallen spruces. To cut an avenue through these was too great a task for the beavers; so with much labor they dug a canal beneath the wide heap of wreckage, and through this, beneath the gigantic fallen trees, the harvested aspens were dragged and piled in the pond for winter food. The gathering of these harvests, even by beavers, must have been almost a hopeless task. In going thus far from water many of the harvesters were exposed to their enemies, and it is probable that many beavers lost their lives.

Beavers become strongly attached to localities and especially to their homes. It is difficult to drive them away from these, but the exhaustion of the food-supply sometimes compels an entire colony to abandon the old home-site, migrate, and found a new colony. Some of the beavers' most audacious engineering works are undertaken for the purpose of maintaining the food-supply of the colony. It occasionally happens that the food trees near the water by an old colony become scarce through excessive cutting, fires, or tree diseases. In cases of this kind the colonists must go a long distance for their supplies, or move. They prefer to stay at the old place, and will work for weeks and brave dangers to be able to do this. They will build a dam, dig a new canal, clear a difficult right-of-way to a grove of food saplings, and then drag the harvest a long distance to the water; and now and then do all these for just one more harvest, one more year in the old home.

The Moraine Colony had lost its former greatness. Instead of several ponds and the eight houses of which it had consisted twenty years before, only one house and a single pond remained, The house was in the deep water of the pond, about twenty feet above the dam. A vigorous brook from Chasm Lake, three thousand feet above, ran through the pond and poured over the dam near the house. The colony was on a delta tongue of a moraine. Here it had been established for generations. It was embowered in a young pine forest and had ragged areas of willows around it. A fire and excessive cutting by beavers had left but a few aspens near the water. These could furnish food for no more than two autumn harvests, and perhaps for only one. Other colonies had met similar conditions. How would the Moraine Colony handle theirs?

The Moraine colonists mastered the situation in their place with the most audacious piece of work I have ever known beavers to plan and accomplish. About one hundred and thirty feet south of the old pond was a grove of aspens. Between these and the pond was a small bouldery flat that had a scattering of dead and standing spruces and young lodge-pole pines. A number of fallen spruces lay broken among the partly exposed boulders of the flat. One day I was astonished to find that a dam was being built across this flat, and still more astonished to discover that this dam was being made of heavy sections of fire-killed trees. Under necessity only will beavers gnaw dead wood, and then only to a limited extent. Such had been my observations for years; but here they were cutting dead, fire hardened logs in a wholesale manner. Why were they cutting this dead wood, and why a dam across a rocky flat,—a place across which water never flowed? A dam of dead timber across a dry flat appeared to be a marked combination of animal stupidity,—but the beavers knew what they were doing. After watching their activities and the progress of the dam daily for a month, I realized that they were doing development work, with the intention of procuring a food-supply. They completed a dam of dead timber.

At least two accidents happened to the builders of this dead-wood dam. One of these occurred when a tree which the beavers had gnawed off pinned the beaver that had cut it between its end and another tree immediately behind the animal. The other accident was caused by a tree falling in an unexpected direction. This tree was leaning against a fallen one that was held several feet above the earth by a boulder. When cut off, instead of falling directly to the earth it slid alongside the log against which it had been leaning and was shunted off to one side, falling upon and instantly killing two of the logging beavers.

The dam, when completed, was eighty-five feet long. It was about fifty feet below the main pond and sixty feet distant from the south side of it. Fifty feet of the new dam ran north and south, parallel to the old one; then, forming a right angle, it extended thirty-five feet toward the east. It averaged three feet in height, being made almost entirely of large chunks, dead-tree cuttings from six to fifteen inches in diameter and from two to twelve feet long. It appeared a crude windrow of dead-timber wreckage.

The day it was completed the builders shifted the scene of activity to the brook, a short distance below the point where it emerged from the main pond. Here they placed a small dam across it and commenced work on a canal, through which they endeavored to lead a part of the waters of the brook into the reservoir which their dead-wood dam had formed.

There was a swell or slight rise in the earth of about eighteen inches between the reservoir and the head of the canal that was to carry water into it. The swell, I suppose, was not considered by the beavers. At any rate, they completed about half the length of the canal, then apparently discovered that water would not flow through it in the direction desired. Other canal-builders have made similar errors. The beavers were almost human. This part of the canal was abandoned and a new start made. The beavers now apparently tried to overcome the swell in the earth by an artificial work.

A pondlet was formed immediately below the old pond by building a sixty-foot bow-like dam, the ends of which were attached to the old dam. The brook pouring from the old pond quickly filled this new narrow, sixty-foot-long reservoir. The outlet of this was made over the bow dam at the point nearest to the waiting reservoir of the dead-wood dam. The water, where it poured over the outlet of the bow dam, failed to flow toward the waiting reservoir, but was shed off to one side by the earth-swell before it. Instead of flowing southward, it flowed eastward. The beavers remedied this and directed the flow by building a wing dam, which extended south-ward from the bow dam at the point where the water over-poured. This earthwork was about fifteen feet long, four feet wide, and two high. Along the upper side of this the water flowed, and from its end a canal was dug to the reservoir.

About half of the brook was diverted, and this amount of water covered the flat and formed a pond to the height of the dead-wood dam in less than three days. Most of the leaky openings in this dam early became clogged with leaves, trash, and sediment that were carried in by the water, but here and there were large openings which the beavers mudded themselves. The new pond was a little more than one hundred feet long and from forty to fifty feet wide. Its southerly shore flooded into the edge of the aspen grove which the beavers were planning to harvest.

The canal was from four to five feet wide and from eight to twenty inches deep. The actual distance that lay between the brook and the shore of the new pond was ninety feet. Though the diverting of the water was a task, it required less labor than the building of the dam.

With dead timber and the canal, the beavers had labored two seasons for the purpose of getting more supplies without abandoning the colony. If in building the dam they had used the green easily cut aspens, they would have greatly reduced the available food-supply. It would have required most of these aspens to build the dam. The only conclusion I can reach is that the beavers not only had the forethought to begin work to obtain a food-supply that would be needed two years after, but also, at the expense of much labor, actually saved the scanty near-by food-supply of aspens by making their dam with the hard, fire-killed trees.

A large harvest of aspen and willow was gathered for winter. Daily visits to the scene of the harvest enabled me to understand many of the methods and much of the work that otherwise would have gone on unknown to me. Early in the harvest an aspen cluster far downstream was cut. Every tree in this cluster and every near-by aspen was felled, dragged to the brook, and in this, with wrestling, pushing, and pulling, taken upstream through shallow water,—for most mountain streams are low during the autumn. In the midst of this work the entrance or inlet of the canal was blocked and the bow dam was cut. The water in the brook was almost doubled in volume by the closing of the canal, thereby making the transportation of aspens upstream less laborious.

When the downstream aspens at last reposed in a pile beside the house, harvesting was briskly begun in the aspens along the shore of the new pond. Then came another surprise. The bow dam was repaired, and the canal not only opened, but enlarged so that almost all the water in the brook was diverted into the canal, through which it flowed into the new pond.

The aspens cut on the shore of the new pond were floated across it, then dragged up the canal into the old pond. Evidently the beavers not only had again turned the water into the canal that they might use it in transportation, but also had increased the original volume of water simply to make this transportation of the aspens as easy as possible.

Their new works enabled the colonists to procure nearly five hundred aspens for the winter. All these were taken up the new canal, dragged over the bow and the main dams, and piled in the water by the house. In addition to these, the aspens brought from downstream made the total of the harvest seven hundred and thirty-two trees; and with these went several hundred small willows. Altogether these made a large green brush-pile that measured more than a hundred feet in circumference, and after it settled averaged four feet in depth. This was the food-supply for the oncoming winter. The upper surface of this stood about one foot above the surface of the water.

Five years after the completion of this dead-wood dam it was so overgrown with willows and grass that the original material—the dead treetrunks that formed the major portion of it—was completely covered over. The new pond was used but one season. All the aspens that were made available by the dam of the pond were cut in one harvest. The place is now abandoned, old ponds and new.

# 19 VANISHED IN THE MOUNTAINS

The Eighteen-Year Search for the Reverend
Thornton R. Sampson, 1915

*James H. Pickering*

*The Reverend Dr. Thornton R. Sampson was an unlikely candidate for mountain tragedy. A professor of church history and founding president of the Presbyterian Theological Seminary of Austin, Texas, Sampson, a master of seven languages, was a scholar by inclination and training. On the morning of September 3, 1915, the day before the dedication of Rocky Mountain National Park, the sixty-three-year-old clergyman started up the Flattop Mountain trail from Grand Lake to attend the festivities in Moraine Park. He never arrived. The story of what happened next first appeared in the Summer 2000 issue of* Colorado Heritage.

Thornton Sampson's love of mountains was not new. During earlier years he had "tramped in the high altitudes of Asia and Europe," as his ministerial colleague Arthur Gray Jones later wrote, and crossed and recrossed the great passes in Austria, Switzerland, Italy, France, and Spain. As he grew older, Sampson continued to find rest and inspiration in his communion with the mountains. ("My husband loved the mountains," Ella Sampson would later tell the press. "He said he communed with the wild things while alone in the depths....")

Arriving in Denver on August 7, Sampson and his wife spent several days at the Metropole Hotel. On the 11th, having moved Ella Sampson into a room at the YMCA, the minister left the city for a fishing and tramping trip through the Estes Park region, planning to return to Denver three weeks later, on September 5. Sampson knew the area reasonably well. He had spent one summer vacation, or possibly two, in the Colorado Rockies, which he boasted he had crossed on foot some ten times.

His vacation ramble began without incident. Within a week after leaving Denver, Sampson had made his way across the Continental Divide through the old silver mining camp of Teller City to Rand, a tiny hamlet in North Park, from where on August 19, he sent Ella a postcard. Two days later, he again wrote from Rand, reporting to his wife that he was staying with a "forest ranger" named Stevens. He had met Stevens, Sampson told his wife, on a previous trip, and the accommodations he offered were "much cheaper and more comfortable than in the miserable little hotel." The only complaint voiced by Sampson was about his encounter with "abominable autos," incursions of civilization which threatened the hunting and fishing. "Tomorrow," he concluded, "I am going up to see some friends who live out of the reach of anybody else, about half a mile from the top of one of the most difficult passes. They say I am the only visitor they have ever had. I shall take up the mail and some fresh meat and spend a night with them, possibly."

The pass Sampson spoke of was doubtless 10,285-foot Cameron Pass, at the entrance of North Park, astride the old wagon road linking Fort Collins and Walden. It was from Cameron Pass, on August 28, that his last communication to his wife was written, though Sampson had apparently left to return south to Grand Lake village in Middle Park before the letter itself was posted. In that letter, the *Dallas Morning News* reported, Sampson told his wife that "he had never felt better in his life and was gaining in strength and health." He also told her that he was "well supplied with provisions for his tramp to the village of Estes Park."

By August 28, the day of his letter, Sampson left Grand Lake, making his way on foot northward towards Squeaky Bob Wheeler's tent resort on the North Fork of the Colorado River (or Grand River, as it was then known), fishing as he went. There Sampson posed for a photographer, wearing his cap, smoking a pipe, holding rod and reel. Five-foot-eleven and 170 pounds, with blond hair, gray eyes, and strong features, Thornton Sampson was a man easily recognizable, as several would shortly testify.

This much of the Reverend Sampson's August 1915 journey we know with reasonable certainty. What happened in the days that immediately followed must be pieced together from a number of published sources, in which the information is often sketchy and at times contradictory.

Sampson apparently left Squeaky Bob's camp on September 2. His announced intention was to make his way by trail across Flattop Mountain to attend the dedication of Rocky Mountain National Park scheduled to take place in Horseshoe Park two days later. The journey before Sampson was some sixteen miles, a strenuous but not terribly difficult trip for anyone in good physical condition. By that night he was back at Grand Lake village. From there the next morning he started alone for Estes Park, taking the North Inlet trail to the broad peneplain that marks the summit of 12,324-foot Flattop Mountain.

On the morning of September 3, 1915, Thornton R. Sampson was on his way to Estes Park. That morning was bright and fair, and with every sign of a good day, Thornton Sampson dressed lightly. He carried only a few provisions, "one full meal and a quantity of condensed food tablets," reported the *Denver Times*, in a small kit. Both his clothing and his kit suggested that he expected to encounter little difficulty in reaching Fern Lake Lodge at the foot of Odessa Gorge, where he planned to spend the night before completing his journey into Estes Park.

Two miles out of Grand Lake, Sampson was overtaken by Clifford Higby, a licensed guide and part owner of Fern Lake Lodge, making his way by horseback home to Estes Park. The two men passed pleasantries, and Higby gave Sampson directions. Higby told Sampson that Higby would leave a cairn marked with a red bandanna to the east of Flattop Mountain, together with further instructions on how to reach Estes Park by way of Odessa Gorge. Higby proved as good as his word, for the bandanna and directions, together with an arrow pointing towards Fern Lake, were later discovered intact, exactly where Higby had promised.

There also was a reported encounter with forty-six-year-old prospector William M. Currence, who had a crude cabin and several claims at timberline on Mount Chapin. Some days afterwards, Currence told *The Denver Post* that he had met Sampson on the trail. According to Currence, a known eccentric—who, it would be divulged some time after, had a long history of mental instability—Sampson introduced himself and asked the way to Fern Lake Lodge. The account, which sounded very much like Higby's, down to the cairn with its attached note, may well have misled one of the rescue parties that later combed the area.

Sampson was last seen alive at 2 the afternoon of September 3 by a party of three women and their guide who were returning to Grand Lake from a trip into the mountains. He was sitting, and evidently resting, in a small Forest Service shelter, 1,500 feet below the Continental Divide, some six miles from the cairn that Higby had marked.

What happened next can only be surmised. It is known that by 4 p.m., at about the time that Sampson should have reached the cairn on the summit and turned down into Odessa Gorge, the weather, always unpredictable in September, had changed for the worse. Thick, heavy clouds descended upon the mountain, rendering visibility extremely difficult, followed by heavy snow and high wind. By the next day the snow across the area had drifted in places to depths of forty to fifty feet.

Though Thornton Sampson missed the appointed rendezvous in Denver on September 5, his wife and friends initially professed no great alarm, for as an Austin, Texas, newspaper noted the following week, the minister "has often taken long jaunts through the woods or mountains alone and frequently makes excursions of this sort when on a vacation." The suggestion was even advanced that Sampson had "lost himself intentionally for the purpose of getting a thoro [sic] rest." This conjecture came from C. B. Kendall, a member of the U.S. Geological Survey, who had accompanied Sampson by train from Denver to Steamboat Springs at the beginning of his trip. The men had talked for two hours, during which Sampson told his companion that "he often lost himself in the hills while on hikes, as he loved the mountains." "Dr. Sampson told me," Kendall was quoted by the *Denver Times* as saying, "that he took this same trip last summer…and that twice before he had traversed this route. He is evidently a good woodsman and could not lost [sic] himself in the forests. I thought him very competent to take care of himself."

Sampson's intended route, Kendall reported, was to take him south of "the Estes region, along the ridge," by which Kendall surmised, "he might have gone south towards Corona," the railroad station at Rollins Pass.

So confident were his friends of Sampson's return that not until Monday evening, September 13, did the first search party headed by Shep

Husted, Carl Piltz, and Ira Coleman leave Estes Park, taking the westward trail up from Horseshoe Park to Lawn Lake, with the intention of searching Hagues Peak and Hallett (Rowe) Glacier before circling back toward Specimen Mountain, and covering the area around Odessa Gorge. A second search party left Grand Lake the following morning to cover the area eastward. It included four men hired by the Denver Rotary Club—in response to an appeal from the Austin, Texas, Rotary, where Sampson had been an active member. Also in this party were Roland G. Parvin and M. E. Rowley of Denver's Metropole Hotel, who were determined to "see that nothing was left undone that might lead to trace of the clergyman."

A third party of mountaineers left that same afternoon. It was led by Denverites Morrison Shafroth, son of former Colorado governor (and by now, 1915, U.S. senator) John Shafroth, and George Barnard, secretary of the Colorado Mountain Club and one of its founders. They camped out the night of the 16th by Bear Lake in more than a foot of snow, waiting for daylight so they could search the foot of the Hallett Peak. "The rocks of this pinnacle [Hallett Peak]," the *Dallas Morning News* reported two days later, "are broken and loose. It is feared that Dr. Sampson climbed Mount Hallett, put his weight upon a loose rock and was cast over the precipice. Mountaineers in Estes Park recall that in precisely a similar manner William [*sic*] Levings, a young Chicagoan, lost his life a few years ago." That reference was to Louis Raymond Levings, who in 1905 had lost his life attempting to photograph a snow cornice on Mount Ypsilon. The same issue of the *News* reprinted a photograph of Lake Odessa with a crude handwritten arrow pointing toward the Flattop trail over the Divide.

By September 18, some fifty people, including many of Estes Park's leading citizens, were involved in the search. Spurred by a $500 reward offered by Ella Sampson for finding her husband dead or alive, *The Denver Post* reported that "Every man who can be spared from work in the stores, hotels and garages in the little town of Estes Park is hurrying off on snowshoes into the mountains to join the search for the body of Thornton R. Sampson."

Of all those offering opinions to the newspapers, perhaps the most compelling came from veteran mountaineer Shep Husted, who, with perhaps the exception of Enos Mills, knew the mountains of Estes Park better than any other individual. Having scoured the deep snows of the Odessa Gorge area, Husted told the *Rocky Mountain News* on September 16 that "he would stake his reputation as a guide upon his belief that the lifeless body of the Reverend Thornton R. Sampson...lies at the bottom of Odessa Lake Gorge, hidden from view by a thick coverlet of snow." "The guide bases his calculation," the *News* writer continued, "upon a three-day search of the region, coyote tracks in the snow and other marks and indications that are nothing to [the] untrained eye, but speak volumes to the mountaineer."

By September 14, Frank Sampson, Thornton and Ella Sampson's only son, a civil engineer living in Orange, Texas, had arrived in Denver to participate in the search. He was soon joined by his brother-in-law, the Reverend E. T. Drake, pastor of the Luther Memorial Church in Orange. The Reverend R. E. Vinson, president of Austin Theological Seminary, was dispatched by the seminary's trustees to aid in the search for their former leader, even though it meant delaying the opening of the school year.

Frank Sampson became the family's spokesperson, and it was from his conversations with the press that the minister's supposed connection with President Woodrow Wilson first surfaced. Within days, the Wilson-Sampson relationship was being reported nationwide as fact: "President Wilson, a close friend and former schoolmate of the Rev. Thornton R. Sampson," the *New York Times* told its readers on September 18, "has requested all government officials in Colorado who might be of assistance to join in the search." This much-repeated connection between Sampson and Woodrow Wilson seemed to rest on the fact that the paths of the fathers of both men had briefly crossed in Hampden-Sidney, Virginia. That Sampson and the President were "schoolmates," much less "close friends," has no apparent basis in fact. If Thornton Sampson and Woodrow Wilson knew one another, it was as very young children.

Giving plausibility to the assertion, however, was the younger Sampson's willingness to produce for the press the telegram he had sent to Agriculture Secretary David F. Houston, his father's former neighbor in Austin: "Father lost in National Park between Grand Lake and Estes Park. Four days' futile search by scouts. Please notify Attorney General [Thomas Watt] Gregory and Postmaster General [Albert S.] Burleson. I go to Estes Park tonight. Will keep in touch with Assistant District Forester [Fred] Morrell." This telegram found its way into a number of newspaper stories, including one by the *Washington Post* on September 17. Strengthening the rumored connection was the telegraphed response, received within days, from Attorney General Gregory: "Am greatly distressed over the news regarding your father. Please advise me by wire if I can be of any assistance."

On September 18, as a report from Fort Collins, published in the *Dallas Evening Journal*, noted: "Twenty Government Forest Rangers left for Estes Park…under orders not to return until they found the Rev. T. R. Sampson." This party, which had been ordered into the field by Houston through Fred Morrell, was divided into four groups of five rangers each, given enough food for five days, and was ordered to rendezvous and report at Estes Park on September 22. Though Frank Sampson, Morrell, and members of the Denver Rotary Club temporarily joined this new search party, the probability was widely shared that Sampson was dead by now. Even the family seemed resigned to the outcome. "No news," Ella Sampson telegraphed a friend in Austin before her son's arrival in Denver. "Sheriff and posse searching. Frank coming. Almost hopeless." Frank echoed his mother's resignation: "Father loved the mountains. He said he communed with the highest things while alone in the depths of wild, rugged country. And if father's time had been allotted, what more could he have asked than to have stood alone with his Maker on the top of the peak and gave [*sic*] his tired spirit to Him who had alone guided him in the night of snow, cold, and peril?"

The rangers and their pack horses returned to Estes Park on September 22. The *Rocky Mountain News* reported that one group, led by Forest Service supervisor Herbert N. Wheeler, had made base camp at the shelter cabin on the Flattop Trail, where Sampson was last seen, and from there spent three days traversing the Continental Divide, north and south, "searching the canon heads and gorge walls which form the precipitous east side of the divide in the Estes Park region…Flattop, Hallett, Notchtop and other peaks of the region." Other groups searched the gorges on the north and south sides of the Estes Park–Grand Lake trail. Dr. Roy Wiest, Estes Park's resident physician, even allowed himself to be lowered by rope into various crevasses on Tyndall Glacier.

Part of the problem facing the searchers, as a subsequent Rocky Mountain National Park historian, William C. Ramaley, has noted—echoing the assertion made by Herbert Wheeler in October 1915—was the condition of Flattop itself, which was literally covered with cairns of one sort or another. "It seemed that almost every visitor must have added one of his own. Thus, this gentle mountain top was turned into a trap for the unwary if the weather was the least foggy, or snowy. Even experienced guides could lose their way in bad weather."

There were clues. Based on fire remnants found on the concrete floor of the shelter cabin, there was speculation that Sampson had spent the night there. On September 24, the *Longmont Call*'s Estes Park correspondent reported that there was evidence that Sampson had roasted some small animal by the fire, and that a piece of coarse brown paper was discovered nearby with the name "Sampson" clearly written, and with other indiscernible pencil marks. The note, the *Call* surmised, "would apparently indicate that the missing clergyman had realized he was lost, and having made a vain effort to leave intelligence of his intensions, had sought shelter from the icy blasts which at this time of year frequently sweep over Flat Top [*sic*] mountain."

Some days earlier, Shep Husted, Sam Service, and John Malmberg of Estes Park had located the ashes of another campfire, this one on the East Slope of the Divide. The fire site was, the *Rocky Mountain News* reported, "in a region into which Dr. Sampson would have gone to get to Odessa and Fern lakes, his destination by a short cut." The site, labeled "quite fresh," was on Mill Creek below timberline and at a place where it was supposed that Sampson could reach without being able to complete his journey into the park. At the fire there was a stick which had been whittled as for toasting a piece of bread, and nearby was a stick of pine whittled as if to get shavings to start a fire. Even more tantalizing was a bit of burned writing paper, also found on Mill Creek. Only one word on the paper was distinguishable— the initial 'Dr.' Interestingly enough, in reporting these facts and conjectures it apparently occurred to no one that if Sampson were trapped by mountain snows on Mill Creek, he could easily have found nearby shelter and refuge at the Mill Creek Ranger Station.

By September 23, although three rangers still remained in the field, the search for Thornton Sampson was virtually abandoned. Three days later, Ella Sampson was back in Austin.

Just then, however, the search was momentarily revived. Newspapers in Fort Collins and Loveland reported that Estes Park grocer Sam Service received in the mail a letter "from the southern part of the state." The author was an anonymous spiritualist who reported "that he saw in a vision the exact spot where the body of the Rev. Thornton Sampson lay and describing in detail the circumstances of the minister's death...." The site, interestingly enough given the earlier discovery, was Mill Creek, and though local residents were, according to the *Loveland Reporter*, "somewhat skeptical as to the mysterious letter having much value, many of them believing the writer to be some crank," they were also determined "to leave no stone unturned to trace the missing man." The search was made by a small party, but without success. As the *Fort Collins Morning Express* concluded with a hint of disdain on September 29, "the unknown author of the letter evidently misunderstood the angel which he declared appeared to him in a dream concerning the exact location of the body, for the directions given failed to reveal the body of the Texas clergyman at the point where the writer said it would be found."

On October 3, a memorial service was held in Austin for the Reverend Sampson. The *Austin Statesman and Tribune* wrote that it was "attended by as many people as could crowd into the University Presbyterian Church" at Highland, where Sampson and his family regularly worshipped. Included among the mourners were "the most prominent people of the city." Principal speakers were Dr. R. E. Vinson, president of the Austin Presbyterian Seminary, and Pat N. Neff of Waco, head of the Texas Conference for Education. Resolutions passed by the seminary's faculty and students were also read.

Frank Sampson was not in attendance. The day before, he had been summoned back to Colorado by a discovery splashed across the pages of Denver's major newspapers. The *Denver Post*, with its typical penchant for sensationalism, summarized that matter graphically: "Animal-Gnawed Skeleton Found In Hills and Is Believed That of Lost Educator." An unidentified body, the story reported, had been found by a stockman from Steamboat Springs while rounding up cattle on Little Rock Creek, twenty-two miles east of Yampa, Colorado, some forty miles west of the search area. The partially eaten corpse had a gray moustache, as did Thornton Sampson.

The *Rocky Mountain News* made even more of the story, giving it front-page attention and bold headlines: "Routt Ranger Finds Body Thought Sampson's/Disappearance of Minister May Be Solved." The story said: "The body of a man, battered by wind and snow, torn by wild beasts—which is thought to be that of the Rev. Thornton R. Sampson of Austin, Texas, was found yesterday.... The body bears many resemblances to the description of the missing minister." While the details reported were basically the same, the *News* added color and plausibility by interviewing Shep Husted, Cliff Higby, and George Barnard, three of the mountaineers who had participated in the original search for the missing minister, and Enos Mills, now back from the San Juan Mountains of southwest Colorado where he had been promoting yet another national park for Colorado. Husted was the most circumspect of those quoted, asserting once again his conviction that Sampson had perished somewhere in the depths of Odessa Gorge. He did allow, however, that "it would have been possible for Dr. Sampson to have wandered to Routt County." Higby, one of the last to see Sampson alive, was far more positive. Without offering any explanation, he volunteered the conclusion that "the body found was that of the clergyman."

The *News* did somewhat better in supporting its hypothesis in its follow-up story the next day: "Mountain guides have said it would have become possible for the educator to have become lost, wandered around aimlessly, struck the wrong trail or have become demented thru exposure and hunger, walked back over a trail he had made from Steamboat Springs to Grand Lake." The residents of Estes Park, however, remained skeptical, logically pointing out that the area in Routt County was some of the wildest territory in the Rocky Mountains, "and [lay] in a direction which no sane man would be likely to take, even if he was completely lost.... Dr Sampson was altogether too good a mountaineer to head for Routt county when he wanted to get into the Estes Park country for the national park dedication."

The story and its premise quickly evaporated. While the body in Routt County was so decomposed that the younger Sampson was unable to make a positive identification, Frank did tell the authorities that on the basis of the corpse's missing teeth, plus the fact that it seemed older and grayer than his father, and that his father had a missing nail on his left thumb, it seemed unlikely that the Reverend Sampson had been found.

Not content to let interesting hypotheses fade away, the *Denver Post* was back three weeks later with a new theory and an even more sensational story. "Dr. T. R. Sampson Murdered by Hermit in Hills Above Estes, Is New Theory," screamed the headlines on October 18. This conjecture had as its source none other than acting park supervisor Charles R. Trowbridge, who the *Post* reported had told his superiors in the Department of the Interior that Sampson had been accompanied on his trip into the mountains by a "queer stranger." Forest Service officials, the story continued, "have learned there was an insane man in the mountains near Estes Park about the time the Texas minister disappeared." Trowbridge, the report said, had learned from Ella Sampson that her husband had written in his letter that "he had taken for a companion on his walking trip into the mountains a decidedly queer man whom he had met along the way." The "queer companion" was never identified, and unless the individual alluded to was the man named Stevens of whom Sampson had written his wife from Rand, the story seems to have been largely fabricated.

This did not, however, stop the *Post* from concluding that Sampson's body was at the "bottom of some prospect hole along the heights of the Continental Divide west of Estes Park." Ending the convoluted story was what was purported to be a direct quote from Trowbridge's letter to Washington: "I can hardly conceive that a man experienced in mountain climbing, as I understand Dr. Sampson was, could be lost. He had been several times thru this range, altho not over this identical trail. No one has been able to find out who the minister's queer traveling companion was."

There the case of the missing minister came to rest. "The supposition is," Trowbridge wrote in his supervisor's annual report for 1915, "he became bewildered after reaching Flat Top [*sic*] Mountain and was unable to locate the trail. It is also possible that Dr. Sampson may have been struck by lightning or may have had an attack of heart failure." In an attempt to prevent further such accidents, Trowbridge "rearranged" the cairns on the Flattop trail, placing them some 200 feet apart, and removed numerous others which could confuse and mislead the unwary. Trowbridge reported at year's end that he intended, "to paint them [the cairns] white with a black circle about one foot from the top."

The following April, Shep Husted was contacted by Frank Sampson who told him "to begin negotiations for hire and equipment of as many men as he considered necessary to go into the mountains as soon as the snow begins to melt on the heights." Such a search, if indeed it was ever initiated, was fruitless.

And there the matter rested for sixteen more years, until July 9, 1932. That afternoon, Meldrum Loucks, a young man from Fort Collins and member of a trail reconnaissance crew, came across human skeletal remains at the base of a cliff at the foot of Odessa Gorge. The left leg clearly showed a shinbone fracture. The upper part of the skeleton was encased in what had been a raincoat. Nearby in a cave-like rock overhang was found a knapsack containing a pipe, leather puttees, a can of tobacco, matches, English-made fishing flies, toilet articles, a few coins, a tattered railroad timetable, a watch (still capable of keeping perfect time), and a frayed diary, the handwriting still legible despite years of exposure. The Reverend Thornton R. Sampson had at last been found.

The diary was of particular interest, for it recorded Sampson's itinerary following his August departure from Denver, as he made his way through Teller City to Squeaky Bob Wheeler's place on the Colorado, where he dutifully noted his expenditures. It also revealed, for the first time, that Sampson had been "slightly indisposed" during the preceding week, suggesting that his trip to Estes Park had begun at Wheeler's and not at Grand Lake. The story of the long-lost minister's journey was now clear enough. He had indeed reached the summit of Flattop Mountain, and then continued on, correctly, to the top of Odessa Gorge, which he needed to descend in order to reach his destination at Fern Lake Lodge. As sunset approached and snow began to fall, travel became treacherous. Lost and confused, perhaps still suffering the effects of his "indisposition," Sampson slipped and fell, breaking his leg. Though he found shelter and perhaps even managed a fire that night, the combination of wet clothes and falling temperatures on a cold September night proved fatal. Thornton R. Sampson fell asleep and did not awaken.

The discovery of the minister was reported across the nation, with the repeated comment that he had been "a close friend of President Wilson." Frank Sampson was called back to the mountains of Estes Park to identify a body. The photograph taken during Sampson's visit at Squeaky Bob's resort was brought forth by Estes Park resident Clem Yore. It clearly identified the clothing that the minister had with him at the time of his disappearance. Even more telling was the pipe found in the knapsack. It was one that Frank Sampson had carved for his father. Equally poignant was the letter found with the body, whose handwriting the younger Sampson immediately identified as that of his mother.

It was the wish of Ella Sampson, then living with a daughter in Toronto, and the family that Sampson be interred in the mountains close to where he had perished. The spot chosen was some five miles distant from the place the skeleton was discovered, in a tomb carved out of a cliff just beyond the Fern Lake trailhead near Moraine Park. There was little more do to, much less to say. "But for the anxiety his disappearance caused his loved ones," Frank Sampson told the press in Atlanta, his home by that time, "I cannot imagine my father wishing for a more peaceful passing—high in the mountains, from which all his life he had drawn his inspiration."

Soon afterwards, a headstone of sorts, in the form of a board with white lettering against a green background, was installed by the place of interment. Though unfortunately not transcribed until years later, when some of the words had become indistinct, its message was clear:

REV. THORNTON ROGERS SAMPSON DD
1852–1915
MISSIONARY EDUCATOR
A RUGGED MAN OF GOD WHO PASSED AWAY AMID THESE
RUGGED MOUNTAINS THAT HE LOVED SO WELL AND WHICH
INSPIRED HIS MANY ACHIEVEMENTS IN THE WALKS OF MEN
[WORD INDISTINGUISHABLE] AND WHERE IT WAS HIS WANT TO [INDISTINGUISHABLE] FOR CLOSE COMMUNION WITH HIS MAKER.

# 20

## SUPERINTENDENT'S MONTHLY REPORT

1915

*Charles Russell Trowbridge*

*On October 4, 1915, a month to the day after the dedication of Rocky Mountain National Park, Charles Russell Trowbridge (1865–1937), the park's first superintendent (he carried the title Acting Supervisor), filed his initial monthly report with his superiors in Washington, D.C. Trowbridge, a veteran of the Spanish-American War, had been hired in 1913 by the Department of the Interior as an "inspector" to help to watch over its far-flung activities, including the national parks then within its care. He arrived in Estes Park on July 1, 1915, with $3,000 to carry the park through to the end of the fiscal year. Although a lover of the out-of-doors, Trowbridge knew little about park management. He knew even less about the 358-square-mile area for which he now had responsibility.*

*Renting a small white building in the village of Estes Park, which he equipped and opened on July 10, Trowbridge then set out by horseback on a leisurely reconnaissance and inspection of the new park. His long and comprehensive report, parts of which are reprinted here, provide a valuable benchmark against which to measure the changes in the century that followed. That some of the road and trail measurements and the dates provided are inaccurate takes nothing away from its author's attempt to provide his superiors with a full and accurate inventory.*

Sir:

Pursuant to instructions of the Department letter of September 24th, 1915, I make the following report of the affairs of the Rocky Mountain National Park.

## GENERAL STATEMENT

The Rocky Mountain National Park was created on January 26th, 1915, on which date the Act of Congress was approved.... This Park is located in the northern part of Colorado and has an area of 358 1/2 square miles, and includes the principal part of the Rocky Mountain Range, the highest point being Longs Peak which is 14,255 feet, and fourteen mountain peaks that are over 13,000 feet above sea level. The park is accessible to tourists and travelers at numerous points on the eastern and western boundaries, where trails have been in existence for a number of years.

There are two roads within the boundaries of the Park which are accessible from the county roads without passing through private property before entering the park. The most central point from which the public can enter the Park to different points therein, is Estes Park, a small village located about three miles from the nearest point to the Park boundary, and approximately 7 1/2 miles from the main entrance where the Fall River Road enters the Park.

The nearest point from the main entrance to a railroad is 29 1/2 miles. The Supervisors Office for the Park was opened on July 10th, 1915, and located at the village of Estes Park, the nearest points to railroad stations from that place, being Lyons, Colorado, 22 miles, Loveland, 33 miles, Fort Collins, Colo. 46 miles and Boulder 40 miles. Automobile stage lines making regular trips between these points and Estes Park with special rates during the tourist season. I assumed charge of the Rocky Mountain National Park as Acting Supervisor on July 1st, 1915, and was unable to accomplish as much as I desired owing to the fact that I was unassisted, no appointments of employees being made until August 10th, when one ranger was appointed, consequently there has been little progress made this season, toward improvements in the Park.

## ROADS

*Fall River Road*

The Fall River Road, which was constructed with State convict labor in 1913, before the National Park was created was built to a point about two miles within the Park boundary. Construction of this road is now being continued to a point three miles distant from where the convict work ended. This work is being done under contract by the State of Colorado at a cost of $18,000, $2,500 of which is to be paid by the Department of the Interior. The contractor commenced under the present contract, on July 2nd, 1915, and expects to complete the work by November 1st of this year. This road when completed will terminate at the junction of the County road, about 9 miles north of Grand Lake, a distance of approximately 19 1/2 miles within the Park boundary and will reach the highest point, when crossing the Continental Divide at about 11,300 feet above sea level.

That part of the Fall River Road which was built by convict labor is in fair condition and requires repairs at certain points. It is entirely too narrow, in some places being only 8 and 10 feet in width. The point known as the second "switch back" which is reached by a 12% grade, was not sufficiently wide for the average vehicle to change direction without "see saw" movement which made the point extremely dangerous, there being no protection to prevent a vehicle from going over the embankment. This defect has been remedied by cutting into the bank, a distance of 8 feet, thereby enabling a large automobile to make the turn. Contract has been let for the construction of a stone retaining wall at this point and when completed all chances of accidents at this point will be eliminated. At the time of building the "convict road" no culverts were constructed and this is necessary at points 400 feet apart where the grade is 5% or more. These culverts should be installed as soon as possible in the spring of 1916, and the gutters opened up. The county road extending into the Park on private holdings is in bad condition. A survey of the balance of the Fall River Road should be made, before any further steps are taken to continue the construction. The survey which was made in 1912, was a preliminary survey only.

### Road to Sprague's

There is a roadway entering the Park running parallel to Glacier Creek approximately 1 1/2 miles in length which was constructed by Mr. A. E. Sprague at his own expense. Access to this road is through private property. The road is in fair condition and an expenditure of $100.00 would improve it considerably.

### Road to Bear Lake

Continuing from Sprague's resort in a westerly direction and extending to within one mile of Bear Lake is a roadway, 2 miles in length, in poor condition. At an expenditure of about $300.00 this roadway could be made passable for automobiles, if a log bridge was constructed across Glacier Creek in close proximity to Sprague's resort.

### Copeland Lake Road

There is a roadway entering the Park near Copeland Laker and extending a distance of approximately 1 1/2 miles. The road is in poor condition and was built by the Arbuckle Supply & Reservoir Co., and is passable for horse-drawn vehicles only and leads to a trail to "Wild Basin."

### Road to Mill Creek Ranger Station

This road runs parallel to Mill Creek and extends about 1/2 mile into the Park. The road is in poor condition and in order to enter the Park it is necessary to pass through private lands, over a road which is exceedingly bad. Very few visitors enter the Park at this point except with saddle horses. This road was repaired within the Park at small expense, but unless the road outside the Park were put in proper condition there would be no object to expending any money on the road within the Park at this point. Most of the traffic over this road is by local residents removing fire-wood which is obtained in the vicinity of the Mill Creek Ranger Cabin and known as the "Pole Patch."

### Beaver Creek Road

There is a roadway which starts from the "High Drive" in Horseshoe Park, outside the National Park and crosses the National Park boundary line in Section 19T. 5N, R. 74W and extends for a distance of approximately 1 1/2 miles. This roadway was built to remove timber sometime in 1910 and is in fair condition, but would require considerable expense to put in proper shape for automobiles.

### Grand Lake County Road

A roadway extending approximately 1 3/4 miles within the Park boundary which is part of the Grand Lake Fall River Road has just been completed under the supervision of the county commissioners of Grand County. The expense of the construction of this road was defrayed with State and County funds. The road runs through timber where a 40 foot right-of-way was cut. It is designated a 16 foot roadway but is considerably wider in many places. The grade is less than 1%. It will eventually connect with the Fall River Road which is now under construction. The roadway at the present time ends in Sec. 24T. 54N, R. 76W. The work was performed by day labor. Corrugated iron culverts were used in the construction. There is considerable timber along the right-of-way which should be disposed of in the same manner as was done with the timber on the Fall River Road.

## TRAILS

Most of the interesting part of the National Park can be reached by trail only, which are in fairly good condition, and if the Spring opens sufficiently early in 1916, they can be put in good condition for use of tourists during the summer season. There are approximately 128.5 miles of trails in the Rocky Mountain National Park.

The principal and most widely known trail within the National Park is the one leading from Estes Park to Grand Lake. This trail enters the National Park 6 1/2 miles from Estes Park and crosses the western Park boundary 1/4 mile from Grand Lake, 18 1/4 miles within the National Park. This trail has been cleared of all timber and with some repair work done above timberline will be considered a good trail.

*Grand Lake Trail (via Milner Pass).*
This trail leaves the Fall River Road 12 1/2 miles from Estes Park and crosses the western Park boundary, 12 1/2 miles north of Grand Lake where it joins the county road. Length of trail 11 miles.

*Bierstadt Lake Trail*
Leaves Flat Top Trail near Mill Creek Ranger Station, follows old saw mill road, full distance. Some of trail is in bad shape and in need of repair. Distance from Ranger cabin to Lake 1 mile.

*Bierstadt Lake Trail. (From Glacier Creek)*

From Glacier Creek to Bierstadt Lake starting at the junction of Storm Pass trail. Distance 1 1/2 miles. Built by the Forest Service, in 1914. Trail in good condition.

*Bear Lake Trail*

Joins the Flat Top trail 1 1/2 miles from Bear Lake. In fair condition.

*Bear Lake Trail*

From "Miners cabin" to Bear Lake. Distance 1 mile. Trail in good condition.

*Loch Vale Trail*

From "Miners Cabin" to Loch Vale distance 3 miles. Trail needs repair. Built in 1913 by the Estes Park Improvement Association.

*Storm Pass Trail*

Leads from Glacier Gorge to Storm Pass, distance 4 miles. Built by the Forest Service in 1914. Trail in good condition.

*Trail to summit of Longs Peak*

Trail enters National Park 1 mile above Longs Peak Inn, and leads to the summit of Longs Peak 14,255 feet high. Distance 6 miles. 1 1/2 miles by foot only. Trail needs some repair.

*From Mill Creek Ranger Station to "The Pool"*

Trail passes over "Steep Mountain" from the Ranger Station to the "Pool," a distance of 2 1/2 miles. Trail in fair condition.

*Trail to Fern, Odessa and Helene Lakes*

From Moraine Park past Fern and Odessa terminating at Helene Lake. Distance 6 1/2 miles. A new trail from Fern Lake to Lake Odessa was constructed in the fall of 1914. This trail should be repaired and extended so as to join the Flat Top trail, passing Lake Helene and Two River Lake.

*Lawn Lake Trail*

Leads from Horseshoe Park to Lawn Lake. Distance 6 miles. Needs repair.

*Ypsilon Lake Trail*

Branches from the Lawn Lake Trail 1/2 mile from Horseshoe Park and extends 4 miles to the Lake. In good condition.

*Crystal Lake Trail*

From Lawn Lake to Crystal Lake. Distance about 1 mile. Trail poorly built and needs construction.

*Tombstone Ridge Trail*

From Moraine Park through "Windy Gulch" to Poudre Lakes. A scenic trail but is in poor condition. Distance 15 miles.

*Lost Lake Trail*

Trail follows the north fork of the Big Thompson river to Lost Lake. Distance about 9 miles, from Park boundary line.

*Specimen Mountain Trail*

From Poudre Lakes to "The Crater," on Specimen Mountain. Trail poorly constructed. Needs considerable repair work. Distance 1 1/2 miles.

*Poudre River Trail*

From Pingree Park to the South Fork of the Poudre River and then up the river to its source at Poudre Lakes. Distance about 15 miles. Little work, other than "blazing" has been done on this trail.

*Sand Beach Trail*

From Copeland Lodge to Sand Beach Lake. Distance 6 miles. Trail in good condition.

*Thunder Lake Trail*

From Copeland Lake to Thunder Lake in "Wild Basin." Distance 9 miles. Trail in fair condition.

*Ouzel Lake Trail*

From Copeland Lake to Ouzel Lake and Ouzel Falls. Distance 7 miles. Built by the Forest Service. In good condition....

## ANIMAL LIFE

*Deer*

Owing to the protection under the game laws of the State, deer have been increasing rapidly, there being about 600 in the Park, and surrounding the boundary. They are rarely seen on account of the heavily timbered country.

*Elk*

In 1912, 20 head of elk were shipped from Wyoming and put into the Forest, a part of which is now the National Park. In 1913, 25 more were shipped from the same place. A portion of these animals died, and at present there are approximately 30 elk in the National Park and vicinity.

*Bear*

There are only a few bear in the Park and these are specimens of the "Common Black" bear.

*Sheep*

The Big Horn sheep are found in considerable numbers and some of them are exceptionally tame, tourists having approached within a few yards of them. From what information I have been able to obtain, the increase for the last year has been exceptionally large.

*Wild birds and fowls*

Game birds are scarce within the Park. The Ptarmigan may be found in small numbers on the range above timber-line. Owing to the open season on Grouse in the State of Colorado, they have become nearly extinct in this locality, but under the protection afforded by the Park Rules these birds will increase rapidly.

*Fur-bearing Animals*

To a person wishing to see Beaver at work an exceptional opportunity is afforded to visitors, owing to the fact that the Beaver are plentiful in various localities in the Park. Other fur-bearing animals are few owing to the fact that they have been trapped in past years, prior to the establishment of the National Park.

### Predatory Animals

There are coyotes and mountain lions roaming within the Park and if they increase to any extent, will become a detriment to the preservation of other animals, when action will be necessary looking toward their destruction....

### RANGERS

There are only three rangers provided for this Park at a salary of $900.00 per annum, which salary I do not consider sufficient to attract the right kind of men, for this class of labor. This is an expensive locality to live and by the time a ranger has subsisted himself and his horse, he has little left for his efforts. In my opinion the salaries should be increased to $1200.00 per annum. A chief Ranger is not required for this Park until the number of rangers has been increased to five or more.

There should be a uniform designated for the rangers for summer use and this matter should be decided before the season of 1916. An olive drab uniform such as used by the U.S. Army, leather leggings, and soft, drab felt hat would be desirable.

### RANGER STATIONS

There are four ranger cabins within the Park, and located as follows:

### Mill Creek Ranger Station

Located on Mill Creek 1/2 mile from boundary line and about 7 miles from Estes Park village. Partly furnished. Connected with telephone.

### Fall River Ranger Cabin

Located on the Fall River Road, 5 miles from park boundary line and about 14 1/2 miles from Estes Park village. About 1/2 mile from terminus of present contract of Fall River Road. Partly furnished.

*Shelter cabin. Flat Top trail*

Located on Flat Top trail, 11 miles from Grand Lake and 13 miles from Estes Park. Not furnished.

*Specimen Ranger Cabin*

Located at Poudre Lakes. Located about 3 miles from the western boundary, and ten miles from eastern boundary line by trail. 19 1/2 miles from Estes Park village. Not furnished.

## CONCESSIONS

No concessions have been granted other than the continuation of the permits for hotels and resorts issued by the Forest Service prior to the creation of the Park.

There are six resorts within the Park boundary as follows:

Summer Hotel and resort at Fern Lake. Higby Bros. permittees. Permit expires December 31st, 1915. Rate per annum $15.00.

Summer Hotel and Camp, at "The Pool." Higby Bros. permittees. Permit expires December 31st, 1915. Rate per annum $10.00.

Summer Hotel building and Fish Preserve, at Bartholf Park. A. E. Sprague, permittee. Permit expires December 31st, 1915. Rate per annum $15.00.

Summer camping grounds at Lawn Lake. Willard H. Ashton, permittee. Permit expires December 31st, 1915. Rate per annum $15.00.

Shelter cabin, at timber-line, Longs Peak. Enos Mills, permittee. Permit expires December 31st, 1915. Rate per annum $15.00.

Summer camping grounds at Bear Lake. E. A. Brown, permittee. Permit expires December 31st, 1915. Rate per annum $15.00.

In my opinion the rates heretofore made by the Forest Service for permits for resorts are entirely too small.

## RESERVOIRS

There are a number of irrigating ditches and reservoirs located in the Park, title to which is in the name of private parties and corporations. This matter will be investigated at first opportunity and report made thereon....

## MINERAL CLAIMS

There are several so-called Mineral Claims within the Park and this matter is now under investigation to find whether or not the claims are valid....

## TRANSPORTATION

There is no transportation furnished this office and it has been necessary to hire an automobile on numerous occasions to make trips to certain points of the Park which are accessible. Had there been available transportation no doubt more frequent trips would have been made, and it might be advisable to consider the purchase of an automobile to be used in connection with the administration of this office.

## CASUALTIES

During the month of August, Bertha Herbaugh of Highland, Ill. Dislocated her elbow on the trail to Fern Lake. Proper action was taken at the time, consequently the affair was not serious.

On September 2nd, 1915, Dr. Thornton R. Sampson of Austin, Texas, left Grand Lake with the intention of going to Estes Park and was last seen on the Flat Top trail about two miles from Grand Lake by a licensed guide. On notification of his disappearance September 14th, prompt action was taken to locate his where-abouts and volunteer searching parties were organized, assisted by Forest Service rangers and Park rangers, but without result. The supposition is that he became bewildered after reaching Flat Top Mountain and was unable to locate the trail. It is also possible that Dr. Sampson may have been struck by lightning or may have had an attack of heart failure.

Since the disappearance of Dr. Sampson the line of cairns which distinguish the trail across Flat Top mountain have been rearranged and numerous other cairns which were in existence have been destroyed. The cairns at the present time were arranged about 200 feet apart and it is the intention to paint them white with a black circle about one foot from the top....

## RECOMMENDATIONS

I herewith submit the following recommendations:

That this office should have the services of a clerk and stenographer at a salary of nine hundred dollars per annum.

That a two seated automobile be purchased for the use of this office.

That the salaries of Rangers be increased to $1,200 per annum.

That the force of rangers be increased to four for the present.

That the legislation be recommended for an appropriation of $50,000 for the continuation of Fall River Road.

That a shelter station be constructed on the eastern slope of Flat Top Mountain.

That the following new trails be constructed, if an appropriation is made sufficiently large for this purpose:

Trail on Tombstone Ridge. Terminating at Poudre Lakes. Distance 15 miles.

Trail from Lake Helene to Flat Top Mtn. Distance 1 1/4 miles.

Trail from Odessa Lake to Lake Helene. Distance 1 1/4 miles.

Trail from Fern Lake to Hour Glass Lake via Sprague Lake. Distance 3 miles.

A trail from "The Pool" through Forest Canyon to Poudre Lakes. Distance 15 miles. This trail would pass through the best timbered region in the National Park.

A trail to Mills Lake and Glacier Gorge. Distance about 3 miles.

A trail from Fall River Ranger Cabin to the northern boundary of the Park at a point where the Poudre River crosses the boundary line. Distance about 5 miles.

Foot trail to Chasm Lake, located at the head of "East Gorge" of Longs Peak.

Note: The average cost of trails in this locality is approximately $150.00 per mile.

> Very respectfully,
> C. R. Trowbridge [signed]
> Acting Supervisor

# 21

## SQUEAKY BOB WHEELER AND HOTEL DE HARDSCRABBLE

*Clark Secrest*

*The former editor of* Colorado Heritage *writes about Squeaky Bob Wheeler's guest resort on the Colorado River. Before and after Thornton Sampson's visit, Camp Wheeler was a popular destination for fishermen and hunters and for those using the nearby trail linking Grand Lake and the Kawuneeche Valley with Estes Park. Today the open clearing where Squeaky Bob's once stood is little more than a convenient place to stop for those hiking the Colorado River trail on their way to the site of Lulu City.*

When the Rocky Mountain National Park was formed in January 1915, a provision allowed private property owners within the new park to retain their land. One such person was Robert Lincoln Wheeler, whose mountain camp north of Grand Lake was among the final locations at which the Reverend Thornton Sampson, subject of the adjacent article, was seen alive. Wheeler was one of Colorado's legendary characters at the turn of the nineteenth century.

Born in 1865, Wheeler—who said he was a cousin of the famed Confederate General "Fighting Joe" Wheeler of the Civil War—moved to Colorado from Michigan at age twenty to work on his brother Luke's ranch in North Park. When he stepped off the train at Fort Collins, he was wearing a tight-fitting striped suit, tan spats, buttoned shoes, long frock coat, kid gloves, and a tall silk hat. The sheriff loaned him a horse to ride the 130 miles to Luke's place, but Bob did not change clothes for the trip.

At Luke's, Bob's dandified way branded him as an eastern "dude" who now became the target of the other cowhands' teasing and practical jokes.

One day in the milkhouse, Bob wearied of being teased about his voice, his small stature, and his traveling wardrobe, and got into a fistfight with two of his tormentors. He prevailed, but by now was fed up with North Park, with the ranch, with the ranch hands, with Colorado, and with the entire West. Luke gave Bob "a couple of horses, a good gun, four head of cattle, and a good-bye." After a few days to himself, thinking it over in the woods, Bob returned to Luke's place and they became ranching partners.

As a lad, Wheeler had incurred the bronchitis attack which produced a distinct "squeak" in his voice, and which persisted for the rest of his life.

Barely noticeable in normal conversation, the squeak got higher and higher as Wheeler raised his voice, which he did often, usually in the course of issuing forth a marvelous stream of profound profanity or a tall tale. It was considered unfriendly on the rugged frontier to nickname a man by a deformity, his unusual behavior, or his strange characteristics, but Wheeler thoroughly approved of being called Squeaky Bob. In later life, he would even sign his checks that way.

In 1898, Squeaky Bob went away to the Spanish-American War, although he never got beyond Jacksonville, Florida. Upon discharge, he returned to Colorado and homesteaded 160 acres at the base of Milner Pass, fourteen miles north of Grand Lake on the bumpy trail over the top of Estes Park. There, he lived a solitary life hunting, fishing, sinking prospect holes, enjoying nature, and occasionally putting up a passing traveler. He named his spread "Camp Wheeler," also known as *Hotel de Hardscrabble*, or especially, as Squeaky Bob's Place.

Initially, Squeaky Bob's consisted solely of his two-room cabin, which had a hard-packed dirt floor covered with bear, deer, and elk robes which lasted for years and were warm and soft as a fancy carpet. Bob piled sod on the roof and eventually grass and flowers grew all over the top. He boasted of owning the first "roof garden" in Colorado. Squeaky Bob did not long have the place all to himself, however. Because it was on the trail between Grand Lake and Estes Park, this became a convenient roadhouse for travelers. In about 1908, Bob built a couple of framed tents to accommodate those staying overnight, and continued to turn out marvelous meals of elk, deer, bear, and sage chicken. Squeaky Bob Wheeler and his bulldog Jack became known as far away as Denver. (Some said that Jack, who could go up and down a ladder like a fireman, was more famous than was Bob.)

As Squeaky Bob's popularity spread, he added tents—eventually there were twenty of them—each one on a platform two feet above ground and furnished with cots and chairs. He had discovered that some city folk from back East had never slept in a tent, and enjoyed it a great deal. Bob issued a brochure which read:

> This is the natural and only stopping place between Horse Shoe Inn in Estes Park and Grand Lake. The landlord, Squeaky Bob Wheeler, aims to host, cook and companion to his tired guests who often sit in the kitchen-dining room and watch him prepare the meals, whetting their appetites and cracking jokes at the same time. Here you may actually eat wild strawberry shortcake and trout just pulled from the stream.

Increasing numbers of customers (including Teddy Roosevelt and wealthy noblemen from Europe) journeyed to visit Bob, stay awhile, and enjoy his wonderful meals. Bob's charges were five to six dollars a day, room and board—a sizable sum at the time. Squeaky Bob's evolved into a desti-nation all its own, and became known, literally, worldwide. Carrie Leimer Vote recalled her 1909 trip to visit Squeaky Bob:

> We had heard a prospector some seventeen [sic] miles away [from Grand Lake], whose name had been swallowed up by the sobri-quet of "Squeaky Bob," and to his place we drove one drizzly morning. Over a road, we trotted along, that was never meant for civilized folks. Huge boulders paved the way, upon which the wheels struck with unabated force, and each time we arose in the air we came down in a new place, but this only served to accen-tuate the glory of the road when we came upon a level spot. Out into the open, where we had a view of the river which had its course changed by the busy beavers, who were then preparing for the winter. At last, when we had given up all hope of ever seeing a human habitation again, we came upon the two-room cabin of

"Squeaky Bob." He was away fishing. His door being hospitably [left] open, we took possession.

"Well," said [traveling companion] Flo, "home was never like this." The interior was as white as soap and water could make it, the ceilings and walls covered with white canvas, the cupboards and table with white oil cloth—the dishes fairly shone.

Our host appeared and was overjoyed to see us. He immediately, as all good housekeepers should do, began to prepare a meal.... Our host dished up a meal that would make an ordinary woman green with envy. While we ate, he talked about his mines, and his voice kept growing higher and higher as he talked about his wonderful properties on the opposite hills.

The house rules were posted in each tent: "Blow your nose and clean your shoes. Use all the grub you need and leave things as you find them." Each tent cabin, people said, "was as clean as your grandmother's kitchen." Soon Bob was making a good living, despite the shortness of the season.

Bob had fun with his guests. A young woman from back East wanted so earnestly to catch a trout that Bob took her to a place where fishing was foolproof. When she caught a six-inch fish, she came running to proudly show it to Bob. Just then, the game warden happened by and told the woman that if the fish weren't seven inches, it would have to be thrown back. Bob told the warden to mind his own business, explaining to the puzzled woman that the man was a harmless maniac wandering the mountains. Others in the fishing party, meanwhile, told the warden that Bob was a desperado who already had killed four men in Wyoming, and that the warden was lucky to be alive. The warden was so frightened that he packed up and departed in the middle of the night.

No woman could keep house to suit Squeaky Bob, but after fifty years a bachelor, in 1915 he married one of his housekeepers, Allie Farquher Corbley. Bob and Allie honeymooned all winter long in their little log cabin in the pines, accepting no guests. She ran a trap line for marten, fox, and bobcat, and Bob measured snow for the government—fifty-three feet before spring.

Squeaky Bob contracted a "leaky heart" in 1926, sold out for $24,000, and he and Allie moved to Denver, where she died in 1933. He lived alone in an apartment at 1851 Logan Street, sadly reflecting: "I'm in the winter of my life now, and, like the sheep, I had to come down from the high country." Gazing upward toward Longs Peak, he wrote: "If one could only stop thinking back, it would help. Oh, I always love the hills and the trees and the streams...."

Squeaky Bob Wheeler died in Denver on January 28, 1945, and was buried beside Allie in Crown Hill Cemetery. Squeaky Bob's Place became the site of the Phantom Valley Ranch, and today has reverted to meadowland, near the trailhead up the headwaters of the Colorado River to the remains of Lulu City, Dutchtown, and Teller City—where Squeaky Bob hiked and fished, and communed with nature.

# 22

# THE TOURIST ON THE TRAIL

## 1916

*Julia Ann Prouty*

*In 1902 Abner Sprague took on James D. Stead as partner in his guest ranch in Moraine Park. Stead's wife, Dora, was Abner's cousin. This arrangement did not last. The two wives, it was said, could not get along, and two years later, in 1904, Sprague sold his interest for $25,000, temporarily exiting the resort business. The new owner changed the name to Stead's Ranch and Hotel and began to significantly enlarge its operations. Two of those who helped were Julia Ann Prouty (1857–1924) and her husband, Fred.*

*The Proutys, who first came from Chicago as guests in 1903, became fixtures at Steads. Fred helped J.D. with his herd of cattle while Julia ran the popular Pine Log Inn, built by Stead on ranch property. A July 1914 advertisement reads: "Prouty's Pine Log Inn. Hot and cold lunches, ice cream, cold drinks, everything for tourists. Moraine Park, Colorado."*

*Julia was a member of the Estes Park Woman's Club. In 1916, when the club decided to raise money for a local library by putting together a small book titled* Little Nature Studies of Estes Park, *Julia contributed an essay titled "Tourists on the Trail," good-naturedly poking fun at both herself and her tourist visitors.*

The tourist is a traveler, and is divided into many classes, being represented by all nations of the world.

A trail is generally a crooked, rocky, narrow strip of land formerly a calf path but always leading somewhere and in it one very often finds mud, water and much fallen timber. No doubt you will find this paper as crooked and disjointed as said trail.

Prouty's Pine Log Inn was established to supply the outer and inner wants of the tourist; also to replenish the money drawer of the firm. Therefore the above subject is probably far more interesting to me than I can make it appear to others.

Mr. Abner Sprague claims to be the first tourist in Moraine Park, coming in 1868 on horseback mostly making his own trail.

The first of September, 1903, Mr. Prouty and myself came to Moraine Park as tourists and guests of Mr. and Mrs. J. D. Stead. Almost immediately a trip was planned to Andrew's Glacier via Lochvale. Let me say right here that in "seeing America first" no more beautiful region could possibly be seen.

Each of us was supplied with a fine saddle horse fully equipped with everything necessary for a four days' journey; and all suitably dressed for same, for Mr. Stead had informed us beforehand just what to bring and I can assure you that no superfluous article was included in the packs. And also, no more tenderfooted tourist ever left the ranch than yours truly!

Our first day was certainly ideal in every respect, but I can truthfully affirm that I discovered the first gray hair the following morning after fording the swollen, rushing stream known as the South Fork of the Big Thompson. At picturesque Alberta Falls we ate our lunch, fed and rested our tired horses and aided the digestion of our lunch by rolling immense boulders into the falls below. The force of the mighty water carried them far below as tho they were mere pebbles.

We reached camp at the lake with the sun still shining, and giving us ample time to pick balsam for our sleeping bags and also to pack wood for the camp fire.

The next day we explored all the different peaks and lakes in the vicinity of our camp. The second day we packed lunch and hit the trail for the glacier, reaching the most beautiful spot just as the snow began to fall—the beginning of the September line storm. We started for camp with many regrets at leaving the glacier so hurriedly, but soon found we were wise, for by the time we reached camp we were in the midst of a severe range storm. We had tired, wet feet and a genuine, mountainous appetite. But we soon satisfied that after much labor (which further aggravated said appetite!)

procuring dry wood for our camp fire. The snow kept falling and hissing into our hot skillet but never before or since has a meal tasted so good as that one cooked in the snowstorm. I will not give you our menu for maybe it was out of season for said grouse and Mr. Thompson[1] might hear of it. Soon after our bounteous repast we sought comfort in our sleeping bags, and not one of us gave the storm outside a passing thot [*sic*].

Early the next morning we woke to find the ground covered with snow six or eight inches deep and fog so thick we were several hours locating our faithful horses. Mr. Stead remarked as soon as he saw the fog, "It's us for the home trail as soon as possible for this is likely to get pretty serious." We let the horses take their own time to pick the way on the trail as best they could. I want to speak a few words about the value of these sure-footed little mountain ponies to the tourist on the trail. Without them, many tourists, especially tenderfeet, would never return. To prove this, when we had gone about two miles we came to a fork in the trail and each trail seemed equally indistinct. Mr. Stead, being in the lead, took the straight one. I was last of the four and my horse, Freckles (being so named on account of her brown spots and white body) absolutely refused to pass the fork in the trail. I coaxed with all the endearing words I could think of, then called to the others, who were by this time quite a distance ahead, that Freckles wouldn't budge. Mr. Stead said quite impatiently, "Oh! Make her! Hit her with your heels." I did so but she paid no attention whatever, only looked wistfully up the other trail. So I called again and said, "Freckles says this is the right trail and you better follow me." And they did and she soon showed us fresh blazes on the trail and proved she could see best even in the fog.

We had no further trouble outside of the severe cold and dampness. However, when we got home a party was coming in search of us.

Business soon called us to our city home but in the days that followed the sound of the wind, even tho coming from beautiful Lake Michigan, seemed but the echo of the pines on the trail. So in just one year from the day we left Moraine Park as tourists we returned as permanent citizens.

Being strictly in business with the tourist, we hear of many curious experiences. We rent riding shirts, slickers, leggings, etc. By the way a slicker is a coat made of heavy cloth and covered with a coating of oil to keep out the wind and rain. The back is cut out in such a manner as to form a skirt on either side of the horse to protect the rider's knees while on horseback.

One morning quite a party came from the hotel to be fitted out for a trip to Odessa Lake. All went well with them on the trail till the return trip. Then at the rockiest possible spot near the Pool[2] a maiden lady of uncertain age, knowing there were two nice looking young men in the party, took advantage to faint—made a feint of fainting, in other words. Two slickers were immediately constructed into a carrier and so she was brot [sic] down to the wagon road, from there a messenger was dispatched to Stead's for a rig. We learned the next morning that she ate a hearty breakfast but the two young men bought bandages and liniments for lame arms before retiring that night.

When the slickers were returned one was minus an arm, a collar, etc. Both skirts of the others were torn as far as the neck. The parties were horrified when asked to pay damages, thinking, I expect, that we ought to be satisfied since they had been torn saving a tourist's life.

This same young maiden lady, this last summer, was being urged by an entirely different party to join them in climbing the Peak. She came to us and said, "Would you advise me to climb Long's Peak?" I said, "Well, no, I wouldn't, if you remember your experience of four years ago." She didn't climb.

Last season a fair young lady from the Brinwood [Hotel] was out with quite a party horse-back riding. The trail was very rocky and quite narrow. There was a tree near the path with branches very low. This lady did not notice an old dead branch, so her hair caught and held her suspended in mid-air as her horse sped on with the rest of the party. No harm done—only a much disordered coiffure!

The tourist on the trail! Since the day of the auto the specie has changed from that of the days of the horse. Then they dressed appropriately—now, very often an auto will stop for supplies, the ladies in light voile dresses and wearing French-heeled slippers and ask the following questions:

How far can we go with the machine?
Is that almost to the Pool?

Do we have much climbing to do?
Do we have to climb any beyond the Pool?

We always answer truthfully, for we realize that, like the cat, they may come back.

The genuine tourist and the tenderfoot differ widely in their selection of things to purchase for a camping trip. The former will rent a slicker, buy two bars of Hershey's chocolate and a package of gum. The tenderfoot will order three kinds of sandwiches, deviled eggs, several kinds of fancy cakes, a bottle of olives, a box of bonbons, rent a slicker, buy leggings, gloves, etc.

We truly appreciate the Outdoor Club's[3] advertising winter sports so widely. We realize how many curious questions it will save us answering. In summer time we never show a snow scene or say anything whatever to remind a tourist of winter, for fear of the following questions:

How early do you have to leave in the fall? (Answer).
Why, you don't mean it!
How do you get supplies in?
Do you see anyone at all in the winter?
What would you do if you should get sick?
Do you get mail very often?
Do you dare go far very late in the afternoon?
Why? Why because of the wild beasts!

When we answer truthfully he or she will look at us in such surprised and unbelieving manner that we actually wonder if Estes is as grand in winter as we picture it.

NOTES
1.   Apparently, a local game warden.
2.   The Pool, a swirling, churning bowl of water on the Big Thompson 1.75 miles from the Fern Lake trailhead, has always been a favorite tourist destination.
3.   An organization formed by Estes Park residents in 1915 to promote winter sports.

# 23

## PUBLICIZING THE NEW PARK

### The Eve of Estes, 1917

James H. Pickering

*In the years after 1916, publicizing the nation's parks was high on the agenda of the National Park Service's founding director, Stephen Mather. Keenly aware that annual appropriations depended upon visitor headcount meant it was necessary to generate publicity whenever possible. Much of this activity was assigned to veteran journalist Robert Sterling Yard, who had been personally recruited by Mather to be his publicist. But Mather's superintendents had a role to play as well. They were expected to make themselves available to the local and regional press on a regular basis and to participate in whatever promotional activities Mather and Yard invented. When the opportunity offered, they were also expected to initiate publicity efforts of their own. Louis Claude Way, the second superintendent of Rocky Mountain National Park and a former army captain used to taking orders, understood the Mather strategy, and showed himself more than happy to oblige.*

*Most of Way's encounters with the press were routine and predictable— often to the point of being innocuous. But on one occasion Way made a tactical error in judgment. In agreeing during the summer of 1917 to participate in the publicity scheme involving the so-called "Eve of Estes," inspired and carefully choreographed by Al Birch, assistant city editor of the* Denver Post, *Way soon found himself caught up in an embarrassing situation which quickly spiraled out of control.*

*The story is told in the editor's* America's Switzerland: Estes Park and Rocky Mountain National Park, The Growth Years *(2005).*

The idea of sending an attractive young woman (or man) into the wilderness to live off the land was scarcely original. It had been tried several times in the sedate and civilized East with varying amounts of publicity success, including an episode involving one Joe Knowles, "the Maine woodsman, who went into the wilderness naked and empty-handed, to come forth again two months later—clothed, vigorous and an infinitely finer man physically than when he went in." But Al Birch, a summer resident of Estes Park, saw in the mountains of his own Colorado, where nature was to be taken rather more seriously, the opportunity to grab a few headlines for his paper while helping to publicize the beauty and outdoor opportunities of the new national park. It also promised to provide stay-at-home readers a bit of welcome relief from the rising tide of war news from Europe, whose indignities and horrors the *Post* was adept at reporting.

Just how, or when, Birch approached L. C. Way with the project he had in mind we do not know. What we do know, as Way apparently did not, was that Birch was a consummate stuntsman, who had already made a career out of thinking up and executing outrageous ways to call attention to the *Post* in its on-going circulation battle with the *Rocky Mountain News*— sometimes with unintended consequences. On one occasion Birch managed to release eight "escaped" monkeys onto the coping of the dome of the State Capitol building, with the intention of having them "captured" by the Denver police and fire departments using extension ladders before a big crowd of onlookers, an episode that ended with the cavorting monkeys pelting a delegation come to visit Colorado Governor Elias Ammons with exploding light bulbs unscrewed from the dome's ribs. Though publicizing Rocky Mountain National Park as a Garden of Eden no doubt initially sounded innocent enough, Superintendent Way clearly failed to understand just how far Al Birch and the *Post* were prepared to go in pushing their stunt. In point of fact, in involving himself with a newspaper that operated a circus, fed itself on contests, promotions, and sensational journalism, and whose part-owner was a friend and sometimes business partner of Buffalo Bill, Captain Way was a man in over his head.

The escapade began with the selection of an attractive young woman to play the role of the "Modern Eve." Birch did not have to look far. At De Lux Studios, located at 1230 16th Street in Denver, which the *Post* frequently used to produce its photographs, Birch found a receptionist named Hazel Eighmy, who he persuaded to assume the role of Agnes Lowe of Ann Arbor Michigan, a young coed from the University of Michigan in Colorado on holiday. Birch introduced her to the world on July 29, 1917, with a story in the Sunday edition of the *Denver Post* written under his own byline. "Agnes Lowe," a young woman of twenty was in Estes Park, together with her mother and her brother, Richard, and was preparing that very morning

> to go off into the wilderness alone and attired in as primitive fashion as was the First Woman, without food, weapons or shelter, to subsist seven whole days thru her skill in woodcraft. She will pick or kill her own food, cook it over a fire made after the fashion of prehistoric man, and fashion a bed and its covering that will protect her against the cold of lofty mountain nights. And at the end of one week she will return to civilization in as good physical condition as when she left, without having lost a single one of her 116 pounds of weight. That is, she will TRY to do all this.

Accompanying Birch's article were several photographs of the blonde-headed Miss Lowe, which the *Post* explained had been taken especially for *The Denver Post* by Bert Blasing of De Lux Studios.

Birch then went on to explain that Agnes Lowe was determined "to do what Knowles had done." For at least a week, she had been "hitting the trails" in preparation, and her mother and brother, knowing the "phenomenal woodcraft" learned from her lumberman father, who had taken her as a child into the "trackless woods," had at length consented to let her go. Miss Lowe had selected the Thunder Lake region of Wild Basin, "a vast area almost virgin to the foot of man," so remote and trail-less that "even the oldest inhabitant of the region—Enos A Mills himself—knows it only hazily."

Lest anyone wonder, Birch assured his readers that

> No advertising "stunt" has impelled Miss Lowe to adopt this "back to nature" outing. She is no actress. She is no candidate for the "movies." She is no writer, about to spring a new book upon a weary public. Neither is she a notoriety-seeking suffragette.

Instead she is just a wholesome, level-headed, healthy young college girl, a University of Michigan co-ed, with a passion for the out-of-doors and an inherited aptitude, wonderfully developed for woodcraft.

With a concluding comment that "The trackless woods are open books to her sympathetic mind," as far as the *Post*'s Sunday readers were concerned the stage had been effectively set.

The follow-up story the next day was once again front-page news. It featured a photograph (by De Lux) showing the "Modern Eve" waving goodbye to mother, brother, and girl friends before departing into the forest, having promised to communicate back in some way. Captain Way and Enos Mills were both on hand for the carefully-arranged send-off. That Mills, an avowed enemy of "nature faking," had also become one of the cast of players speaks worlds about the skill and the persuasiveness of Al Birch.

To the surprise of everyone, though clearly planned to stir still greater interest, Agnes Lowe was quickly back. After some 36 hours in the woods, "hungry, drenched and nearly frozen" she suddenly appeared at the Babcock cabin on the ledges north of Longs Peak Inn, tearfully asking to be cared for until mother and brother could come for her. By the time of the article, Agnes Lowe, pneumonia avoided by effective home remedies, had been re-united with family and friends at Clem Yore's recently-opened Big Thompson Hotel, where, "if sufficiently recovered" she was expected to address the Colorado Campfire Club the following evening on her "adventure."

*Post* readers opening their papers the next day, August 1, 1917, found the "Modern Eve" once again front-page news. Agnes told of her Sunday night ordeal in the rain near Thunder Lake where wet wood prevented a fire. Beginning to get a cold, the "level-headed" college girl "decided to give up and go back to civilization. I trust I am not fool enough to stay out in the wilderness when common sense says to come in." With a hint, unmistakably placed in the story's headline that the "'Modern Eve' May Try Again Life of Primitive," Agnes Lowe then briefly disappeared from the *Denver Post*.

This was Wednesday. On Saturday, August 4th, L. C. Way arranged his work schedule so that by 3 p.m. he was at his office in Estes Park village to greet the returning Agnes Lowe. The second arrival of mother and daughter had been carefully designed by Al Birch to provide the carnival-like atmosphere missing the week before. The previous evening both Miss Lowe and her mother were "royally entertained…at various hotels in Estes Park" including the Stanley Hotel where they were given a dinner and, later, at the Big Thompson Hotel, where they were guests at a dance at which "Mr. and Mrs. L. C. Way and other park officials were present." The next day, "the 'movie' operator insisted upon Mayor Roy L. Wiest and Supervisor Way, with C. H. Bond, Samuel Service and other leading citizens, getting out in the center of the main street in front of the post office and posing shaking hands with Miss Lowe." From the village the Lowes were then taken to Longs Peak Inn to spend the night, where Enos Mills was expected to devote "most of his time to final coaching of the girl for her arduous and risky adventure." Lest anyone fail to understand that the doings of the "Eve of Estes" were by now big-time news, Birch referred to "the sizable and energetic press delegation" which had attached "itself temporarily to her household" and to the fact that the "translation of her resolve into action is being telegraphed to every corner of America, and every handshake and smile are following by special delivery post to periodicals everywhere."

By now L. C. Way was no doubt becoming increasingly uncomfortable with the fraud he was being asked to help perpetuate. He had been forced to pose for any number of contrived photographs, to attend a dance where Miss Lowe was the center of attention, and play the onlooker as Miss Lowe's "mother" and "brother" expertly supervised the public relations surrounding the young woman's every move and kept her on schedule. The whole affair—innocent as it must have at first seemed—was getting out of hand.

The second departure was carried in Monday's *Post* with two farewell photographs: the first, the one taken on Saturday in the village, showing Miss Lowe alighting from her automobile to greet Superintendent Way and Mayor Wiest; the second, taken a day later against the background of Longs Peak Inn, showing the smiling, skin-clad "Eve of Estes" saying goodbye before plunging into the wilderness. According to the story accompanying the photos, a crowd of "nearly 2,000," including L. C. Way and Enos Mills, together with a "battery of cameras" had turned out for the event.

Birch's prose was becoming increasingly more purple and tongue-in-cheek, no doubt to make sure that even the most trusting readers were now in on the game.

Al Birch was by no means through. As was the case with his Denver monkeys, Birch had a knack for knowing how and when to ratchet up his promotions to the point of absurdity. "Well, folks—here's Adam!" he began his story the following day, August 7th, introducing a letter purportedly received by the *Post*, written from Greeley the previous day:

> Dear Sirs—You think you have did a smart thing sending "Eve" such far into the mountains but such shall avale you nothing. I must find her. These national park policemen shall not keep me from this fare young Eve were there numbers as mighty as the sunbeams, for I have had a vision from heaven while I sleep directing me to what I shall do. Go find Eve, if you do not I shall. Vision says so. Tremble and obey heaven's vision. This command comes from heaven, in the vision—tell fare young Eve I am coming. I am onto you. Before you get this I shall be in Rocky Mountain National Park. These devils, park policeman cannot stop me. I send picture of myself in ceremony robes as directed by vision.
>
> Yes sir,
> George Desouris
> Adam the Apostle

With the article was a photograph of "Adam (Himself)" and a "dispatch" from Rocky Mountain National Park to the effect that "park officials will not tolerate the girl being molested" and that "if captured [Adam] will be hurled out of the park upon his ear." A determined L. C. Way is also quoted as announcing: "Adam won't think he's in the Garden of Eden if he comes up here...."

Much to Birch's delight, the story of Miss Agnes Lowe was being picked up nationally by a press amused by the goings on in Colorado. To illustrate Birch's column of August 8th the *Post* reprinted a cartoon from the *New York Evening Telegram*. It showed a group of middle-aged males lined up to make travel arrangements, one saying "Hey I want one to Estes Park in hurry. Physician's Orders." According to Birch, "Papers from every section of the United States and Canada, from Portland, Maine to Portland, Oregon, from Hudson's bay to Key West, Florida have been publishing 'Miss Eve's' adventures, and have been telegraphing frantically to Denver and to the national park for photographs of Miss Lowe and her primitive costume." As if to mollify Captain Way and his Park Service bosses in Washington, who were by now decidedly not amused by the high jinx in one of the most popular of their parks, Birch assured his readers that "The Rocky Mountain National park—and for that matter, the whole of Colorado—received more advertising from the exploit of this pretty young girl than this region has received from every other source in many years. The eyes of the whole of North America are upon Colorado. The story of the 'modern Eve' has given that essentially human note to this state's advertising that nothing before has contained."

Despite Birch's claims, in Colorado at least, the saga of Miss Lowe was becoming a bit stale. For all the story's supposed nation-wide importance, it was now being carried by the *Post* as page 13 news. Not content simply to report his own success, Birch kept the story alive by inserting into his story of August 8th two additional pieces of information. The first indicated that Miss Lowe had kept her promise to communicate. A message written in charcoal on "three bits of aspen bark" had been found by tourists (miles from Thunder Lake) near the Longs Peak trail:

1—Nearly froze last night.
2—Tempted to give up, but didn't.
3—Have fire now. Feeling Fine.
—A. L.

The second bit of news had to do with George Desouris, the self-styled "Modern Adam." He had been captured by rangers after a "strenuous fight" as he was trying to enter the Thunder Lake region clad "in a moth-eaten bear hide." There were no photographs of the capture, or its purported aftermath when the rangers escorted Desouris down to Estes Park village and handed him over to the town marshal who, before the jeers "of a great crowd on the main street," hustled him out of town "on a big automobile stage filled with New York tourists."

Though one-time *Post* writer Gene Fowler, in his 1933 history of the newspaper and its famous owners, Frederick Bonfils and Harry Tammen, would claim that Desouris was a telegrapher on vacation from Omaha who Birch corralled into being photographed in a bearskin before being dispatched into the national park, there is no actual record that the "Modern Adam" was anything more than a photograph and a brief story. Fowler has L. C. Way calling down to Denver to inform a startled Birch that "There's a nut up here…who claims you appointed him as Adam to find your Eve. I tried to argue with him and he put up a fight." Fowler's story, like others in his book, is apparently apocryphal, and seems to have been largely constructed from the details of Birch's original story.

Captain Way and Enos Mills were not through participating in Birch's escapade—in name if perhaps not in fact. According to yet another story, two days later, on August 10th, both men "ran across" Miss Lowe near the trail along the Roaring Fork (a small stream near Longs Peak Inn). They were promptly invited to her "den" for an impromptu lunch. Since Birch identifies her camp as being about a hundred feet above Thunder Lake, the ten or so mile walk deep into Wild Basin that followed no doubt allowed the two men to work up sufficient appetite to attack the luncheon that Miss Lowe "quickly prepared" and served. Consisting of pine bark soup, mountain trout, mushrooms, chipmunk peas, wild honey, and choke berries, it was a meal, Way and Mills admitted, fully "the equal of some meals they have paid good prices for in city hotels." By now Miss Lowe had "adroitly" solved the problem of clothing and was wearing "crude but serviceable" sandals made of aspen bark tied on with cords of "wire grass" and, in apparent deference to the sensibilities of her male guests, a pair of leggings made of "tough" leaves. Birch also indicated that park rangers were having a difficult time keeping curious tourists ("both men and women") from "penetrating the Wild Basin section of Thunder Lake to get a glimpse of the 'modern Eve.'"

Agnes Lowe returned from her "adventure" on cue, arriving back at Copeland Lake at noon two days later, where she was photographed and quickly taken away. By mid-September Birch had his sequel ready, a long three-part Sunday magazine-section article written by Agnes Lowe herself providing a detailed day-by-day record, with photographs, of "How I Proved to Science that Modern Woman Can Live Like Mother Eve." The first installment was accompanied by a shorter piece by Mrs. H. R. Lowe, titled "Why I Let My Girl Go Back to Nature." There was, of course, the obligatory bear story—"one of the big brown bears that inhabit the Rocky Mountain heights, the most vicious of all the bear family." He had been encountered in a cave, where Miss Lowe had sought shelter from a lightning storm on the night of day two. Before she escaped by playing dead "He bushed and snuffed at every inch of my body" and, " with a grunt, threw me over on my back."

The first of these articles appeared on September 16, 1917; the second and third on successive Sundays. In the third, written with the same kind of histrionics as its predecessors, Miss Lowe told of her encounter with the original Adam, the Greek from Greeley named George Desouris. She had been warned of his approach by a note, "written on the back of a ranger's notebook," telling her that the "religious fanatic" had been sighted in Estes Park where, after having frightened tourists "into an embryo panic" with his ravings, he disappeared into the wilderness. Their encounter, which reads like a chapter from a pulp novel of the cruder sort, gives way to a madcap "panic-stricken" chase which ends with a second note informing her that a search party led by "Mr. Mills, the naturalist; L.C. Way, the park supervisor, and chief ranger Frank Kennedy" have "rounded up" Adam and taken him to the "Estes calaboose" (a convenience which, in 1917, did not yet exist). The story ends with a brief paragraph recounting her return from "voluntary exile":

> A great cheer went up. I saw my mother stand in an automobile to wave her handkerchief. It seemed *so* strange they should be glad to see me. If they knew how unhappy I was at the thought of the gown and corset and shoes and stockings and furbelows with which I would have to go into the hotel for dinner, they would be as downcast as I was at heart.

To this final chapter of Birch's publicity-hoax was appended a photo of Mills and Mrs. Lowe welcoming Agnes back to civilization, accompanied by a three paragraph note "By Enos Mills (The World-Famous American Naturalist)" stating, incredibly enough, that "I wish other girls could take a leaf from the record of Miss Lowe's experiences and go and do likewise...."

Whatever their degree of actual involvement in the episode of the "Eve of Estes," it was not Enos Mills' or L.C. Way's finest hour. Mills, of course, was answerable only to himself, and perhaps a sense of humor allowed him to dismiss without regret Birch's humbuggery, some of which had clearly been at the expense of his own reputation as a respecter of nature's integrity. After her brief moment of fame, which was followed by an invitation from the Fort Collins Commercial Club to attend the annual Labor Day Poudre River Picnic, Hazel Eighmy returned to receptionist duties at De Lux Studios, where she remained at least through the following year. Way, on the other hand, was not his own agent. Within a week of Birch's first *Post* columns, he had been called on the carpet by Washington and asked to explain his participation in this "frame-up for publicity purposes." Way weakly responded that he felt that the *Post*'s stories, and those that they had triggered, "will result in very valuable publicity...bringing hundreds of people to this park." Al Birch had already preempted that argument and Horace Albright, speaking for the Park Service in Mather's absence, responded that Way's involvement would "surely bring adverse criticism upon park management" and that "a national park is not the stage for even this sort of thing."

Equally incensed was ranger Dixie McCracken, who had been detailed to meet Agnes Lowe on the trail near Longs Peak Inn and deliver her clothing. Following orders, McCracken found himself "right in the middle of it." Realizing that Way and Birch were in "cahoots," he confronted the superintendent and angrily accused his superior of advertising the park "by something that wasn't so." "I blew my stack," McCracken later recalled. "We didn't need that kind of stuff." According to McCracken that incident, "for some reason," soured their relationship, and from that moment on Way didn't like him. Soon afterwards McCracken resigned his post and spent nearly two years in southern France as a volunteer scaling lumber in the forests near the Pyrenees. When he returned to Estes Park after World War I and found Way still in charge, McCracken decided not to take up his old job, though he stayed close to Rocky Mountain National Park for the rest of his life, because "I just had to see a pine tree grow up somewhere.''…Fortunately in terms of his own career prospects, Captain Way was having greater success on other, less controversial, fronts.

# 24

## "CHARLIE, DID I EVER TELL YOU..."

The Death of Agnes Vaille, 1925

*Walter Kiener*

*On January 12, 1925, Agnes Wolcott Vaille, the thirty-five-year-old daughter of one of Denver's pioneer families, died alone on the Boulder Field of Longs Peak, following the first successful wintertime ascent of the 1,160-foot East Face. Her companion, a young Swiss mountaineer named Walter Kiener (1900–1959), had left the exhausted woman in a vain attempt to secure help. As in the case of the eerily similar death of Carrie Welton four decades before, the question of just who was responsible was openly contested. Was it the headstrong Agnes Vaille, a veteran member of the Colorado Mountain Club, who in many ways personified the "new" American woman of the 1920s? Or did the fault lie with Walter Kiener, the experienced mountaineer whom Agnes had apparently chosen as a companion precisely because of his expertise? The question was revived some months later with the discovery of the body of Herbert Sortland, the caretaker at Longs Peak Inn, who as a member of the rescue party summoned by Kiener had also perished.*

*For his part, Walter Kiener remained reticent, responding to the questions of authorities, but keeping the larger issues, including many of those that the public most wanted to know, to himself. He waited for six years, in fact, until the evening of December 21, 1931. Sitting before the blazing fire at Hewes-Kirkwood Inn, Kiener turned to his host and friend, Charles Edwin Hewes, and said, "Charlie, did I ever tell you the story of Agnes and my ascent of the East Face in 1925?"*

*Hewes proved both a good listener and amanuensis. He put down on paper what Keiner told him that evening, but then, for reasons not clear, consigned*

201

*the thirteen-and-a-half-page document to an old desk where it remained hidden and undiscovered until the late 1970s. The present editor reprinted it in* Colorado Heritage *in 1990 in an article subsequently included in* Western Voices: 125 Years of Colorado Writing, *published in 2004 by the Colorado Historical Society.*

Our inclination to climb the East Face of Longs Peak came when Mr. and Mrs. Herman Buhl and ourselves had just ascended Mt. Evans early in the fall of 1924; and while resting on the summit of that peak, we looked off north and beholding the grand appearance of Longs, we resolved to climb its East Face in the near future. With the reputation that Agnes enjoyed in the Colo. Mt. Club as the equal of any member, man or woman, for daring endurance, and other qualifications of an able mountain climber, and my own experience in both Switzerland and America, we felt that we could make a successful winter climb, as the previous ascents had been made in late summer or early fall when the face of the mountain was about as dry and free from ice and snow as it ever gets.

One Sat. evening in the following Oct. we made the first attempt. Motoring to and camping on the Longs Peak campground in Rocky Mt. National Park, above Hewes-Kirkwood Inn, we took the trail to Chasm Lake and proceeded on up the glacier to the foot of Alexander's Chimney.[1] The going was good despite the snow which covered the glacier. My examination of the Mt. in that vicinity convinced me that we should advance up the glacier to its junction with Broadway then proceed along that ledge until we found an opening above it which looked promising as leading to the summit. Agnes, however, got so interested in the chimney that I gave way to her desire to explore it. Upon entering we were soon involved in difficulties—the interior was lined with ice and for nearly every foot we climbed, steps had to be cut in the ice. Finally in order to get around and up over a mass of rock which blocks the upper end, we had to cut niches in a vertical wall of ice, and tho succeeding at last in gaining the top of the wall, I dropped my ice axe which made further progress impossible. Calling to Agnes, I told her the situation and that we must return. Having a very precarious footing on the steeply inclined wall, I succeeded in finally lodging my partner in a place where she could hold on; then, for the second time in my life—the first time, a tight place in Switzerland—I loosened the rope from my body so that in case I slipped and fell she would not be dragged down. On account of the long time we had been employed in cutting steps in the ice, darkness had come on, and I soon realized that I was in a difficult situation. Soon, however, my body was wriggling over the edge of the wall, with fingers clinging to the slight indentations in the rocks and with my feet finally finding the niches previously cut in the ice I made my way down to safety and we returned to camp.

The next trip was made in the following Nov. We had taken a couple of Agnes' friends, two young ladies, with us up on the first trip, who remained at the camp while we were on the mountain; and we were accompanied by Carl Blaurock, a fellow Mountain Club member, on the second trip. Although the weather was fine and the going good, such serious errors were made in choosing the route involving a long and protracted retreat to cover the true course, that night was upon us almost before we realized it; and after a laborious descent in the darkness, in which the rope was resorted to until we reached the glacier, we again gave up the task and returned to Denver.

The following Dec. Agnes and I motored to the campground again and ascended to the foot of the East Face through a heavy blizzard; but admonished by one of the strictest rules of mountain climbing to attempt no difficult ascents in adverse weather—and there being no prospect of any abatement of the storm, we turned back for the third time.

At this juncture a sort of disagreeable, unhealthy situation developed in our East Face efforts. Agnes became the object of considerable adverse criticism on the part of those who tried to dissuade her from any further attempts to climb the East Face. Members of her family, fellow Mountain Club members, friends and others contributed to this—and with the highest motives, the belief that the climb was too dangerous, until they became a unit in asserting that it was impossible to ascend the East Face of Longs Peak in winter. In opposition to this was Agnes and myself, both of us believing that it could be accomplished. Thus a regrettable but definite challenge arose in the matter which we proposed to meet; although, moving in almost wholly different strata of society from hers, I was not subjected to this criticism as she was, and I too endeavored to dissuade her from going again, stating that when the talk quieted down we could slip up to the peak and make the ascent almost before anyone knew we were going. To these remarks, however, she was not favorable; and although not feeling happy over the situation, I accepted her invitation and the following January again found us on the mountain.

Upon this fourth, and last, and successful attempt so far as attaining the summit was concerned, we encountered new difficulties, for there had been a heavy wind and snow in the region since our last visit, drifting the roads and forcing us to park our car several miles north of our former campground, about a mile below Bald Pate Inn; and from that point we skied to the timberline cabin on the old Longs Peak Trail, arriving there well after midnight, Sunday morning January 11. Our companion on this trip was Elinor Eppich. There was a strong wind blowing and we spent the balance of the night dozing in our heavy clothes around the old stove there. When daylight came the prospects for the ascent were not favorable for there was a heavy gale blowing and lifting the snow considerably. After eating breakfast, and joking and visiting awhile, Elinor gave a sudden exclamation and told us to look out of the window at the peak, for as if by magic the wind had ceased and the appearance of the mountain was so magnificent that every drop of blood in my body anticipated its conquest, with the girls equally enthusiastic. The storm over and the sky clear, we said goodbye to Elinor who returned down the trail to Longs Peak Inn where she was to wait until we came back.

Although we made a late start I felt that we could attain our object if we could maintain a reasonably rapid speed. Reaching the glacier we climbed to Broadway and traversed the ledge to its junction with the Notch Couloir, the galley which descends from under the great notch of the peak of the east side. The day remained calm and beautiful but the couloir was filled with snow and ice and we spent about four hours in cutting our steps up its steep incline. Then another two hours was occupied in getting from the top of the couloir north on the face of the mountain to a point that had been selected from which we could finish the climb up through the little notch to the summit. It was four o'clock in the afternoon and darkness had set in, and although I felt strong and fit for the remainder of the ascent I was greatly perturbed and grieved to note that my companion's strength was about spent. For some time I had noticed that she was far from being in the wonderful form and endurance that she was noted for, and for the past two hrs. she had been almost helpless; and often as we paused she complained and apologized for being such a burden on my hands. Although I had long since abandoned all hopes of rapid ascent, I tried not to betray it, and encouraged her all I could; but it was soon evident that she was helpless to proceed, and for close to twelve hours I had to cut the steps alone, handle the rope, and pull, lift, and assist her, until we finally reached the summit about four a.m. This last twelve hours of the climb was made in complete darkness, and the way exceedingly tantalizing, for the face of the mountain at this point is a series of projections, like great steps; and at this time of year being covered by a blanket of snow and ice, one step would be on the sheer rock face just under a thin covering of ice, and at the next we would sink to our waists in snow—thus every step we advanced became an effort won only by dogged labor. We lost our two lanterns on this slope, and here I took the only thermometer reading of the trip— 14 degrees below zero. We found it fairly quiet on the summit and Agnes suggested that we register as proof we had made the ascent, but anxious to get off the mountain on account of her exhausted condition and fearing a now gusty wind would bring in something stronger, I said jokingly "What's the use? Of course it would be proof we reached the summit, but by which side and that's the point. Let's go on." By this time the summit began to be enveloped in clouds; we lost our way, we wandered off toward the northwest, when a fortunate opening in the clouds occurred just at day break and I got our location exactly seeing Mount Lady Washington to the east, the Boulder Field below me, and our route down the north face. My joy and exultation in this observation were suddenly dispensed, however, when the light of dawn revealed the features of my brave companion; for they were those of one who was doomed—that most appalling lines of suffering, anguish, pain, haggard and deep drawn, had developed in the countenance of that heroic woman; her eyes were fearfully bloodshot and she talked in tones that seemed supernatural. I did my best to conceal my own intense agitation and despair; but even as far advanced as she must have been into the spirit, kept still on earth by her dauntless will and courage, she read my glance, and then there was born a friendship in the presence of death that must have risen to God as a thing immortal. The apologies she sought to make for being in such a condition were heart breaking, but I passed them over by asking as gently as I could, if she felt that she could go on; and nodding in the affirmative though she seemed on the verge of actual dissolution, we started down the north face near Chasm View for the Boulder Field below. Reaching the point where a large rock jams the long lateral crack where the cable is now, I tried to get her to go around instead of over it, but probably too far gone to heed the suggestion she went over the top of it, and slipped, as I feared she would, she fell and skidded a long ways down over the smooth, snowy slope, and lay there until I could descend. It was broad daylight now with the wind steadily rising from the west, and as the sun rose over the distant plains we discussed the situation. She was so weak that she could not hold onto me, and I was so far gone that my knees shook and I fairly tottered; and all the time she was insisting, in that supernatural voice that smote and terrified me, that a half hour's sleep would restore her. Assisting her to some rocks that seemed to offer protection from the wind, I put her knapsack under her head as a pillow, placed her ice axe in her hand, for she seemed to cling to it as a treasured thing; and then with all the speed at my command I started across the Boulder Field for help. It was not long before I was brought up quick by two or three terrible falls made between the great boulders which were covered with the treacherous snows; and as I lay recovering in one place, I wept at my miserable weakness and helplessness; and debated whether to return and die with her, or push on for blankets, restoratives, and aid to bring her off the Boulder Field; and as the latter plan offered the only fighting chance for life there was, and hoping that she still had enough endurance left to last until I could return with the cherished aid, I went on. This was about 11 o'clock Monday morning, the twelfth. By 1 p.m. I managed to reach the timberline cabin and found to my great surprise and joy that a rescue party had been organized by Miss Eppich, who had become alarmed at our long absence and the rising gale, and which consisted of Hugh Brown, his son Oscar, and Herbert Sortland, the caretaker at the Longs Peak Inn, and Jacob Christen, all of whom had been putting up ice at the inn. I told them the situation, we took the blankets and restoratives they brought and the elder Brown, Sortland, Christen, and myself started for the rescue. By this time the wind had risen to a terrible gale and it was intensely cold. On account of being so poorly dressed, Brown had to give up and return within a short distance; then Sortland called out that he could not stand it, and he left us; but as I remember, the timberline cabin was still in view, and both Christen and I thought he could make it, never dreaming that it was the last time that anyone would see him alive.

When Christen and I reached Agnes she was dead and frozen, but during my absence she had partially risen, turned over and was lying face downward still clutching her ice axe. The gale was raging in unabated fury, driving the cold against our bodies without cessation or mercy—there was nothing to do but return, for we could not carry the body; later, when it was recovered, it took eight men in calm weather to carry it. We would do well if we got back alive ourselves. How many times I fell on this last journey I could not tell. It was one long, horrible nightmare of slip, plunge, groan, prostration, painful recovery among the jagged boulders and again staggering on with the aid of the brave Christen. There was no visibility—all was one vast welter of blinding snow; but the way was downward and that was our cue. My knees were battered to pieces it seemed to me and I could feel the blood trickle down them, and stiffen, and freeze. My feet had long since ceased to have any feeling. They were just stumps that I tried to balance myself on against the wind like a pair of stilts; and my hands were gone with the fingers frozen and rattling like icicles whenever my gloves fell off. The wind never let up, but roared and beat upon us like a furious monster that is determined to kill and devour his prey. About half way back my eyes began to freeze and I could not see, and Christen had to lead me by hand. When I fell he would help me up. Sometimes he would get ahead, and then when I fell I hoped he would never come back it seemed so restful as I lay upon the snow and rocks; then when he did come back yelling, and shaking me, I was glad when I got up again. I had no real sleep since the previous night—had worked under heavy nervous strain and exposure for the past 36 hours, and it was now late Monday afternoon—I was a wreck. For the last mile or so Christen had to lead me by the hand for I was blind and almost helpless. Finally reaching Timberline Cabin about 7:30 p.m. and sitting near the fire that had been built on the stove, it looked only like a dim candle seen far off. The National Park Rangers arrived at the cabin three hours later. The next morning Mr. Toll, the superintendent, came. He was a cousin of Agnes and his official report tells the balance of the story—how I was badly frozen and taken to a Denver hospital; the disappearance of Herbert Sortland, whose remains were found near Longs Peak Inn six weeks later; and the recovery of Agnes' body by the rangers a couple of days later when the storm was over. (Here ends Kiener's personal narrative as told by him to Charles E. Hewes, the evening of December 29 1931 in Hewes['s] cabin near Longs Peak.)

NOTE

1.   Alexander's Chimney was named for James Alexander, the Princeton professor who made the first successful ascent of the East Face on September 7, 1922.

# 25

## THE HIGHEST HOTEL IN THE WORLD
1927

Merrill J. Mattes

The years 1925 and 1926, those immediately following the death of Agnes
Vaille, were the busiest in Longs Peak history. Superintendent Roger Toll,
who was, ironically, Agnes's cousin, took a number of steps to increase safety
on Longs Peak in the hope of avoiding future tragedies and facilitating rescue
work. These included opening a new, quicker route to the summit by installing galvanized-iron cables on the ledges of the North Face above Chasm View,
laying out a new trail from Jim's Grove to the middle of the Boulder Field,
and constructing a small cylindrical granite shelter on the narrow ledge just
below the Keyhole to offer refuge to climbers. The shelter was built with funds
from the Vaille family.

The major project of these years, however, was the story-and-a-half rock structure five hundred feet below the Vaille shelter built in order to provide a
secure overnight stopping place for those bound for the summit. Officially
named the Boulderfield Shelter Cabin, it became known as the Boulderfield
Hotel when Toll agreed to allow it to operate as a small hotel under a concessions agreement. Robert Ripley, in his syndicated "Believe It or Not" column,
later dubbed it the "highest hotel in the world."

During the summer of 1929, one of the young guides employed by National
Park Service concessionaire Robert Collier was Merrill J. Mattes (1910–1996),
who would go on to enjoy a thirty-year NPS career during which he wrote
extensively about the history of the American West. In 1986 Mattes published
the essay included here in Colorado Heritage, recounting the brief seven-
year history of "the highest hotel in the world."

209

Boulderfield is exactly what the name implies, a gently inclined alpine pla-teau of about 1,000 acres of erosional debris—chunks of granite accumu-lated over millions of years (in 1873 Isabella Bird, the first woman to climb Longs Peak, called this "the Lava Beds"). Looming above the plateau is the great, square-topped crown of Longs Peak, looking like a primeval mon-ster luring flatland tenderfeet to their doom. Boulderfield lies just below the abrupt North Face of Longs; just around the corner, to the left, one can get a glimpse of the awesome upper part of the East Face, the gigantic vertical "Diamond" which can be seen up to a hundred miles away from the Great Plains. Straight ahead as the climber approaches is a knife-like ridge that connects Longs with Storm Peak, a relatively modest mountain to the right. In the center of the ridge is a huge, oval-shaped aperture called the "Key-hole." To the left, as climbers enter Boulderfield from Granite Pass, is another lesser elevation, which for some obscure and illogical reason is called Mount Lady Washington. From the ridge between this small mountain and Longs there are stunning views of the East Face and its Chasm, as well as Longs' companion of respectable height, Mount Meeker. The shelter cabin was in the approximate center of the Boulderfield, where it was convenient to two climbing routes—either directly up the North Face or along a circuitous route via the Keyhole.

Boulderfield was—and still is—reached by a trail measuring over six miles from its start at the present Longs Peak parking area, the site of our 1929 base camp. It zigzags through a pine forest, emerges from timberline, and makes another zigzag ascent to the crest of a lateral moraine left by the immense glaciers that scooped out the Chasm to sculpture the East Face. At the end of this moraine the trail divides, one branch heading toward Chasm Lake to the left, the other swinging to the right along the flanks of Lady Washington to reach Boulderfield at Granite Pass. From this point there is a trail that ends at the site of the 1929 shelter cabin. It is marked by daubs of black paint to facilitate passage through this labyrinth. Between the site of the shelter cabin and the Keyhole, and also approaching the North Face, there are no prepared trails; climbers must simply pick their way over and through a sea of rocks.

To understand how the Boulderfield Shelter Cabin came to be built in the first place—and why it was obliterated ten years later—one must understand the shifting sands of bureaucratic thinking, the mystic psychology of the breed known as "technical climbers," the simple expectations of ordinary visitors wanting only to climb a mountain safely, and the impersonal realm of geological dynamics.

People have been climbing Longs Peak (though never in great numbers) ever since Denver editor William N. Byers and the one-armed explorer John Wesley Powell went all the way to the summit in 1868. Byers's lucid description of his exhilarating experience, appearing in the September 2, 1868, edition of the *Rocky Mountain News*, could have been written by a climber of 1986, for though people and times change, the mountain never does—at least in the minuscule time-frame of human history. Members of the Colorado Mountain Club, organized in 1914, were frequent climbers, leaving their names on a tablet in a brass cylinder, which they had chained to the highest point of the summit. They and other hardy souls sometimes climbed the difficult North Face and the much more precipitous East Face. The less daring used the longer and somewhat precarious Keyhole route, which was made less precarious in 1922 when a rough trail along Longs' steep west slope, overlooking Glacier Gorge, was hacked out.

The twin concepts of a shelter cabin at Boulderfield and a safer method of climbing the North Face resulted from a tragedy that occurred in January 1925—the deaths of Agnes Vaille and Herbert Sortland, and serious injuries to others. Vaille and a Swiss emigrant, Walter Kiener, had the temerity to climb the East Face in mid-winter. While descending the North Face they were caught in a subzero blizzard. Vaille slipped and fell about 150 feet; because of injuries, exhaustion, and exposure, she was unable to go on. Kiener hurried down the long trail to get help, but when a rescue party finally reached Agnes Vaille she was predictably dead. Sortland, one of the would-be rescuers, got lost, his remains missing until the following spring. Later that year Agnes's father had a granite memorial in her honor—intended as a storm shelter—erected at the Keyhole (elevation 13,200 feet). This has been described as the highest man-made structure in the National Park system.

Agnes Vaille was a cousin of Rocky Mountain National Park superintendent Roger W. Toll, which may have been one of the factors in his subsequent resolve to prevent such tragedies in the future, or at least minimize them, by four improvements: 1) laying out a reasonably smooth trail to the middle of Boulderfield, 2) erecting a shelter cabin there, 3) stringing a telephone to the cabin, and 4) installing a cable up the smooth 60-degree incline of granite that is the most difficult part of the North Face climb— at or very near the place where Agnes Vaille had fallen. (According to the *Estes Park Trail* of August 21, 1925, this cable was recommended to Toll by her companion, Kiener, who claimed that such climbing aids were used at "dangerous places" in the Alps.) A hardbitten but reliable ranger, Jack Moomaw, was responsible for constructing the trail, telephone line, and North Face cable. All of these projects, accomplished in the summer and autumn of 1925, are recounted in his *Recollections of a Rocky Mountain Ranger* (Longmont, 1963).

The concept of the Boulderfield Shelter Cabin was not without precedent. In 1908 Enos Mills built his Timberline Lodge a short distance off the present Longs Peak Trail, near Jim's Grove, along an earlier and steeper trail to Granite Pass. This was a frame building twelve by twenty-four feet, which saw much use by climbers and vacationers until 1925 when Mills's widow abandoned it to the custody of the National Park Service. It served as a shelter for the rescue party of the Vaille episode, and later for Moomaw and his work crews. However, it was in ruins in 1929, and later obliterated. Another Longs Peak shelter, built in 1931 and still standing, is a small and seldom-used masonry affair on the trail to Chasm Lake.[1]

The officially designated Boulderfield Shelter Cabin—unofficially our beloved Boulderfield Hotel—was designed by the Landscape/Engineer branch office of the National Park Service in San Francisco and was built by contractor M. L. Laursen for about $5,000. Work on the shelter did not get started until August 1926 because of delays in funding. Early autumn storms prevented its completion until June 1927.

This structure has one room measuring eighteen feet square and a windowed attic. Its principal features were concrete foundations and footings on a bed of boulders leveled by dynamite, massive corner-buttressed walls of boulders from the immediate vicinity, and a timbered roof held down by more boulders, all of them wired together. The structure was further strengthened by interior tie rods. The stout door opened upon an intimate view of the North Face, while the three metal-paneled windows looked upon the Boulderfield approach, the Keyhole, and Storm Peak, respectively. The work was hampered by transportation problems (everything but the boulders had to be brought up by horses), ice storms, and winds of hurricane force that tore off the first three roofs before one of sufficient strength was finally devised.

Superintendent Toll at first intended that the shelter was to be simply that. It would be open to the climbing public for free use as occasion might arise, but these high-altitude pilgrims would have to provide their own bedding, victuals, and utensils. Later Toll decided that a case could be made for a concession there that would provide ready-made meals, lodging, and guide service on the peak—all for approved posted fees. The concession went to Robert Collier, Jr., of Denver. In all probability it was the energetic Collier himself who planted the idea of the Boulderfield operation in Toll's head.

When provided with furniture and cooking facilities, the barren shelter cabin was transformed into a kind of hostel like those in the Alps and the Himalayas. In the *Estes Park Trail* and in circulars left at hotels Collier advertised its unique charms: "No modern facilities, no mosquitoes, no hay fever," among others. While the accommodations could only be described as primitive, group reservations were accepted by mail and the place was in touch by phone with the outside world. It also afforded some of the most spectacular scenery in North America. To the unsophisticated 1929 crew it seemed to have all the important features of a resort hotel except for indoor plumbing. Indeed, one of Ripley's "Believe It or Not" features labeled this "the highest hotel in the world," while the superintendent's annual report for 1927 referred to it as "a small hotel or lodge."

After completion of the shelter cabin, work began on a nearby stable for the horses that brought tenderfeet up from below. This was a rectangular masonry structure eighty-five feet long with a latrine at the far end. At the near end, a shed was designed for use as tack room but on occasion served as dormitory for Boulderfield guides and overflow guests. Because of this ambiguity, we called it the "bridal suite." The stable itself was open on the downslope side. Since there was no way to keep its roof from blowing off in mid-winter gales, a special roof was installed in 1930, designed so that it could be removed at the end of the climbing season and reassembled at the beginning of the next one.

Although the Boulderfield Hotel was destined to be short-lived, it was my good fortune to be on its staff during its heyday. In 1929, just before the stock market crash, it was enjoying its third season and was well patronized by dudes who wanted to climb one of Colorado's most famous mountains. It was ironic how I—a boy from the prairie flatland—became an instant Longs Peak guide. After working for a summer in 1928 on a ranch near Cheyenne Wells, Colorado, I had toured Rocky Mountain National Park in an open-air bus and got my first close glimpse of Longs Peak. To my eyes it was the most beautiful and seductive thing—in the category of scenery—that I had ever seen. Consequently, when Robert Collier came to my hometown of Kansas City, Missouri, the following winter to lecture about the lure of Longs Peak, I was ready to follow him back. After hearing his lecture, I expressed my interest in working for him during the next season. He was noncommittal at that time, but to my great joy he later wrote and offered me a job as a guide at Boulderfield. Even more implausible, when I then recommended my equally inexperienced Kansas City friend Melvin Wickens for a similar job, Collier agreed to hire him as well. LaSelle Gilman, the third member of the crew that year, came from Nebraska, not a terribly mountainous state either. He aspired to be a novelist, and during off-duty hours pounded out page after page of lurid prose on his portable typewriter.

I still have my license as a Longs Peak guide, duly signed by then park superintendent Edmund Rogers. While this sudden conversion from neophyte to mountain guide may seem a bit preposterous, Melvin and I were not expected to do any tortuous pathfinding or technical rock climbing. Once familiar with the prevailing route, all we had to do was to escort parties up, over, and down the mountain. True, some clients, because of overweight or awkwardness, had to be pushed, lifted, or led by the hand. Some fainted from altitude sickness, and we had to administer first aid, usually by breaking an ammonia capsule under their nose, but specialized mountaineering skills were not a requirement. All that Collier wanted were healthy fellows willing to work seven days a week for one dollar a day, and we filled those specifications.

Melvin Wickens and I rode the rails to Denver and then a bus to Estes Park, where Dorothy Collier met us. After being processed at park headquarters we went on to base camp, located at the place now occupied by the Longs Peak parking area, the head or beginning of the Longs Peak Trail. That year Collier had under construction there a frame building to serve as a seasonal warehouse and quarters which became later the first Longs Peak ranger station. Before its completion we sheltered in tents. A bonus was the privilege of eating occasionally at the Hewes-Kirkwood Inn, now identifiable as the Rocky Ridge Music Center just off State Highway 7.

Robert Collier, who in the off-season taught chemistry at Denver's South High School, was a serious, competent, and businesslike boss, on occasion given to sardonic humor. He got the Boulderfield concession on the strength of being a genuine licensed mountain guide in addition to having respectable old family connections in Denver well known to Superintendent Toll. Dorothy Collier was quite competent in the provisioning and cooking side of the business and had an outgoing personality that offset her husband's seriousness. A magazine article about her Boulderfield enterprise was entitled "Uncle Sam's Hostess to the Hardy." This was not entirely a figure of speech, for the Park Service made her an "honorary ranger," the first woman to be so designated. She was also a mountain climber in her own right; in 1931, in company with Wickens and others, she made the first recorded nighttime ascent of Longs' East Face.

We three apprentice guides learned that our first major assignment was to pack burros with equipment, fuel, and provisions, and then to take them up the six miles to Boulderfield. Melvin Wickens was the first one up, to help Collier open the cabin, the first to climb the peak, and the first to stay overnight by himself at the "Hotel" in the middle of the rock-strewn desert, an eerie experience he recalled as "like being alone on the moon."

Soon it was my turn to rope and load the burros, using a diamond hitch, something a good deal more complicated than anything I had learned as a Boy Scout. Then the idea was simply to escort the burros uphill, encouraging them as needed with a sawed-off broomstick. These two loveable animals were named Jack and Cootie. They normally did their job without complaint, though they sometimes declared their independence by bucking and throwing off their packs. When this happened on the trail, the driver was on his own and somehow had to repack the animals despite their efforts to skitter out from underneath. One way or another the job was done. It usually took several hours to make it all the way to Boulderfield. In rain the trip was wet drudgery, but in clear weather and with well-behaved burros, it was an exhilarating experience. Once above timberline I felt that I was walking on top of the world.

Arriving at Boulderfield our little caravan was greeted by marmots—dark brown, yellow-bellied, hibernating animals up to twenty inches long, resembling oversized and overweight prairie dogs. They would pop up from behind the rocks and emit warning whistles, or they could be seen scampering away in the distance. It is difficult to imagine how any form of wildlife can exist in those sterile heights, mild enough in mid-summer but most of the year subject to snow, sleet, howling winds, and temperatures which plummet to sixty degrees below zero. But this was rightfully marmot territory, and we were intruders.

After we unloaded and became acquainted with the Spartan amenities of the Hotel, Collier gave me a fast lesson in how to become a bona fide guide, accompanying me on my first ascent of Longs Peak via its North Face, which towered 1,500 feet above Boulderfield. We had with us our first party of awed customers, who paid $2.50 apiece for the privilege of professional guide service. As far as Chasm View the climb was nothing more than a scramble over rocks, but where the cable began, on the sheer granite, the going required more concentration. Climbers had to hoist themselves slowly skyward, making sure that they did not slip or step on someone else's hands.

Standard equipment for guides included hobnailed boots, an ice axe, and a coiled length of rope for use in emergencies. By mid-July most of the snow on the cable route had disappeared, and the ice axe was useful mainly to impress the dudes. I had to use the rope only once on a routine climb. This was early in the game, when an overweight young woman missed a handhold on the cable and started sliding toward the brink of the East Face. Somehow—whether the result of mutual prayers or her own weight—she slowed to a stop, and I was able to rope her back up to the cable.

The North Face was just the beginning. On the flat, rock-strewn summit of Longs, on a clear day, the scenery is fabulous: one can see all the way from Pikes Peak to Cheyenne and from Denver and the Great Plains to the Never Summer Range. The hidden hazard on the summit is lightning, which has been reported on clear days as well as stormy ones. People have been killed or injured by lightning, so the rule is, Don't linger! (In 1928 guide Hamilton Hatfield reported that his party, while on the summit with blue skies above, was knocked down and slightly injured when lightning struck nearby.) From the summit, after everyone entered his or her name on the register, we returned to Boulderfield down the south side by the steep, granite-plated Homestretch, the aptly named Narrows, the long, snow-filled Trough, and Fried Egg Trail along the mountain's west slope. (This last part isn't a trail so much as a rough shelf slanting alarmingly toward the awesome 1,600-foot depths of Glacier Gorge. It gets its name from painted bull's-eye guide symbols.) At the end of this trail, passing through the Keyhole is like entering Alice's magic mirror, for there, about a half mile downhill, is Boulderfield—and there, in 1929, was the welcoming Boulderfield Hotel, smoke curling from its chimney.

Accommodations at this "highest hotel in the world" were all supplied by the concessioner. On the main level was a double-deck bunk, table, benches, storage boxes, coal and kerosene stoves, and a ladder to the attic or loft. Upstairs furniture consisted solely of two rows of contiguous floor-level bedding. While the place was designed to accommodate twelve people in addition to the crew, there were times when we made room for over double that number—on one occasion, I believe, squeezing in over forty. Certainly no one was ever turned away from our door to catch his or her death of pneumonia from freezing nighttime temperatures. While the resultant crowding would seem to have inhibited sleep, fatigues of the day ensured deep slumber, even for those compelled to stretch out on the concrete floor.

The bulk of our guests came by horseback from Longs Peak Inn, Columbine Inn, or Hewes-Kirkwood Inn. Staying overnight, including supper and breakfast, was part of their tour package. but there were also a fair proportion of free-lance hikers whom we called pilgrims. In 1929 over 1,700 people registered their names on the peak. Of that number, probably half stayed with us overnight....

While things became crowded enough during the evenings with the overnighters, the big rush hour was around noon, when overnighters down off the peak needed nourishment before hitting the downward trail, and new parties coming up from below drifted in to climb the peak that afternoon or lay over until the next day. With the limited kitchen facilities and eating space, they sometimes had to be fed by platoons. While either Bob or Dorothy Collier presided as chef, the all-purpose guides became waiters, dishwashers, and information clerks.

While the standard scheduled climbing time began right after breakfast and ended at noon, the guides were on standby for those who wanted to get to the summit in the afternoon. Frequently, therefore, we led climbing parties twice during the day. This was no strain on us, once adjusted to the rarefied altitude. In fact, at times, when business was dull, we would scramble up and down the North Face by ourselves—between the hotel and the summit—to see who could make the round trip by that route in the fastest time. I don't know who holds the record for this non-Olympic event, but in a letter sent home at the time I reported doing it in a little over an hour.

Aside from their own competitive climbing and tall-tale swapping, the only entertainment available to the guides was to play records on a wheezy wind-up phonograph. Songs by Rudy Vallee were played so often that they squeaked and would drive me out into the night to contemplate the starry heavens. Another unforgettable platter was John Philip Sousa's "Stars and Stripes Forever." Collier used this to wake up the help about 4:00 a.m., yelling, "Get up! It's darn near noon!" His voice seemed loud enough to echo off the East Face, but sometimes this routine failed to penetrate the ears of guides sleeping in the neighboring "bridal suite." Then he would wake up these delinquents by throwing a handful of rocks on the top of the shed's tin roof.

There was no reportable crime on Boulderfield, but because of his accumulated cash from the day's receipts—and the fact that the cabin, by law, could not be locked against anyone—Collier kept a .38 caliber revolver under his pillow at night. Normally the people who stayed overnight arrived before sundown, but sometimes slow hikers would turn up in the night, disturbing the general tranquility. Collier's daughter "Tiny" recalled that once about 2:00 a.m. "a rough looking crew drifted into Boulderfield and opened the door to the cabin. Daddy pulled out the long flashlight and shone it in their faces. Mother woke up and screamed, 'Good Lord, Bob— Don't shoot!' We didn't see them again until well after daylight the next day. Daddy said that he had a permit to carry the .38 on condition that he shoot nothing but tourists."

Collier had quite a number of such memorable sayings. When asked about the weather he would invariably reply: "Only tourists and fools try to predict the weather." (The fact is that Longs Peak weather seemed to me to be fairly predictable. Mornings would be normally calm with clear blue skies, and in the afternoon, at least half the time, it would get windy and cloud up, with rain or drizzle, occasionally with thunder that sounded like cannonballs in a heavenly bowling alley.) Another popular tourist question was something like this: "How many times a year do folks die up here?" Bob's stock reply: "Only once." A question in this same category would be prompted by the coiled rope carried by the guides: "What's the rope for?" Answer: "To measure how far folks fall when they are careless." This type of rejoinder had a virtue of putting the customers in a cheerful mood, with no further naïve questions.

While eating, packing, and guiding—seemingly in that order—were our principal occupations, a few incidents outside of the job routine are etched vividly in my memory even after the passage of over half a century. I would rate my near miss by lightning as the foremost, followed by an attempted rescue of two climbers stranded on the East Face after their companion had plunged to his death. On August 18, 1929, free-lance climbers descending from the North Face had reported hearing cries for help from the East Face. They had not seen anyone, however, which suggested that the party in trouble was not on the sheer wall but probably in the vertical chute called the Notch Couloir or Chimney. Collier sent LaSelle Gilman and me to the summit to attempt a rescue. This, I recognize now, was most unwise on his part because neither one of us had ever climbed the East Face and did not know the proper exit route from Notch Chimney. Nevertheless undaunted, each loaded with a hundred feet of rope, we quickly reached the top and began to look for a logical descent. Edging ourselves out on the steeply sloping curved wall above the Couloir, we soon found ourselves almost stranded below the great Notch itself, a distinctive feature on the skyline south of the Longs Peak summit. Far from becoming rescuers, we ended up almost in need of rescue ourselves. Yet by careful maneuvering from one horizontal crack to another, we managed to work our way off this blind slope, then back to the top, and down to Boulderfield to confess failure.

Soon a trio of rangers led by the locally famous veteran, Jack Moomaw, arrived with the proper knowledge and equipment. Because of the late hour they decided to wait at the cabin until dawn. Their rescue of Dr. Stacher and his wife and the recovery of the shattered remains of Charles Thiemeyer at the foot of East Face was fully reported in the Denver and Estes Park press, which gave undue credit to the well-meant but ill-advised efforts of two Boulderfield guides. Moomaw's vividly caustic account of the tragedy and rescue missions is told in his *Recollections*....

Far less dramatic but scarcely less dangerous than fooling around on the East Face was the episode of the 1929 Fourth of July fireworks. Shooting off fireworks from the summit of Longs Peak was a promotion of the Estes Park Chamber of Commerce. The National Park Service now forbids all fireworks within its domain, however patriotically motivated, but in 1929 this government agency was more relaxed in its wilderness ethic. Collier, at any rate, was agreeable to the idea, and said that if fireworks were delivered to Boulderfield his stalwart crew would pack them to the summit and ignite them according to plan. Each of us packing about sixty pounds of combustibles and a box of matches, we scrambled up the mountain, blithely indifferent to the fact that none of us had ever handled big, professional-type rockets. The result was several scorched fingers and eyebrows as well as a glorious display that could be seen, presumably, from all over central Colorado. Certainly it was seen in the park headquarters village, where the *Estes Park Trail* referred to Longs' colorful "eruption."...

The Boulderfield concession was in actual operation for nine years, from 1927 through 1935. The shelter cabin, our 1929 "Hotel," was condemned in 1936 because of structural deterioration. The next year it was dynamited into oblivion, the boulders of which it was composed being scattered to blend in with its original landscape. It seems the Boulderfield Plateau is a "rock glacier" resting on a substratum of ice. Its slow but inexorable shifting fractured the cabin's walls, and through the cracks blizzards drove the snow that piled up and had to be shoveled out each spring. There was simply no way this building could be stabilized. Its companion structure, the horse barn/privy/dormitory, of course, also fell into ruin. Today its remains are the setting for hitching racks for the horses that—in fewer numbers—still plod up to Boulderfield....

NOTE
1.   The Chasm Lake Patrol Cabin was destroyed by an avalanche in March 2003.

# 26

## THE REMARKABLE STETTNER BROTHERS

1927

Dougald MacDonald

*On September 7, 1922, James W. Alexander, a thirty-four-year-old assistant professor of mathematics at Princeton, climbing alone, made the first recorded ascent of the rugged East Face of Longs Peak. Three days later, Elmira Buhl, climbing with a party made up of seven Colorado Mountain Club members, became the first woman to achieve that goal. This was the accomplishment that Agnes Vaille and Walter Kiener were intent on repeating in wintertime less than three years later.*

*The other notable achievement of the 1920s belonged to Joe and Paul Stettner, two brothers from Chicago. In September 1927 they found yet another new route to the summit, one described by Colorado mountain historian William Buehler as then "perhaps the most difficult climb in the country" and "certainly the most advanced, not only on the face, but in all of Colorado, until after World War II." Another, more recent historian and climbing veteran, Dougald MacDonald, describes the Stettners' climb to the summit by way of the series of ledges that now bear their name.*

Toward the end of the 1920s, one pair of European climbers launched Longs Peak climbing toward the future. The route they pioneered on the East Face demonstrated that difficult rock could be climbed safely with the right skills and equipment. By eschewing the easiest way up the mountain, their route was a precursor of all modern climbing, and their low-budget, anything-to-climb trip to the Rockies presaged the climbing bums of today.

The route they established in 1927 was easily the hardest rock climb in North America.

Joe and Paul Stettner were born in Munich, and they learned to ski and climb in the Alps. They emigrated to America in 1925 and 1926 and settled in Chicago. Joe, older by five years, was a metal smith; Paul was a photoengraver. Almost all of the climbing they accomplished in the West was done in short vacations from work.

There were no interstate highways in 1927, and much of their vacation time was eaten up just getting to the Rocky Mountains. In early September, packing a handful of pitons that had just arrived from Germany, the two mounted their Indian motorcycles and hammered along dusty roads for five days before reaching the mountains. They camped along the way and were slowed by breakdowns, flats, and storms. Both men crashed repeatedly on the rutted and sandy roads of Iowa and Nebraska, though neither was badly hurt.

They traveled first to Colorado Springs, where they rode their bikes to the top of Pikes Peak and did some practice climbing on the sandstone fins of the Garden of the Gods. Then, riding north, they searched in vain for a climbing rope to buy. ("This surprised us," one of the brothers said later. "In Germany and Austria you can always get a rope in the mountain villages.") At the Longs Peak Inn, the resident guide wouldn't loan them his rope, saying it was too late in the year to climb the East Face. This did not surprise the experienced climbers. "As we used to say in Europe, 'You don't loan a climbing rope or a girlfriend,'" recalled Paul Stettner. Eventually they were able to buy 120 feet of half-inch hemp at the general store in Estes Park. It would have to do.

On September 14, after spending the night at the ramshackle Timberline Cabin ("much worse than the huts in the Alps, but better than our pup tent"), the two hiked to the base of the East Face and, with binoculars, searched the wall for a new route to the right of Alexander's Chimney. They spotted a line of angling corners and cracks, just to the left of the unbroken, water-streaked Lower East Face. There appeared to be icy patches here and there, but Paul said, "We can worry about that when we get there."

These were the days when shoulder stands were still considered essential climbing techniques. At least as Colorado climbers practiced it, belaying was virtually useless. Yet the Stettners' alpine techniques were advanced. They had pitons and carabiners to anchor themselves to the rock. They knew how to belay each other with the rope, and they carried ice axes and crampons and knew what to do with them. They wore boots to the base of the cliff and then, like modern climbers, switched to specialized rock-climbing shoes—or, in their case, "climbing sneakers." Of course, they did not have the comfortable climbing harnesses, or belay devices used by today's rock climbers, to say nothing of sticky-rubber climbing shoes or chalk to dry sweaty hands.

Paul led the entire climb. Joe occasionally carried both of their knapsacks, and Paul hauled their packs hand over hand up the rope to pass the most difficult stretches. Burdened by his pack, Joe fell from an overhang at one point, but Paul successfully held him with the rope and lowered him 20 feet, the rope painfully cinched around his waist, so he could try again.

To protect his passage up one short corner, Paul had to hammer several pitons in a row. This tough stretch, now rated 5.8, is Piton Ladder—the section that gave me fits during my own climb.

It has long been presumed that the Stettners traversed left on easy ground near the top of the face, but in 1996 Joe Stettner said they climbed straight to Broadway, apparently finishing on a climb now called Hornsby Direct, also rated 5.8. No pitons were found on later ascents, he said, because the only piton Paul placed fell out as he was climbing.

The two men continued up Kiener's Route and summited around 5 p.m. in a snowstorm. They ate a meal—their first of the day—of bread and sardines, and then raced impending darkness down the North Face.

This was an extremely bold climb. The two men had never seen the face and knew almost nothing about the climbs that already existed on it, yet they pioneered a route so far ahead of its time that nothing harder on Longs would be climbed until the 1950s. Over the next 19 years, Stettner Ledges was only repeated twice, and one of those ascents was led by Joe Stettner.

The Stettner brothers made numerous other important climbs in Colorado and Wyoming, and they maintained a lifelong association with Longs

Peak. On the Fourth of July, 1930, Paul proposed to his wife, Ann, on the summit after climbing the East Face with her. "I threatened her if she didn't I would leave her up there," he joked.

In 1936, depressed after the break-up of his marriage, Joe climbed a second new route on the East Face all alone. So difficult was the climbing that many have not believed he climbed the direct route he described and must have traversed off to one side. But in the late 1970s, climbers discovered a 1930s-era piton on this climb with just its tip hammered in, right where Joe said he used one for a foothold.

# 27

## WINTER PATROL

c. 1928

Jack C. Moomaw

*Every national park has its iconic, larger-than-life ranger. In Rocky Mountain National Park that honor belongs to Jack Moomaw (1892–1975) who served as the park's east side ranger from 1922 until his retirement in 1945, much of the time making his home at the Bighorn Ranger Station near the Fall River entrance. Over those three decades there was hardly a major event or undertaking in which the versatile Moomaw was not involved, from installing cables on the North Face of Longs Peak to laying out new ski trails in Hidden Valley. Moomaw, an expert climber, also found himself participating in any number of search and rescue operations, including the futile attempt in 1925 to save Agnes Vaille. Outspoken and opinionated, and known for both his wit and wisdom, Moomaw was a man of many talents. He painted, was an active amateur archaeologist, and wrote poetry. His three volumes of published verse earned him the title "Poet of the St. Vrain."*

*Some two decades after his retirement, Moomaw wrote and published his personal recollections as* Recollections of a Rocky Mountain Ranger *(1963). In the essay reprinted here, Moomaw recalls a winter trip on skis across the Continental Divide to Grand Lake Village during the late 1920s in the company of fellow ranger John Preston and a man named Walker, presumably a ranger as well.*

Six o'clock on a January morning in the late 20's, a biting breeze whispering through the pines around Horseshoe Park Ranger Station, a ragged moon hanging low over Trail Ridge; ghost-like peaks of the Mummy Range outlined against the glittering stars, and a hint of dawn in the east.

John and I loaded our skis and packs into the Ford pick-up; fourteen miles through snow drifts and over wind-swept roads we hurried through the cold grey dawn to Bear Lake. Other rangers would come up and take the car back. Walker was waiting near the Ranger Station, and with the remark that it looked a little fuzzy on top, we strapped on our skis and donned our packs.

The fire-scarred valley was deathly still and cold as we mushed across the lake and zigzagged up the rough moraine to the base of Flattop Mountain.[1] From far above came the faint moaning of the wind in the crags. Out across the sea of hills and canyons, low-lying clouds on the eastern horizon, one hundred miles away, turned into a riot of gold and red. And soon the sun, a great bronze disk, jumped into the blue-green sky. The peaks above turned from lifeless grey to rose and pink, and shadows in vale and canyon from dusk to mauve and cobalt blue. For a little while the scene retained the flush of morning, then turned into a world of sparkling whiteness, and a frigid breeze with spirals of snow came sifting down from the barrens.

The snow grew deeper and deeper as we climbed higher into the forested part of the mountain. A fresh coyote track led straight up the slope toward the pass through the criss-crossing of squirrel and snowshoe rabbit tracks. The going was good, from one to six feet of old, hard snow with a fresh thin surface of new snow on top. The sun had warmed the air until it was just comfortably cool. As we neared timberline, the snow was piled in great drifts among the stunted trees. At timberline the going got rough, and we had to pick our way through the tops of the scrub trees and rock slides. Ptarmigan, like fluffy balls of snow, sprang from almost under our ski tips, fluttered and floated to another snow bank and disappeared again in the whiteness. Soon there was not enough snow for skiing, so we took the "boards" off and carried them, scrambling over the rocks.

Up, up we climbed, to eleven thousand, then twelve thousand feet above sea level, and higher. Colder and colder grew the wind, ten, fifteen, possibly twenty below zero. Gusts of fine snow that stung like wind-driven sand swept across the peneplain. Little dark fluffy clouds were forming as if by magic just over our heads, and scurrying away to the east. The wind was ripping through the gorges below. With a bang it would slap against some cliff, and pieces of snow like white rags would shoot far above the brink and dissolve in the gale.

The Continental Divide was just ahead, some of the smaller parts of it were leaving for the plains. We hurried over, leaning with our carried skis into the wind. The land sloped gently down to the westward for a mile or more, covered with great snow fields that were almost as hard as rock and fluted and carved into fantastic designs by the ceaseless winds. In the distance, as far as the eye could reach, lay scattered, forested, snow-clad ranges like the billows of some mighty ocean tossed and left frozen.

We hardly paused to admire the view. Little white spots began to appear on the faces of the boys, and every few minutes we would have to turn our backs to the wind until the spots would disappear. John lagged behind. We slowed up and, when he reached us his lips were blue, his face grey, and there was a bleary look in his eyes—sure signs of altitude sickness. As we were going down now, I knew that he would get better as we descended. He said his feet were a little cold, and we often stopped to swing our arms and beat our fingers.

We came to the edge of the peneplain. A deep gorge led steeply down to the timber. At the head of the gorge was a large cirque almost filled with snow. We strapped on our skis and I led off. There were no shadows, what appeared to be a steep slope turned out to be almost level, and sometimes places that looked level turned out to be steep slopes. Often I ran into a side slope when expecting level footing. Suddenly the surface would seem to drop from under one as he entered an unseen depression, and it would just as suddenly seem to bulge up as one crossed a hillock that had looked like a smooth place. A few times before, I had experienced this phenomenon of white light in the high country. The boys following my tracks were bothered but little except when they slid out into untracked snow. John, running out into virgin snow at about thirty miles an hour, ran into a drift, spilled and came up with a sprained ankle. We had to go slow because of John's ankle but soon reached the timber and in a little park below came to the shelter cabin that was almost buried in the snow. I asked John how his feet were, and he replied that they were all right now.

It felt good to take off the skis and packs. We soon had a fire going in the stove and were melting snow for drinking water. (Often I am asked about the hardships of skiing in the high country in winter, and my reply is, that there are none except for the lack of water.) We took an hour or more to eat our lunches, rest and smoke.

It was almost warm in the heavily-wooded canyon. There was no wind and only a few fleecy clouds in the sky. We expected to reach Grand Lake Village, nine miles down, in a couple of hours, but the snow soon grew deep and soft and we could make but little over one mile an hour. Walker and I took turns breaking trail. John was favoring his ankle and still had a touch of the altitude. The sun went down but the peaks above still gleamed in the sunlight as we mushed along, slower and slower. Twilight crept into the canyon, but the reflected light from the peaks above caused it to linger for a long time. The blazing stars came out, they seemed just above the mountain tops, blue, yellow, red, and white ones. We lost the trail, and floundered on down the valley. A coyote wailed from the hillside. The air grew bitterly cold and our skis squeaked in the snow. Zigzagging and with the aid of our flashlights we found and followed the trail again. John spilled in a narrow canyon, lost a ski pole, and hurt his ankle again. Slowly, silently we mushed on and down the now almost-level valley floor. After what seemed hours, a cabin light gleamed through the trees, and the bark of a dog shattered the stillness. People who live in the crowded marts do not know the joy and thrill of a light in some distant cabin window.

In the cabin, we drank glass after glass of water. McLaren, the Grand Lake ranger, was at the Inn and, after a brief rest, took us in his car to the Ranger Station. It was ten o'clock and we were more than ready for sleep, but when John took off his shoes, his toes and part of his feet were frozen. The feet were beginning to pain him and we spent hours soaking them in cold water until some of the color returned.

Dawn broke, cold and grey. John was complaining about his toes. We took a look. They were purple and swollen. We prepared and ate a hasty breakfast. The nearest doctor was at Kremmling, forty-four miles away. We put heavy woolen socks on the frozen feet, bundled the cripple into a car and drove through a storm over snowy roads to that doctor. The doctor treated and bandaged the toes, said that he did not think John would lose any of them, but that he would be unable to wear shoes for a month or two. The following day we sent the cripple to Denver by car.

Grand Lake Village was thronged with ski runners and jumpers from all over the State, and many visitors who had come to take part in and see the annual Ski Tournament. We helped with the management of the events, but when asked to take part in the races, had as an excuse that a forty mile trip back over the Range via Fall River Pass would give us all of the skiing we desired.

We started for the Ranger Station when a reporter from a Denver newspaper asked permission to take a few pictures of us and said something about a feature article.

In the evening we went down to the Village for some fresh supplies. The streets were deserted but the Community House was lighted up like a theatre. We slipped in. A banquet was in progress. We seated ourselves quietly by the door so as not to disturb the speaker, who was a visiting lady skier. As she sat down amid much applause, the toastmaster turned and said that one of the men who had just come in, mentioning me, would now favor the crowd with a speech. I mumbled a few words about the excellence of Grand Lake snow and Grand Lake skiers and, feeling rather embarrassed, sat down.

The morning dawned clear and bright. After an early breakfast, and setting the Station in order, we skied up the long broad valley of the Colorado River. After a few miles of good skiing, "Dad" Henderson, in a sled drawn by two plunging horses, overtook us and we accepted his invitation to ride on to his ranch a mile or two up the road. He insisted that we stop and have some of his homebrew and an early lunch with him. He was rich in the lore of the surrounding country and it was hard to break away.

After a few hours of almost level, untracked skiing we came to where the trail leaves the valley and starts up toward Milner and Fall River Passes. We tried the horse trail, but the snow was soft and deep in the woods, so we tacked over to the road, where the sun and the wind had settled the three feet of snow a little. Circling and zigzagging, we mushed on and up. The sun was nearing the ivory domes and spires of the Never Summer Range. Looking down one could see our ribbon of ski track one thousand feet below, winding along the floor of Phantom Valley. Several times Walker stopped and listened, saying that he thought he heard voices. Sometimes when air conditions are right, as one passes through the high country in winter, these faint voice-like sounds can be heard, but if one stops and listens, there is only the wind in the trees or rocks, that indescribable sound of sifting snow, or just dead silence.

The sun went down. Fleecy clouds gathered over the Never Summer Range, and the chill grey of winter twilight settled over the vast panorama. Then suddenly the clouds turned yellow and the snow-mantled peaks were bathed in a flood of golden light. The alpine-glow lasted for several minutes, then slowly faded as the first stars began to twinkle over the Front Range.

On we pushed, on into the night. But night in the high country in winter does not mean darkness; there is always a sort of dim, filtered, elfin-like light. And presently, tired and hungry, we came to Poudre Lakes shelter cabin.

The snow was drifted almost to the eaves of the cabin and it took us several minutes to shovel out a passageway to the door, but we soon had a gasoline lantern lit and a cheery fire crackling in the stoves. As we were leisurely eating supper, three feet of snow on the roof slid off with a startling roar. When we looked out of the doorway, the passage was completely filled up. Luckily we had brought the shovel in with us.

The morning dawned fair, but before we had gone a mile, wicked-looking clouds came rushing out of the west from over the distant peaks of the far-flung ranges, and snow squalls mixed with slanting sun-bursts were racing across the sea of hills and valleys. When the wind soon struck the tops of the surrounding peaks, long snow streamers waved far out over the canyons. Soon the wind was howling in the highlands ahead, but in the forested valley the air was calm. The sky turned gray and one could hardly tell where the mountains stopped and the sky began. Snow began sifting down through the spruce and pine. A frozen, lifeless region it seemed until with a whirr of wings a fierce-eyed hawk swooped and banked through the trees, and startled grouse sprang from nowhere and scattered into the woods. Fresh tracks of a snowshoe rabbit crossed the trail. No doubt he was watching us from some vantage point, but because of his white winter coat was invisible to us.

In a little while we reached timberline. During a lull in the storm we could see the Pass ahead. The swirling snow and clouds soon blotted it out, but there was time enough to get our bearings and set a course. Often we stopped to get our breath, as the air is very thin at twelve thousand feet above sea level. Soon the rocks and then the bare ground began to crop through the snow, and we took off our skis. The Pass on the west side is nearly always swept clean by the wind. All we could see of the flat-topped stone shelter-cabin, just over the brink of the Pass, were the roof and eaves, so we strapped on our skis and eased down past the snow gauge which registered fifteen feet, and on to the shelter cabin on the wind-swept point half a mile below. The wind fairly shook the rock-ballasted roof and much fine snow had drifted, and was drifting, in through the cracks around the windows and doors. However, it seemed comfortable after what we had passed through during the past two hours, so we made a fire in the sheet-iron stove and ate our lunches.

It took only a few minutes to glide down to Willow Park and then into the timber of Fall River Canyon. Again the storm was above us, and the snow drifted gently down through the trees. We began to catch glimpses of Horseshoe Park seven miles below. Although the snow on the old road began to get too thin for good skiing, we felt that we were almost home. Due to a lack of snow we soon were forced to take off our skis and walk.

Just as darkness settled down, the lights of Horseshoe Park Ranger Station shone through the trees with a welcome gleam. And once again came that thrill and charm that can be found only in the light of a cabin window at the weary end of a long journey.

NOTE

1. The reference is to remnants of the great Bear Lake fire of 1900.

# 28

## CCC DAYS

1933

*Dorr G. Yeager*

*If Jack Moomaw was the living epitome of the park ranger, his literary proto-
type was Bob Flame, the fictional hero of four novels published between 1934
and 1946 by Dorr Yeager (1902–1996), Rocky Mountain National Park's first
chief naturalist. Arriving from Yellowstone in June of 1931, Yeager quickly
made his presence felt. Among his accomplishments were the exhibits he
designed for the new museum in the former recreation hall of the old Moraine
Park Lodge (today's Discovery Center) and the formation in 1931 of the Rocky
Mountain Conservancy (formerly the Rocky Mountain Nature Association)
to support the park and its programs. Yeager's stay was relatively short. In 1935
he was transferred to the Park Service's Field Division in Berkley to continue
his museum work, the next step in a long and distinguished career.*

*Bob Flame became Yeager's vehicle for providing an honest, if somewhat
romanticized, look at ranger and park service life. As he explained in* Bob
Flame, Ranger *(1934), the first in the series, "The story of Bob Flame is the
story of any Ranger. I have told of the commonplace as well as the extraordinary; the bitter as well as the sweet; for they must all be taken together before
the picture is finished."* Bob Flame, Rocky Mountain Ranger, *published
a year later, finds its protagonist, like Yeager himself, personally involved in
establishing its first Civilian Conservation Corps camp in Little Horseshoe
Park. As with all of Yeager's Bob Flame novels, most of the events described
can be documented from Park Service sources.*

*Two of the chapters in* Bob Flame, Rocky Mountain Ranger *are devoted
to the work of the CCC in Rocky Mountain National Park, whose first camp*

*was established in Little Horseshoe Park on May 12, 1933, in the immediate aftermath of a spring snowstorm that dumped twelve to eighteen inches in the area. In addition to Bob Flame, the characters in the excerpt reprinted below ("The Conservation Army Takes Over") include park superintendent Wentworth, assistant superintendent McDonald, U.S. Army captain Benton, and his assistant, Lieutenant Anderson (referred to as "Fritz"). Remarkably, even then, author Yeager was fully aware that the CCC was "an army whose name would live long after the economic forces which gave it birth were forgotten."*

Noon came and they went to lunch in shifts in order that someone would be on hand when the army arrived. One o'clock came, two, and two-thirty. At three an olive drab car pulled up and came to a stop in front of the building. Two officers climbed out, stretched their stiff muscles for a moment and then came up the steps. Bob noticed the insignia at once. One of the men was a captain and the other a second lieutenant.

Wentworth came out of his office as they entered. "Captain Benton?" he asked, holding out his hand.

"The same. I suppose you're Wentworth. Lieutenant Anderson, Superintendent Wentworth. Gad, that fire feels good." He slipped out of his service coat and held his hands before the fireplace. "Come over and get warm, Fritz. We've got a job when those trucks get in. Well, Mr. Wentworth," he continued, turning to the superintendent. "We've had the devil's own time getting here. Trucks slipped off the road, cars got stuck and we ran out of gas."

The superintendent laughed. "This isn't a very cordial reception, Captain, but we're not responsible for the weather." The captain shrugged his massive shoulders.

"Don't let the weather worry you," he responded cheerfully. "I've soldiered in a lot worse weather than this. We'll make out okay."

"By the way," said Wentworth, "we've made arrangements for your men to sleep in the bunkhouse tonight. They'll be comfortable enough out there, and it's getting pretty late to set up camp, even if there wasn't a snow."

The captain smiled. "That's mighty kind of you, Mr. Wentworth. Fritz," he said, turning to his lieutenant, "there *is* a god that watches over soldiers like us!"

"You and the lieutenant can stay at the hotel in town if you like. You'll find the accommodations comfortable enough, I think."

But Benton shook his head. "Not for us. We'll stay with the men. When it's smooth going it's all right to live apart from them, but when it gets tough I'll take it with 'em. What about you, Fritzy Boy?"

"Right with you, Captain." Wentworth called McDonald and Bob and introduced them.

"You'll see quite a bit of them this summer, Captain. In fact, you'll probably see them more than you do me." They chatted for a moment together and then the captain glanced out of the window.

"Well, Lafayette," he chuckled, "I see we've arrived."

Bob saw a huge army truck parked behind the captain's car. The box was covered by an arched brown canvas and in the cab he saw figures in the uniform of the army. There was something about the sight of that truck, waiting there in the snow, that gave him a thrill. On the side, in neat white, appeared the letters U.S. C.C.C.—United States Civilian Conservation Corps. Another truck rolled in and took its place behind the first. Then another and another until a long line of them was parked along the curb. There was an atmosphere of silent efficiency about these great trucks loaded with equipment and supplies. Bob had been too young to join the army during the war, but he remembered seeing long lines of trucks, similar to these, pulling in and out of the cantonments. Now he suddenly realized that another army had been recruited—an army which would fight as valorously as any other army had ever fought, but with different weapons and for a different cause.

Not until this moment did the realization of a conservation army crystallize in his mind. He had read correspondence and the neatly mimeographed instruction sheets in their crisp manila folders, but they had done little toward aiding him to formulate a picture of actuality. Now he was looking out of the window at a long line of businesslike trucks—the advance guard of an army to come. Suddenly he knew that this was big. He sensed the magnitude of this project which was to place thousands of men in the field armed with picks and shovels and axes. They were fighting not alone for the conservation of forests and streams and wild life. They were fighting for the conservation of American ideals, fighting with a weapon the extent of whose power and influence was not realized even by the men who created it.

But now was not the time for musing. Wentworth was speaking.

"Mac," he said, "suppose you and Bob show Captain Benton the bunkhouse and see that they're comfortably settled."

Within ten minutes the fleet was under way again and the long line was rumbling down the road in the direction of Utility.

"This is mighty nice of you," Benton said after the trucks had been lined up in front of the bunkhouse and necessary equipment and supplies transported into the building. "It *would* have been rather a tough beginning to have to put up canvas in this snow."

"We're glad to do it," McDonald replied. "By the way, what time do you want to pull out in the morning? The place is about five miles from here."

"What's the weather going to do?"

McDonald squinted at the sky. The snow had ceased and it was becoming conspicuously lighter in the west. The thick cloud blanket which had hung low over the range had lifted, and the peaks, white with fresh snow, were visible.

"Say!" exclaimed the captain with enthusiasm, not giving the other the opportunity to answer his question. "That is a sight. This assignment may not be so bad after all. Living with that makes up for a lot of things."

McDonald smiled. "We think so here. Why it's safe to say the storm's over and you'll have a clear sky in a couple of hours. And I'm not a fool either," he added, winking at Bob.

The captain looked at him curiously.

"We have a saying that only fools and tenderfeet predict weather up here," Bob explained....

The following morning the fleet of trucks left Utility in a long line and wound up the road toward Little Horseshoe Park. The snowplow had worked the previous night and the road was clear, but the warm sun was rapidly converting the snow into rivulets which flowed down the highway in ever-increasing streams. Half an hour later they pulled into the isolated mountain valley which was to harbor the conservation army for many months to come. The drivers pulled their trucks up in a line and awaited orders.

Benton and his lieutenant stood beside Bob and McDonald surveying the scene. The little valley was a beautiful spot with its level floor bordered by white-barked aspen, and the Mummy Range lifting itself majestically beyond its rugged slopes, enhanced by the robe of fresh new snow. At that moment, however, the captain was unable to concentrate upon the scenic values of the spot. For several minutes he stood gazing at the eighteen inches of wet soggy snow....

"Well," he said suddenly. "I've got work to do. Much obliged to you for showing us in. Give us twenty-four hours and you won't know this place. Come on, Fritzy, let's move."

He began barking orders. Men poured out of the trucks and immediately there was a scene of apparent confusion. As Bob watched, however, order began to disentangle itself from chaos in response to the captain's sharp commands. Men with shovels began clearing the snow, others unloaded tents and equipment, while trucks were dispatched to the village for supplies. They were still watching the activities when Brent drove up and climbed out of his car with photographic equipment. While the naturalist shot scenes of the work, McDonald and Bob returned to the office. Interesting as it was to watch the establishment of the first C.C.C. camp in any national park,[1] the regular duties must be carried on.

Later that afternoon they drove back to Little Horseshoe. The change was astonishing. Captain Benton, no longer in full uniform, hurried here and there, an apparently tireless machine. He was coatless, his sleeves were rolled up and his shirt was open at the neck. On his head he wore a battered old campaign hat. He saw them and came up.

"Well, how does she look now?"

"Different!"

"Oh, we'll get lined out. Sorry I can't chat with you but I want to get these tents up before dark."

He hurried away to supervise the raising of another of the brown army squad tents. One by one they had gone up in a double row on the spot which had been cleared of snow. Smoke drifted up from the camp ovens as cooks prepared the evening meal. Equipment and supplies had been neatly stacked and covered with heavy tarpaulins.

"I had never thought he'd be that far along," Bob admitted as they drove back to town.

"I guess Benton's able to do anything," McDonald replied. "I've heard of him before. Understand he's a slave driver but the men worship him. He's been working under pressure today though. Hadn't counted on the snow, and it set him back several hours. He'll be ready for them just the same."

By ten o'clock the following morning the village of Estes Park found itself completely occupied and taken over by the Conservation Army. Busses and trucks packed the streets, loaded with men fresh from the process camp at Fort Logan. There they had spent several weeks training, eating rough but wholesome food and acquainting themselves with camp life. There had been a weeding out process and only those who were capable had been assigned to duty. These men, most of whom were under twenty-five years of age had enlisted in the Corps for a definite period. They received one dollar a day and a certain amount of their monthly earnings was sent to dependents. But they did not care if the pay was small, or if the work was difficult. They had jobs, they were living in the open, and they were, as one was overheard to say, "having a whale of a time."

It was a howling, carefree lot that the busses carried up the road into the camp at Little Horseshoe. Many of them had never seen snow and the majority had viewed mountains only from a distance if, indeed, they had seen them at all. The combination of snow and peaks, of streams and forests, loosened the wild reckless spirit of youth on a holiday, and even the commanding officers were helpless to quiet them. Not until the busses rolled into the awaiting camp did the noise subside.

Bob stood beside McDonald and watched them unload. Sergeants called off names and the men were quickly formed into groups. Each group was escorted to its proper tent. As the procession passed by him Bob studied the faces of the boys. Every class was represented. There were boys who had never before been off the city streets, and there were boys who had never been on them; boys from farms and ranches; boys who had hitched and boys who had ridden the rods from Maine to California. Bob thought he had never seen such a heterogeneous group as the men who followed the sergeants to their respective quarters. Every race, every color and every creed seemed represented. He wondered what was going on in the minds of these boys as they trudged down the avenue of brown squad tents with their duffle bags slung over their shoulders.

Here was such an army as had never been recruited under the flag of any nation before. It was an army of construction instead of destruction, an army whose name would live long after the economic forces which gave it birth were forgotten. Bob's mind drifted back to the wording of a bronze plaque which commemorated the first Director of the Service—"There will never come an end to the good that he has done." And it seemed to the man as he stood there watching that line file past him that the words were equally applicable to the men of this group. At that moment Captain Benton came up to them.

"Well," he smiled, "what do you think of them?"

"Looks like they've all come," McDonald remarked. "I never saw such a mixture of color and race in my life."

"It is a mixture," replied the captain slowly, "but it's a good mixture, and a democratic one. I got to know some of them pretty well at Fort Logan before they came up. We have college graduates in that outfit and we have boys who have never seen the inside of a schoolroom. This life is going to teach them both something, and it's going to be a great leveling experience. It'll bring some of 'em up and some of 'em down. Good thing to let one half know how the other half lives, occasionally."

"N.P. 1-C.," mused McDonald as he looked over the brown tents. "National Park Camp One. The first to be established in a park."

"And," the captain added proudly, "we're going to make it the best camp in the outfit."

As they drove back to the village that evening Bob was strangely silent. The thing which he had seen that day affected him greatly, and the pink reflection of the sun on the peaks had driven him into still deeper silence.

"Why so quiet, old man?" McDonald asked at length. "Anything wrong?"

Bob shook his head. "Nothing wrong, Mac. I've just been thinking over what I've seen today."

"Makes one think, all right. It's a great undertaking."

"It's greater than we think, Mac."

"What do you mean?"

"That's what I've been thinking about," Bob replied. "Up to now we've been looking at this from a purely get these boys off the street, to give them jobs and at the same time get something useful out of them. We've been thinking in terms of erosion control and fire lanes and roadside clean-up."

"Well?"

"Well, this thing's bigger than that. That's not what's going to live after these boys go back to their homes. The big thing—the thing that will live and the thing that will be felt for years to come—is what they learn. Listen, for twenty-five years we've been preaching conservation, and how much progress have we made? Mighty little. But think what it's going to mean to the country to have half a million boys go back into circulation who have *lived* conservation for all these months. They've lived it, and every mother's son of them is going to help for the rest of his life. Can you imagine any of those boys, after they've spent a year like this in the hills, who won't be a booster and who won't back up park policies for all he's worth? That's what I mean when I say we haven't been looking deep enough."

"Gad," McDonald remarked softly, "I never thought of it that way, Bob."

Both men were silent for the remainder of the trip while the pink on the peaks gradually faded and night settled down on the mountain country.

NOTE

1. In fact, N.P. 1-C was the first camp in a national park west of the Mississippi River.

# CONQUERING THE DIAMOND

## 1960

*Stephen Trimble*

*Major Powell in 1868, Professor Alexander in 1922, Vaille and Kiener in 1925, the Stettner brothers in 1927—all big moments on Longs Peak. But there was one more climbing prize, the Diamond on the East Face. It proved to be both tempting and elusive. Paul Nesbit, in his 1964 climbing guide, put it well: "A virgin wall to be wooed and won by he who could demonstrate superior prowess. Thus the Diamond came to symbolize the hardest climb on the mountain and displayed it provokingly. It was the mountain's dare."*

*For a time the Park Service stood in the way. In 1954, when two experienced climbers announced their intention to make the ascent and began training, it declared the Diamond off limits. Other would-be climbers applied for permission; all received the same response. Finally in 1960, the decision was made in Washington to open the route. All those who had been refused were, simultaneously, issued application forms. Two Californians, Bob Kamps, an elementary school teacher, and David Rearick, a mathematics PhD, led the way. After an arduous three-day ascent, August 1–3, 1960, the prize was theirs. Historian Stephen Trimble describes their achievement.*

On the topographic map of the park, Longs Peak fits under a single handspan. The Diamond shows as a tiny brown splotch where the contour lines bunch up on top of each other. It begins at 13,110 feet and rises unbroken for 945 feet, nearly to the summit.

Rearick and Kamps intended to climb the wall "direct," in an elegant straight line from Broadway right up through the center of the face to the summit. With the help of their support team they carried their gear up to

Broadway via North Chimney, and began to climb on August 1. They pushed the route up four pitches (the distance climbed by a leader on a 150-foot rope before stopping to belay the second climber), climbing free where they could, using direct aid when necessary. They rappelled down to Broadway for the night, and climbed back up their ropes the next morning to continue the ascent into new territory. To climb fixed ropes they used prusik slings, friction knots that slide upward but hold tight when pulled downward.

The next 400 feet leaned outward, and the two climbed *behind* a steady sprinkle of wet water from melting ice in a chimney near the top of the Diamond. They reached a ledge about three hundred feet above their previous day's high point, and pulled up their bivouac gear from "The Ramp" 225 feet below. They spent the night of August 2 here, on a perch two feet wide and seven feet long. Before dark they were able to climb 809 feet above the ledge, again rappelling down fixed ropes.

Rearick described their night:

> Back on the ledge it was getting cold, and we put on all our clothes, ate some food, and tied in for the night. I sat in a cross-legged position all night, while Bob was able to recline partially. The night was clear and we watched the shadows from the moon creep stealthily along the slope of Lady Washington below us and across the shimmering blackness of Chasm Lake. We both managed to doze for a few hours....

The next morning:

> ...we had to make a crucial decision, as our fixed line ran diagonally upward and outward to the left. We could leave a fixed rope from the upper bolt to the bivouac ledge. Otherwise, when we stepped into our prusik loops and swung into space, retreat would be impossible. Should we cut off our retreat and find that the water-flowing upper chimney was impassable, it would be up to our support party to help us.

Choosing to cut off retreat, they moved on. They negotiated the icy chimney and reached the top of the Diamond at 1:15 p.m.

The sheer competence of Kamps and Rearick and the other climbers who would follow them up the Diamond disguises the incredible adventure of what they do. When they write about the climb, bold and exhausting moves over hair-raising exposure come across as laconic, technical summary.

We can feel with Elkanah Lamb the whoosh of cold air and the biting crystals of the snow as he slides down the mountain.[1] We can struggle on through the cold blast of a blizzard with Agnes Vaille. But the Diamond remains the accomplishment of its climbers in a uniquely personal way.

They come down from the mountain with grins, but with few words. Rearick and Kamps describe a possible bivouac ledge above the "ramp…18 to 24 inches wide, quite level, and about 15 feet long." They advise the next party to "have a generous supply of angle pitons of the inch and larger variety." They state that they placed four bolts for belay and rappel anchors, not for direct aid. But they waste no words on whys and wonderings. Royal Robbins has said: "…we climbers are endlessly asked by nonclimbers, 'Why do you climb?' The proper answer is, 'If you have to ask, you'll never understand.'"[2]

The world below the cliffs, however, remains determined to partake vicariously in the adventure of the Diamond. Though reporters dashing up and down the mountain during the Kamps-Rearick climb wrote most vividly about their own hardships, the two climbers were feted everywhere from the Estes Park Rooftop Rodeo Parade to *TIME Magazine*.

The Diamond was an ultimate—the biggest, highest, steepest, most tantalizing wall in all the Southern Rockies. To the non-participating watchers below, its first ascent was a magnificent conquest—a word climbers themselves would hesitate to use.

Another word that climbers avoid is "impossible." They hungered after the impossible Diamond, climbed it, then repeated the climb time after time. Non-climbers size up such an undertaking and say "out of the question."

Layton Kor spoke for all climbers each time he discovered a difficult and unlikely new route and said flatly, "It's got to be climbed."

NOTES
1. The reference is to Lamb's perilous 1871 descent of the East Face.
2. Royal Robbins, like Layton Kor, were expert Longs Peak climbers in the decade that followed.

# 30

## THE TUNDRA OF TRAIL RIDGE

1972

*Anne Zwinger and Beatrice H. Willard*

*The complex and fragile tundra along Trail Ridge Road is a world that many visitors simply pass through on their way across the Continental Divide, perhaps stopping briefly at the Alpine Visitors Center, the highest facility of its kind operated as a concession by the National Park Service. For those willing to invest the time and effort, the alpine tundra exhibits to be found at the center are particularly rewarding because of the window they offer on one of Rocky Mountain National Park's most special and endangered places.*

*It is this world that naturalist Anne Zwinger (1925–2014) and her botanist coauthor Beatrice H. Willard (1925–2003) write about in their 1972 book* Land Above the Trees: A Guide to American Alpine Tundra. *Of the two authors, the award-winning Zwinger is, of course, the better known. Her many books dealing with the natural history of the Rocky Mountain West have been widely praised. However Willard's published work, though less in quantity, has been equally influential, particularly in terms of the management of Rocky Mountain National Park's high altitude tundra plant life. Her contributions are remembered in the Beatrice Willard Alpine Tundra Research Plots at the Rock Cut and at the Forest Canyon Overlook, both of which are listed on the National Register of Historic Places.*

Following a path on Trail Ridge in the Colorado Rockies that moccasined feet padded thousands of years ago, one can gain not only a vast view of tundra slopes but of other mountain tops. Prehistoric man used this ridge as an east-west traverse across the Front Range during the summer, hence the name Trail Ridge. The narrow single-file path has been used for at least 6,000 years, and some archaeological evidence suggests that it may have been in use as long as 15,000 years ago. It was a trail used mainly by women and children and is an easy passage over the top of the Ridge. But so slow is tundra vegetation to recover from disturbance that the trail is still clear, raveling across the landscape like a brown thread, even though it has been little used in the nearly forty years since the modern paved road was laid.

At the base of the slope the trail crosses a fellfield paved with lichened rocks and small gray-green plants set in hard soil. A little higher up a tumble of boulders contain pika, usually seen and always heard. Alpine coral bells, cinquefoils, alpine sorrel and an occasional dwarf bilberry grow in the rock's protection. A Parry primrose, usually found along subalpine streams, shelters beneath an overhang. Leaning down to enjoy its resonant magenta color one gets a sniff of its resonant odor instead–a pungent and distinctive smell.

Pussytoes fringe a rug of kobresia. A pocket-gopher worked area is dotted with bright blues and yellows of sky pilot and Rydbergia and chiming bells. Going up takes an inordinately long time because there is so much to see: an iridescent beetle riding a curled rock sedge leaf like a roller coaster; a cluster of wand lilies just out, a willow area where ptarmigan roosted during the last storm, the last harebells of summer and the first arctic gentians. I cannot help but wonder if the Indian women and children who tested this part of the trail enjoyed the plants that they saw, if they had names for them, and if so, what they were. And I wonder, when they walked towards the plains at the end of summer, if they too felt a sense of sadness at a summer's ending.

On the top of the Ridge, the wind birrs across, swooping up from the deep dark green valley below. There is something about an alpine wind: it can blear the eyes and chill the fingers and be exceedingly irksome, but it seems to come from the back of beyond, carrying tangles of trees and warps of willows in its passing. Across the valley, other tundra areas seem close enough to step to, cleanly outlined in the alpine light. It seems unreasonable to have to accept that they are separated by miles of arduous hiking. It is an untouched and untroubled landscape, a peaceful one in spite of the restless wind, an uncluttered landscape, a landscape of ultimate isolation.

In a sheltered niche, back to a warm rock, under the wind, I watch the paved highway winding across the Ridge, its firm sinuous curve to contrast to the wavering foot path. The cars look no bigger than the beetle I watched on the way up, and their sound does not carry this high. But their swift purposeful going is a reminder that Trail Ridge is one of Colorado's alpine areas where man's presence is heavily felt.

Over a million people visit Trail Ridge in the summer; nearly 400,000 travel the road to the summit of Pikes Peak. Visitor pressure concentrates where there are parking areas and scenic overlooks. With overcrowding, parking areas are sometimes full, and more and more people pull off to the side of the road and walk out onto the tundra on their own. There are almost no signs telling them not to. But there are other clear signs for the knowledgeable to read.

When the present Trail Ridge Road was built, the Old Fall River Road was blocked off where it crossed the tundra. It was scarified and all attempts were made to delete any evidence of its presence. It is protected from use. In the nearly forty years since, it is still visible. Strips of sod along the new road, laid to stabilize cut banks, are still almost separate as the day they were laid, the dirt lines between them empty of vegetation.

Enclosures were established by Dr. Beatrice Willard in cooperation with the National Park Service in 1959 in order to measure the recovery of alpine plant communities that have been intensely trampled or destroyed. The study has documented the recovery rate of damaged plants and areas, and is a technique which has value in other heavily used natural areas. In the short time between May 30 and August 25, 1958, the path people made cross a fellfield removed two-thirds to nine-tenths of the pad of cushion plants. It requires only eight weeks to abrade cushion plants to the crown with trampling, and only two weeks for the top horizon of thin fellfield soils to begin to erode. If, after one season of trampling, the fellfield is protected, recovery begins within the month, but it is not complete for more than two decades. Longer degradation causes even slower recovery. Notably missing for many years are the important soil-building and soil-holding ground lichens and mosses.

At Mount Rainier some of the heavily used high subalpine and low alpine slopes have been webbed with paths. In spite of established trails, hikers take the shortest distance between two points, or simply strike off on their own. Attempts are being made to reestablish vegetation by scarification, reseeding and replanting, blocking the paths off and covering them with mesh and burlap to prevent washing. It is necessary to restore their original aspect since any trace of a path is an invitation to use it again. The Park Superintendent estimated that $250,000 is needed for two seasons for full restoration, requiring five men plus machines, plants and water.

It seems obvious that it is easier to prevent damage on the alpine tundra than repair it. Where plants and animals grow at the outer limits of their existence, recovery is marginal and extremely slow.

Not all alpine areas open to automobiles are so fortunate as to have a paved road. The road to the summit of Pikes Peak is a dirt road, excellently maintained. It is wide, safe, constantly checked for washing and erosion, continually patrolled. But it is gravel and dirt in a windy area. On the downslope side of the switchbacks, the plants are so coated with dust that they are almost invisible, and in most places the constant sliding of the fine loose gravel soil has simply inundated them, reducing the slopes between to the most impoverished and constantly eroding scree slopes.

Since the Pikes Peak Highway is well patrolled, cars remain on the road. But in the remote interior passes roadsides are often crisscrossed with four-wheel-drive tracks, made by drivers who take off across the tundra with no thought except of pitting their vehicles against nature, with no realization that their tracks may remain for years and centuries, causing erosion and damage not only to the immediate but to nearby areas.

In recent years, access to high mountain country has been made possible by four-wheel-drive vehicles, trailbikes, and in the winter, snowmobiles. Areas previously closed are now open all winter, and the invasion of noise and people into previously cloistered areas has disturbed both larger animals and ptarmigan, pushing them out of previously peaceful winter pasture and disrupting breeding areas. And during fall and winter, when tundra plants are at their most fragile, vehicle tracking is most damaging.

The litter barrels on Trail Ridge are stuffed with refuse. It is an almost impossible task to keep them emptied. Paper plates, paper towels, disposable bottles and cans are easier to throw away than wash up or return. Some

National Forest areas have tried removing all containers and posting the entrance with notice that everyone is responsible for carrying out his own trash. This is so recent an idea that its effectiveness is not known. The more usual method is constant pick-up; this fall, members of the Sierra Club anticipate picking up between 10,000 and 15,000 pounds of litter along the Adirondack hiking trails. A helicopter goes into the Mount Whitney area to lift the trash out. The *in loco parentis* philosophy of the Park Service and conservation organizations does not encourage personal responsibility. The mother who always picks up after her children soon finds that that is all she does.

In the lowlands, a crumpled cigarette pack would probably decompose within the season. On the tundra, it will take several summers. Meanwhile it cuts the light to the plants it covers, killing them within a few weeks. When it blows a few inches away, it leaves a dead plant and a bare spot. A bottle cap encompasses a nascent cushion of moss campion. Bottle caps and metal cans do not disintegrate for at least a hundred years on the tundra. Fifty to one hundred years of plant growth can be snuffed out by a beer can....

The West has been populated largely by people who originally lived in the East, where revegetation took place in a matter of weeks, recovery in a matter of months. Western mountain slopes still bear the scars of timbering and mining of a century ago because reforestation is so slow in the cool, arid climate. The alpine tundra is fragile far beyond all forests. The tenacity of alpine plants, their adaptation for endurance and survival, is tremendous, but they cannot withstand mass abuse.

The wilderness has never been thought of as a museum in which the treasures of the natural world are preserved, against which man can measure himself and see how human habitation alters his environment. Wilderness has been ours to enjoy and use, and often misuse. There was always more. Until recently, no one ever thought of wilderness as an irreplaceable, exhaustible resource. Now we know that the wilderness can be exhausted, and this is most poignantly true of the alpine tundra.

# 31

# THE WHITE-TAILED PTARMIGAN

2003

## SueEllen Campbell

*SueEllen Campbell is a professor of English at Colorado State University where she teaches courses in nature and environmental literature, as well as creative nonfiction. She also is codirector and founder of CSU's Changing Climate Program.*

*Ms. Campbell writes lyrically about the world of nature. But she does so with the accuracy of someone for whom the details of the natural world are supremely important. In the essay excerpted here from her 2003 book,* Even Mountains Vanish: Searching for Solace in an Age of Extinction, *she tells of a day in early June when, as a way of overcoming her winter vision of spiritual and ecological loss, she sets off in search of white-tailed ptarmigan in the tundra of Rocky Mountain National Park. What she discovered that day not only tells us a great deal about this elusive bird, but brings spiritual renewal. "The Earth is old," she writes.*

> *Nothing lasts.... Ours is an age of extinctions; ours are the hands of the destroyers. Grief and beauty are knotted together. Curiosity and imagination are fundamental human forces. So are fear and hatred, passion and compassion. None of this is surprising.... But scale matters.... When I focus on smaller things, the picture changes.*

*This is how nature, responding to human curiosity in encounters with small things in unexpected places, serves us all. As for the ptarmigan, its "bracing lessons are all about staying engaged and active in the world, however cold or dark it might be."*

June seventh, Trail Ridge Road, Rocky Mountain National Park, just before noon. Ptarmigan Day.

I had offered to drive because I love this road, have loved it my whole life, how it swoops and twists and climbs so high so quickly that driving feels like flying, flying through rising layers of worlds, a new one every few miles: low meadows purple with wild iris, grassy stand of ponderosas, dense woods of Douglas fir, lodgepole pine, new-leafed aspen, two miles above sea level, snow still deep along the roadside, bands of slender Engelmann spruce and subalpine fir alternating with broad-fingered limber pines, each layer a world of more light, stronger winds, sharper colds, deeper winter, then, just below treeline, Rainbow Curve, a spot wide enough for a score of cars to pull off…and all at once the day was turning into a small adventure.…

Even now, a week into June, winter wasn't over. The road had opened for the season only two weeks ago…snow had fallen yesterday, as it would keep doing nearly every day for a while longer, and Trail Ridge was closed again from here on up until the plows could finish their job.

Closed, that is, to everyone else. I was following the man with the key: Ken Giesen, a Colorado Division of Wildlife biologist who was teaching today's class about white-tailed ptarmigan. We'd spent the morning at park headquarters looking at slides, and now, in a caravan of two, we were inching through the crowd [of cars at Rainbow Curve] while my passengers joked through open windows with the folks we were leaving behind us, and we were heading into the sky.

From here, it didn't take long to get through the last of the forest. We passed the site of an old fire, where a few trunks stood white, stark, and solitary more than a century after they burned. As a child I'd been impressed by these mountains, which my father said had looked about the same when he first came in the 1930s, and I marveled yet again at this sign of the harsh climate, how it slows new growth nearly to nothing. Beyond the burn, the trees grew fewer, shrank and twisted and became more picturesque, until each one might have belonged on a postcard. Finally the forest withdrew into tiny low islands of survivors, cushions a few yards across and just hip high. This was krummholz, a good word to pronounce; in German, it means crooked wood. Here one tree might be three feet tall, ten feet across, and many hundred years old.…

Leaving these trees behind makes some people uncomfortably exposed, I knew, but it always exhilarates me. As I drove through the krummholz and out into the tundra, I felt as if I were crossing over an edge, away from any ordinary protection and into some radical and cleansing kind of openness.

From here on for nearly ten miles, the road would stay above the trees, a sinuous thread across the gently rolling uplands that top this part of the Front Range of the Rockies. We were retracing an ancient migratory and hunting route between the Great Plains and the green valleys to the west, one used by elk, deer, bighorn sheep, and people, most recently Ute and Arapaho women and children, then tourists, hikers, ptarmigan searchers. Not far past Rainbow Curve, I'd heard, if you walked uphill and looked very carefully, you find the remains of a game drive system several thousand years old, where hunters once funneled animals into a narrow space and then ambushed them—three long lines of rock that don't quite match their surroundings and a scattered handful of stone blinds; later this summer, I resolved, I'd try to find this site for myself....

Just past the Alpine Visitors Center, Ken pulled over to park where the road hairpins to the south, at the spot the maps call Medicine Bow Curve. I think of it as Poetry Curve, myself, for all the places with good names you can see from here: the Medicine Bow Mountains, the Snowy and Mummy Ranges, the Rawahs, the headwaters of the Cache La Poudre River and the Colorado. And just to the west are the Never Summer Mountains. As a child growing up in Denver, I'd always waited eagerly for my first glimpse of this range, hidden from my home by intervening peaks, visible only when we'd reached the highest point on this pass. I'd been eager for the view itself. A spectacular jagged ridge of white, but also for the chance to savor the name, the best one of all, the way it enticed me to imagine a land of endless winter, of remoteness, cold, and snow. It pleased me today that our search for the elusive and iconic ptarmigan was beginning just here.

A few minutes later, out of the car and newly wrapped in several layers of warm clothes, sandwich in my pocket, I was diving over the high pile of plowed snow at the road's edge. The trail was more than half white, the deeper snow at that stage of invisible melting where every step I took my boot was equally apt to stay on top of the crust, slide out from under me, or sink through the ground. The sky was a hybrid, too, mixing blue with clouds likely to bring more snow, and while the sun felt warm, the breeze was chill. I was toasty from the car, my feet almost hot from under heavy boots and thick socks. But I knew this comfort wouldn't last.

Ken carried a small tape recorder in one hand, an odd-looking fishing pole in the other. Since he'd been banding white-tailed ptarmigan up here for years, he knew just where they'd be getting ready to nest and seemed confident we could find one today. But I couldn't quite believe it.

It wasn't that I'd never seen these birds.... All three of these encounters had been accidental, even startling. More than that, really. For me these birds had become emblems—of high mountains, of the perfect matching of creature to place, of self to its world, and of the potential everywhere for a moment of pure surprise, the sudden appearance of what had been hidden but was always there. And this morning's class—the science, charts, numbers, maps, details—all this had only honed the mystery, given me a glimpse of what this bird knows. Such intricate ways to survive hard winters, in fact to thrive in them. I could hardly believe that we could park our cars, walk a bit, and find one to catch, just like that.

Ken stopped and switched on his tape recorder. Static in the background, a welcoming tumble of low-pitched charters or chuckles. Then, in a switch of tone so sudden it made me jump, two or three short, ear-piercing screams—the sounds of a male ptarmigan announcing his presence.

"This time of year," Ken had told us earlier, "if you play the tape early or late in the day, often a bird will fly right at you." I struggled to quiet my breathing—the air here is noticeably thinner than where I live, nearly seven thousand feet downhill, and even on a level trail the snow made walking harder. I listened. Nothing. "There!" he said, and pointed. "Here it? Down there." He played the tape again, waited a minute, then plunged off the trail.

I hadn't heard a thing except Ken, his tape, the wind in my ears, my own lungs and heart. But I took the leap of faith and followed....

In no time, it seemed, my classmates and I were huddled around Ken, kneeling and sitting on a cold, wet patch of bare ground, watching him handle a bird with careful assurance. He'd caught this one with little trouble: because white-tailed ptarmigan evolved where there were few large mammalian predators, they're generally unwary of humans. Of course, before you can get close to them, you first have to see them; that's the hard part and the reason for the tape recorder. When the bird responded to the recording, Ken had walked quietly toward it, then lowered the noose at the end of his fishing pole carefully over its head. He'd slowly tightened it until he could draw the bird to him, and since they tend to freeze when something unusual happens nearby, it hadn't struggled to escape and thus was unharmed. This was a new bird, still unbanded, not yet entered into his roster of Trail Ridge inhabitants, so there were measurements to be made, notes to be taken.

Ken shrugged off his pack and opened it. He turned the bird in his hands and looked at it carefully, reminding us as he worked of what he'd covered in the morning's lecture. Sex? Female: easy to tell just now, when only the females are in full summer plumage. Age? He straightened out a wing and measured its primary feathers: two years old. Weight? Out came a small scale: just about twelve ounces, the same as a city pigeon. He clipped on the set of expanding plastic bands that would identify this individual bird, two on each leg, each a different color. All this he recorded in his notebook, part of the database he'd been building for more than two decades.

This was a beautiful bird. Her feathers perfectly matched the landscape around us, on this day caught between seasons—her body the mottled browns, blacks, and creams of spring, the colors of lichen, rocks, and matted tundra grasses, her wings and tail the clear white of the winter's snow. Her eyes were black, shiny, intense, each arched over with a thin red line like an eyebrow. Hidden inside her chest would be an enlarged heart, expanded and strengthened to deal with the demands of a life spent entirely at high altitudes where oxygen is scarce.

By now, she would have spent nearly a month on this hillside getting ready to breed. Devoting up to two-thirds of every day to foraging and eating: it takes a lot of protein to make a whole new set of feathers and then lay eggs. As the summer arrives, ptarmigan shift their diets away from willow, their staple during most of the year. They look for new greens of all kinds and especially for new and highly nutritious flowers, and with eyes ever sharper than mine and a much more focused need, they find them. Then they snap the blossoms right off....

Less than two weeks from now, the bird in Ken's hands would be sitting on her nest, somewhere on the ground where the snow had melted, hidden from the wind against a rock or at the edge of a willow patch. She'd lay six or seven eggs. Then, for the next twenty-three days, she'd leave them only to feed, at dawn and dusk. She'd sit so tightly and be so well camouflaged that a hunting weasel might pass right by and never see her. Still, nearly half of the nests are lost to predators, and with such a short season, few ptarmigan manage to lay a second batch of eggs. After her chicks hatch in mid-July, she'd guard them closely, too, especially through their first, riskiest month. The three or four that made it to fall would likely have a long life, maybe as many as a dozen years.

Ken was finished with his measurements, and now it was our turn. He explained how to hold her, firmly but gently, by her lower legs, so that she couldn't take the jump she'd need to fly. We wouldn't be hurting her, he promised; her heart rate would have risen only a little, and when we let her go, she would simply fly a few feet and get back to her meal. Then he handed the ptarmigan to the woman on his left. I watched her face: intent, a little scared, a flash of surprise as the bird stretched her wings, then delight.

Sometimes the world paints its canvas with the indifference of an axe or a blowtorch, lopping off whole branches of life with a single blow, incinerating vast landscapes in an instant. I'd been bent under the weight of this story, the long, tragic saga of extinction. But I was beginning to comprehend how evolution always follows with her intricate creative brush, a point as fine as a single hair, her unequaled attention to detail, her endless inventiveness, new ideas to try, minute changes to make, an extra mitochondrion here, a curling white filament there. Even in this hard, spare place so recently buried under ice, a landscape I imagined might resemble the aftermath of cataclysm. And I thought now, even at the worst moments in the earth's long history, when some massive disaster had brought an end to life on an unimaginable scale, something intricate and beautiful had surely been happening, as it would happen again.

I'd known that these lovely birds changed their plumage for winter and stayed high in the mountains, but I'd had no idea until today just how thoroughly they were adapted to what I would usually think of as harsh conditions. *Adapted*: the word is precise, but we use it so often it has lost some of its force. Ptarmigan don't just adjust their attitudes when the cold arrives.

They don't even much adjust their behavior. By evolving in artic and alpine climates, they have become what they are by virtue of surviving for countless generations in an icy world. They're made in every detail to thrive in a life of winter. If the marmot speaks of retreat and repose, of peace to be found in seclusion or at home, then the ptarmigan's bracing lessons are all about staying engaged and active in the world, however cold or dark it might be.

As the bird made her way slowly around the small circle of careful hands and hushed voices, I remembered what I'd learned today about the likely shape of her life. And I thought about what she would do once her chicks were fledged and she could leave her nest.

In late July, his territoriality forgotten, her mate would gather with the other local males below late-lying snow somewhere further uphill, where it's cool and moist. Soon she and her fast-growing offspring would join them. On the tundra's warmest days, if she felt too hot, she'd move into the shade or the wind, maybe take a bath in snow crystals. Or, she'd pant, mouth wide open, moving the air through her neck where it could cool her blood. In late September, she would begin to change into her winter plumage. As she became whiter, she'd move to snowier areas, shifting her ground in small increments so that she could continue to match her surroundings.

Finally the ptarmigan would move to where the snow lies deep and willow bushes are abundant. Her mate would travel only a mile or so and winter with another four or five birds. She'd go farther, ten miles, twenty, even thirty. She'd winter in a larger flock of females, likely thirty to fifty, maybe many more.

How would she spend her days? Eating. More precisely, eating the buds and twigs of willow bushes, the single highly nutritious food that would make up nearly all of her winter diet.... As Ken had put it, ptarmigan are voracious feeders. At the opposite extreme from marmots, they carry almost no body fat, and so they have to eat nearly every day to survive. She would do this so well that she'd actually gain mass during the winter, while nearly every other living creature would be losing it.

When evening fell, she would work her way into the snow until she was entirely invisible and covered with a thick layer of insulation, enough to maintain an inside temperature of twenty to thirty degrees Fahrenheit, even while outside temperatures dropped to twenty or thirty degrees below zero. On really cold days, which for a ptarmigan means below zero, cloudy, and windy, she might do the same, removing herself just for a little while from the hazards of the surface. Her main danger would be a mild season without enough snow to serve as camouflage, sleeping bag, and temporary sanctuary.

This bird knew just how to behave in the winter. Along with the tundra's other survivors, plants and animals both, she also had the right body. Like the weasel's white fur, her winter feathers would work as both camouflage and heat collectors; on chilly days, she could find a patch of sunshine, fluff herself out, and let the rays of the sun penetrate the hollow shafts and reach her skin. The feathers covering her body were double, too, each carrying a second downy branch called an aftershaft, for extra insulation. In short, she was feathered all over. Feathered nostrils would keep the snow and ice from impeding her breathing. Feathered eyelids would do the same for her vision. Feathers would keep her legs warm, so much so that in winter, when all coats are thicker, she would look like a bird walking around on a rabbit's legs. And feathered feet and soles kept her on top of the snow, doubling the weight each foot could carry without sinking, aided by a kind of fringe that grew along the sides of her toes and her long black toenails: built-in snowshoes.

I'd planned, of course, to be a diligent student and examine the bird we captured for all these details. But from the instant my fingers wrapped around her legs, I forgot everything practical, everything about the context of what I was doing, my desire for facts, any sense of my own body's limits, sore knee, short breath, weak eyes, the thick bundles of clothing I needed to stay outside in this weather, the dark season's sadness. I forgot myself, my self-consciousness, my separate, thinking, human self, and found instead, only for this short moment, the immediate. *This wintry place. This ptarmigan in my hands.* As I received her from my neighbor and she felt the brief freedom of her legs, she stretched out her wings and neck, thinking to fly. But with some instinctive response, my own grasp grew quickly more certain and she settled back again.

Some of the ingredients of this moment are visible in a pair of

photographs someone took of me holding the bird. As I write these para-
graphs many months later, I study them to help me remember, my glasses
off, the prints held close to my eyes, one, then the other, then the first....

Her visible wing is slightly spread, the white primaries sharply lined,
and her neck stretches out. In one photo her head turns towards me and
her eye is hidden. I'm holding her low across my chest, so her back shows,
and my hand, four fingers curved so that just their tips touch her feathers,
so lightly. I look down at her with a goofy little grin. In the other photo, I'm
holding her at shoulder level, her head in front of my chin, and she shows
off her perfect profile, her eye smooth and black. There is no other way
to tell what she is thinking or feeling. I study my face. It is in shadow and
more than half hidden. I look happy. I look absorbed, tender.

What I remember most vividly, though, no photo could reveal—that
sensation of something quivering behind my ribs and in my throat. It
wasn't fear or even nervousness. It was anticipation and care, that rare jump
of the heart that comes with wonder, the sheer thrill of holding this wild
life against my skin, muscle, nerves, bone. I could feel in my own body the
bird's banked energy, her softness and light warmth. I could feel the way
she gathered the seasons to a point, the long ages of ice and the fleeting
summer, the quiver of her heartbeats, her big strong heart.

I was the last in the circle. When I handed the bird to Ken, he let her go.
She flew a few feet away and began pecking at the ground, looking for a
blossom to nibble.

# 32

## ELK IN ROCKY MOUNTAIN NATIONAL PARK

Dynamics and Management, 2014

*Michael Coughenour*

*The Earl of Dunraven found Estes Park and its adjacent valleys a hunter's paradise. So did its early settlers. Their profligacy soon took its toll. By 1878, pioneer Abner Sprague tells us, the elk were largely gone.*

*The issue of elk, and their absence, was revived by talk of a new national park in the years after 1909. The Estes Park Protective and Improvement Association took the lead. In 1913, and again in 1914, this community-wide organization raised funds to purchase two small herds from the Yellowstone region of Wyoming and had them transported by rail to Lyons. From Lyons they made their way to Estes Park on Stanley Steamer Mountain Wagons equipped with special cages. Acclimated in the village, the elk were then introduced into the future park.*

*In the absence of hunting and significant predators, they quickly multiplied. By 1931 elk were regularly leaving the national park, signaling the beginnings of the long debate about their management. The essay included here, one specially commissioned for this volume, reviews Rocky Mountain National Park's history of elk management. Its author, Michael Coughenour, a Senior Research Scientist in the Natural Resource Ecology Laboratory at Colorado State University, has carried out extensive studies relating to the elk-carrying capacity of the park.*

North American elk (*Cervus canadensis*) likely arrived in North America around 15,000 years ago by crossing the Beringia Land Bridge from Asia.

Humans probably arrived in North America by the same route and during the same time period. Carbon dating has shown that elk reached Montana as the Pinedale ice sheet retreated, about 12,000 years ago. Archeological evidence indicates that elk were present in the Yellowstone area at least 9,000 years ago.

It has been suggested that the prehistoric game drive systems discovered at high elevations within Rocky Mountain National Park were predominantly used to hunt elk, mule deer, and bighorn sheep. Radiocarbon dates at one such site places these artifacts at 2,610–4,590 years before present (BP) and at 2,200–4,310 years BP at a second. It is likely that elk were hunted in the late summer and fall, especially during their migrations from summer to winter ranges. While bison were also likely present, Jim Benedict, who has authored the most authoritative archaeological studies to date, argues that the configurations of the game drives, their topographic locations, and the absence of reworking tool flakes that one would expect to be present if animals as large as bison were butchered, indicate that it is unlikely that these game drives were used to hunt bison. These findings point instead towards elk hunting, and thus, the presence of elk in the area during late summer and fall.

There is a considerable amount of historical evidence of local elk presence prior to European-American settlement. Notes made by J. A. Loring of the U.S. Biological Survey in the spring of 1893, following a week-long field trip to Estes Park, observed, "That at one time elk were abundant is evident from the large number of horns that may be found in the timber." According to Fritiof M. Fryxell's 1928 account of the 1914 visit to Estes Park by two elderly Arapaho (ages sixty-three and seventy-three), both men had many vivid recollections of hunting bison in the Estes Valley and Rocky Mountain National Park area in their youth, which would have been between 1855 and 1870. Oliver Toll, who authored the only published report of their pack trip, mentions that the party found a large hunting camp with elk and bison bones at Tuxedo Park. Tuxedo Park is only hundreds of meters east of Moraine Park which is on the current elk winter range. On the basis of interviews with a number of Estes Park's old timers, including Abner Sprague, Howard and Homer James, and Pieter Hondius, Fryxell compiled a list of the physical evidence of bison presence in the area. His interviewees told him that many bison skulls had been found throughout the area at an early date.

Rufus Sage visited North Park, an area just northwest of the current Rocky Mountain National Park, in 1842. He noted that "the entire country was crowded with game, in countless numbers, both of buffalo, elk, and deer." The first settlers of the Estes Valley Joel and Milton Estes arrived in 1859. They found abundant elk and deer. Heavy hunting occurred through the 1860s and early 1870s to provide meat to supply mining camps. Wagonloads of elk and deer were regularly delivered to markets in Denver. Abner Sprague recalled that in 1875, elk came down from the mountains by the thousands and were met by hunters. During the winter that followed hunters continued to kill elk and deer indiscriminately and cart them to markets in the valley towns. The next winter few elk came down, and by 1877, even fewer were seen. The last one he killed was in 1878.

Elk were reintroduced to the area in 1913–1914 and Rocky Mountain National Park was formally established in 1915. During the period of elk hunting, extirpation, absence, and recovery (1875–1930), herbaceous vegetation was heavily grazed by livestock. Livestock were present on what is now elk winter range within the park boundary, as well as throughout the Estes Valley. Humans occupied and altered what is now core winter range inside park boundaries. Wet meadows were drained and willow was cleared to provide hay fields and livestock pastures. Livestock were grazed on the park winter range until the 1930s. In Moraine Park water was diverted from streams and used for irrigation of the hay fields, and later, a golf course. Numerous structures were also built on the winter range, including sizeable hotels, resorts, and homesteads. The last resort buildings and the golf course in Moraine Park were not removed until the 1960s.

Though it is unclear what land elk actually had access to in the years immediately following their reintroduction, the total area available was certainly less than that available prior to settlement. Furthermore, livestock grazing and haying would have reduced available forage biomass, effectively making only a fraction of that land available for elk foraging. In an ecosystem modeling assessment of the 1912–1948 time period, it was assumed that elk were mainly restricted to the area east of the park's current eastern boundary during the period between 1912 and 1931. Although the eastern park boundary in 1915 was considerably west of the current boundary, a Colorado State Game Refuge was created in 1919 along the east boundary, and probably included much of what is now within the current boundary, but outside the 1915 boundary. Elk probably did not have access to the core grasslands in Moraine Park and Horseshoe Park (west of the current boundary) because these were being grazed by domestic stock or hayed. The total winter range was thus about 100 square kilometers, in contrast to the 165 square kilometers available earlier.

In 1925, Superintendent Roger Toll stated that the present number of elk was as large as could be supported without supplemental feeding during winter. Yet, in 1925, there were at most 200 elk. These elk were raiding haystacks and crops in times of heavy snowfall. By 1928 there were numerous reports of elk damage. As early as 1929, concerns were raised by park personnel about negative impacts of elk on plants and range condition. Given their relatively low numbers, but the mounting negative impacts on vegetation and hay and crop raiding, it became clear by then that elk did not have access to sufficient land or forage. Conflicting human land uses were clearly to blame. In 1931, field biologist Joseph Dixon recommended that additional lands be purchased by the park to provide a larger winter range, arguing that "the present winter range is entirely inadequate for the elk and deer now on hand." At that time there were 200 to 300 elk and 800 deer. Eight years later, in 1939, Dixon sounded an even louder warning: "now elk have reached and passed the carrying capacity of the winter range in the park and are destroying it through over-browsing." By 1938–1939, the elk herd reached an estimated peak of 900 to 1,100 animals.

Early wildlife policy for America's national parks was developed following Dixon's 1930–1932 field surveys in Rocky Mountain National Park. That policy clearly stated that the number of native ungulates on a deteriorated range should not be allowed to exceed its carrying capacity, and that the size of the herd should preferably be kept below that carrying capacity to allow range recovery. Given the date and size of the elk population, it is likely that this policy was aimed at repairing damage done by prior livestock grazing. The elk population continued to climb, and from 1925 to 1941 there were repeated and consistent observations of further range degradation. By 1939, it was decided that the elk winter range within park boundaries was seriously overpopulated and that the herd needed to be reduced. National Park Service biologist Victor Cahalane, who inspected wildlife conditions in 1943, subsequently commented that "most of the elk and deer remain within the park and are not subject to hunting," thus justifying the need for direct reductions (culling) within the park. The first substantial direct elk reduction followed in 1944–1945 when 301 elk were removed, reducing the population to some 500.

Though there was little active management during World War II, by 1949 concerns about poor range condition had risen again, and another cull of 340 elk brought the population back down to approximately 500. Three hundred fifty elk were removed in 1949–1950. Between 1944 and 1953, 1,045 elk and 318 deer were removed. By 1950, a program of annual herd reductions was in place and between 1950–1959, 507 elk were removed and the population was maintained at 350–800 elk through 1960. Lethal reductions within the park ended in 1960. They were discontinued principally in response to the large public outcry against the lethal elk reductions that took place in Yellowstone National Park during the winter of 1961–1962.

This backlash contributed to the adoption of a "natural regulation" policy in Yellowstone. It probably also catalyzed action on an interagency agreement for cooperative elk management at Rocky Mountain National Park. That effort began in early 1961 when Colorado Game and Fish and Parks called a meeting with park officials to discuss the possibility of hunting in the park. Though that suggestion was rejected, a decision was reached to undertake a cooperative elk study program. In December 1962, the CGFP, the National Park Service, and the U.S Forest Service signed a memorandum of understanding to begin cooperative investigations to determine if ways could be found to control elk by methods other than direct reduction. A winter hunting season east of the park was initiated in January 1963, with the hope that hunting outside park boundaries would be sufficient to keep the elk population in check. Subsequent studies documented elk movement in and out of the park, so expectations of success were high.

Beginning in 1968, elk in Rocky Mountain National Park were managed in an experimental "natural regulation" as in Yellowstone. This management approach was based on the hypothesis that large herbivores are naturally regulated by food limitation. This idea also aligns with the fact that national parks in the United States were directed to "conserve the scenery and the natural and historic objects and the wildlife therein" (National Park Service Organic Act of 1916); "preserve vignettes of primitive America" (the Leopold Report, *Wildlife Management in the National Parks*, 1963); provide the American people "with the opportunity to enjoy and benefit from natural environments evolving through natural processes minimally affected by human actions" (National Park Service Management Policies, 1988); and maintain all the components and processes of naturally evolving park ecosystems, and rely on natural processes to maintain native species and natural fluctuations in populations whenever possible (National Park Service, Management Policies, 2001). It has also been argued that national parks serve as important baselines for discerning the impacts of humans on ecosystems.

Thus beginning in 1968, the elk herd was managed only by sport hunting outside park boundaries. This proved to be largely ineffective, for by 1975 the population had increased markedly to 1,000 or more animals. On average, 442 elk were harvested by hunting each year through 1987; however, increasing elk use of private lands reduced hunting offtake and the harvest was reduced to an average of 302 from 1988 to 1998. At the same time, elk increasingly began to winter outside the park boundaries in the town of Estes Park, where they also largely escape hunting. The Estes Valley elk herd has come to consist of three sub-herds with fidelities to their own winter ranges and to their own migration corridors leading to a combined summer range. Between 1998 and 2001 the park elk population was estimated to range from 730 to 1,418, an average of 1,012. The town herd segment has been shown to be demographically distinct from the two park herd segments that winter inside the park. During that same three-year period, the town herd grew to an average size of 2,000 animals.

During the last three decades of the twentieth century, concerns about elk impacts on plants and other components of the ecosystem heightened considerably. Elk impacts on aspen and willow were of particular concern. Aspen were being damaged by elk as early as 1929, and more recent studies show that elk browsing has contributed to an aspen decline on the core (lowest elevation) elk winter range. Since the 1930s, heavy browsing of willow and declining willow abundance have also been observed. Since the 1940s, these decreases have also been linked to a marked decrease in beaver numbers. Though the exact cause of the beaver decline has not been demonstrated, since willow is a primary source of food and construction material for the beaver, it has been suggested that in large part that decline was the result of increased competition from elk for willow.

Concerns about high elk numbers not surprisingly resulted in criticism of the park's elk policy, most notably by Karl Hess in his 1993 indictment of park management. Such criticism led the agencies involved to re-evaluate their approach to elk management. That same year, in fact, park superintendent James Thompson requested the U.S. Geological Survey's Biological Resource Division to conduct a problem analysis of the elk situation and submit a proposal to carry out a thorough research study. Between 1994 and 1999 the BRD and scientists at Colorado State University, in cooperation with the National Park Service, conducted a number of subsequently published research studies to assess the elk population status, trends and spatial distributions, and to assess vegetation condition and trends on the winter range and the extent to which they were being affected by herbivory, precipitation, ground water, experimental clipping, and fire. Individual studies focused on riparian, willow, and upland herbaceous and shrub-dominated plant communities. Twelve large fenced elk exclosures (or vegetation "enclosures") were constructed in willow stands, and artificial check dams were installed to simulate the effects of beaver dams on ground water. Four additional exclosures were also constructed in upland shrub communities. These studies culminated in a major final report in 2002 by Francis Singer and Linda Zeigenfuss.

Individual studies documented high levels of herbivory on upland herbaceous and shrub communities, large declines in willow structure and growth attributed to elk browsing. Studies of aerial photographs showed that during the last fifty to sixty years streams have become less sinuous and that water surface areas in Moraine and Horseshoe Parks have been reduced primarily because of the decreased numbers of beaver. Still other studies found that aspen stands on the winter range are not regenerating and, consequently, that aspen clones on the winter range will eventually die off. Ecosystem modeling predicted that wolves would significantly reduce elk population sizes, that protected willow stands would over a number of years increase plant size, and that ground water conditions would have to be improved and elk numbers reduced to achieve sustainable tall willow communities. Modeling also predicted that aspen could regenerate if protected from herbivory, and that if elk numbers were reduced aspen could persist.

Based upon the results of these and other studies, the National Park Service developed and released a draft *Elk and Vegetation Management Plan/Environmental Impact Statement* for public review in April 2006. This also began a formal seventy-five-day comment period that ended on July 5, 2006. Comments were received from the public, various organizations, and the U.S. Environmental Protection Agency. The National Park Service responded to substantive comments and provided clarifications. The final plan was released in 2007 along with a *Record of Decision* published in early 2008. It is conveniently available on-line (www.nps.gov/romo/parkmgmt/elkveg_mgmt_plan_feis.htm). The plan examines several different management alternatives ranging from no action to actions involving lethal elk population reduction, fertility control, fencing of willow and aspen, herding, adversive conditioning, and wolf reintroduction. The preferred alternative calls for gradual lethal reduction to achieve a population size of 200 to 400 elk within the park and 1,000 to 1,300 elk in town. Both numbers are at the high end of the natural range of variation (if predators were present). Fertility control is to be implemented if an effective and logistically feasible agent becomes available. Because of the higher elk population target, aspen and riparian willow enclosures are to be erected on both the primary summer and winter ranges. Wolf reintroduction was ruled out because it would require a high level of wolf population monitoring and management and because of a higher level of uncertainty that wolves could effectively control elk and achieve vegetation management objectives in the current environmental setting. Since 2008, the park has fenced 190 acres, 45 of aspen and 145 of willow, amounting to 5% of the entire winter range. An additional 16 acres is fenced on the summer range. The fences are meant to be temporary, but will likely need to be in place for 20 years or longer until the vegetation management objectives are achieved.

In February 2009 the first lethal elk reduction took place. Reductions are carried out by certified and regulated sharpshooters and not by public hunting, which is prohibited in national parks. In the winter of 2008–2009, 33 elk were culled, in the winter of 2009–2010, 40 were culled, and 50 were culled in winter of 2010–2011. By late 2011 elk numbers had declined to an acceptable range, so no elk were culled in winter of 2011–2012.

Currently, there are fewer elk wintering in the park than there were in the 1998–2001 period; however, this decline is not due to culling. Between 2001 and 2008, park elk numbers declined from about 1,000 to about 600. In 2011 there were estimated to be 634 elk, a number at the low end of the target range of 600–800. It is unclear why the population has declined, but it is likely related to changing winter weather conditions and increased numbers of elk migrating to lower elevations since 2001. In 2011 it was predicted that with no further culling, elk numbers would only rise to 696 by 2013 and that an annual cull of 50 adult females would result in 630 animals by 2013. Based on this modeling work, it is likely that no more than 50 elk, and possibly none at all, will need to be removed each year in order to keep the elk population within the target range. Vegetation conditions within the fenced enclosures are being closely monitored, and initial evidence points, in fact, to signs of aspen and willow regeneration.

# 33

## THE PIKA'S LAST STAND

### The Effects of Alpine Climate Change, 2014

*Thomas D. Gootz*

*Elk management is but the most visible of the current issues faced by the park's natural resource scientists. The multidisciplinary* Natural Resource Condition Assessment for Rocky Mountain National Park, *published in July 2010, documents a broad range of scientific issues and concerns summarized under the headings Air and Climate, Water, Biotic Integrity, and Landscapes. All are directed to answer a single question: "What are current conditions for important park natural resources that should direct the attention of park managers?"*

*Not surprisingly, one of the important habitats examined was the alpine tundra, a complex ecosystem that, like the other life zones within the park, is multidimensional and subject to any number of variables. A key variable is, of course, climate change, one of the issues specifically identified in the 2010 report, and the "uncertainty of long-term sustainability and sensitivity to climate change for native species such as the pika."*

*Pika and climate change is a subject that Dr. Thomas Gootz, a retired research scientist, sets out to explore in his book* Transformation in Rocky Mountain National Park: The Effects of Climate Change and Human Interference *(2014), a chapter of which has been edited for inclusion here. A current resident of Estes Park, Gootz has a long-standing interest in wildlife and wild places, particularly with respect to the global threats to the environment that endanger both.*

There is no better example of an animal in Rocky Mountain National Park (RMNP) threatened by climate change than the pika. The American pika (*Ochotona princeps*) is a small member of the rabbit and hare family. While the pika is not considered a "keystone species," its restricted alpine habitat makes it an important sentinel species for the effects of a warming climate. This diminutive animal lives in a limited environment at the highest elevations in the park. The pika has an unusual metabolism and a relatively high body temperature of 104°F, making it sensitive to outside temperatures above 75°F. Furthermore, the pika does not hibernate in the winter months. These characteristics account for its status as an indicator species for the effects of warming temperatures at high elevations. As a result of its life in remote areas, few visitors glimpse a pika. One of the best places to see them is along the talus rock slopes found in the tundra regions of Trail Ridge Road. It has adapted well to such rocky tundra habitats which also help it to elude predators. The pika accomplishes this by hiding under loose talus piles, often less than one acre in size. Talus is composed of medium-sized broken rock, some of which may interlock, giving the pika plenty of places to hide. Tourists may encounter the pika during rest stops along Trail Ridge Road.

The first alert of the small creature comes from its high pitched "eeep" call. This is most often used to warn neighbors of approaching danger. If one looks carefully toward the direction of the call, the source may be seen scurrying among the disorganized piles of talus, in search of food or shelter. Obtaining a photograph of the pika is much more challenging, since its small size and high octane movement leaves little opportunity for a pose. The much larger alpine marmot may also be the source of the sound. They share much of the same habitat as the pika. However, the marmot is not as habitat restricted as the pika and can sometimes be found in more open alpine meadows as well as in sub-alpine and montane zones. Although the pika often goes un-detected by most park visitors, there is real concern about its future across much of the mountainous West. The pika is being extensively studied to better understand the potential harmful effects on its distribution from increasing temperature.

## THE PIKA'S UNIQUE CHARACTERISTICS

The pika's species name comes from a Latinized version of the Chipewyan Indian name, "little chief hare." They are small (4–6 ounces), rounded in shape, and about the size of a young guinea pig. They have short, rounded ears, thick fur, and a tail that is not visible externally. Fossil remains suggest that pika migrated from Siberia to North America, some 500,000 years ago, across the land bridge linking Asia to Alaska. From that time to approximately 7,500 years ago, pika enjoyed a much greater distribution than today, because of the colder climate of that period. As the earth warmed over the ensuing thousands of years, pika were forced to live among alpine rock features. Talus fields were often found down slope from melting ice which created moist habitats that supported lush regions of grasses and sedges. This slow, incremental upslope migration of pika across western mountain ranges resulted in its overall restriction to a rather narrow habitat composed of loose rock, at elevations generally above 9,500 feet. Recent scientific studies indicate this upward migration is a result of the pika's unusual intolerance of summer temperatures above 75°F. This heat intolerance has restricted the pika to a much reduced range, sometimes referred to as "mountain islands." Today, distribution of O. princeps in North America includes the Northern Rocky Mountains of central British Columbia and Alberta, through Idaho, Wyoming, Montana, and the Ruby Mountains of Nevada, as well as mountainous regions of Colorado. Their distribution is becoming increasingly limited to mountain ranges at higher, cooler elevations.

The specific adaptations of pika to their alpine habitat make them one of our most sensitive sentinels of climate change in the West. Pika have dense fur to protect themselves against extreme cold periods during the long alpine winters. Two fur molts occur each year, during the spring and summer. The cinnamon-brown midsummer pelage is worn for only a few weeks. The pelage during the winter is grayer and longer to provide greater insulation during the bitterly cold months. This adaptation of thick fur is necessary for winter survival. Pika do not hibernate over the winter, as many rodents do. They remain active amid the talus structure, insulated from the most extreme cold temperatures by the thick layer of snow typical at high elevations. Pika cannot dig den holes in the dirt beneath the talus;

however, they are able to dig snow tunnels in the winter, to gain access to surface plants and lichen.

Pika give the impression of living life in the fast lane, moving quickly from rock to rock while eating and collecting grass. They are strict herbivores, eating a variety of grasses and forbs (low-growing, short-stemmed plants) such as cushion plants, which grow around the talus. Living in an extreme environment with a long winter, they have an industrious habit of harvesting different plant species. These they dry in the sun and cache in "hay piles" under the talus rock to serve as food and bedding for winter. In severe circumstances, hay piles may be the only source of food over the winter. Some of these caches are up to a bushel in size, to allow survival over the coldest months. If sufficient snow cover occurs, pika can run among the talus through snow tunnels to feed on forbs remaining on the ground or lichen growing on rocks. Pika hay piles comprise forbs and small shrubs that contain acidic phenolic compounds. These chemicals make the vegetation unsuitable to eat in the summer, but they break down over time, while serving as preservatives to inhibit the growth of bacteria in the stored hay pile.

During summer months, pika must feed on fresh grass and forbs to replenish nutrition. They spend a significant amount of their feeding day "haying" to build their stock for the winter. Pika know which herbaceous material is most nutritious for eating and which are best harvested and stored in the hay pile. They often use different parts of the same plant for summer grazing and storage as winter food. Pika will both eat material, and cut it to carry more than a mouthful away for winter. While this activity can be comical to watch at close range, it is a matter of life and death for the pika. They have evolved as masters of their harsh alpine climate. Much eating and stockpiling must be completed during July and August, to permit survival through the winter months.

Pika scurry about during the day, since there is much to be done to survive in this harsh environment. Pika rarely travel more than about thirty feet from talus while grazing. In addition, the pika must hurry, since when exposed, it is at risk for predation by its greatest enemy, the weasel. Weasels are particularly efficient predators, since their long, narrow bodies allow them to chase pika under the rock talus spaces. Pine martins, coyotes, hawks and eagles also feed on pika. The alarm "eeep" is an important communication tool for the pika to warn all in the talus habitat that danger is near.

The pika's extreme sensitivity to temperature is becoming a greater liability, since as temperatures warm across the West's alpine regions may be affected most. Such warming leaves the pika vulnerable to extended exposure to sun and heat as it feeds and gathers food for its winter hay pile. There are many reasons for pika to hurry across their talus home, making sure that they do not spend excessive amounts of time in the open. Some studies have found that pika spend up to 30 percent of the day outside of their rocky burrows, but they are generally restricted to their mountain homes and do not usually disperse over distances greater than 0.5 to 1.2 miles to find improved living conditions. The inability to travel across distances in their landscape makes the pika vulnerable to limited genetic variability, which may affect its ability to sustain a healthy population. This lack of genetic diversity could further compromise their ability to adapt to a warming environment.

## THE LIFE OF A PIKA

The pika lives in a restricted range of remote habitats of RMNP and other mountainous regions across the West. Pika inhabit a narrow area of talus at elevation, in what scientists call a meta-population. A meta-population consists of spatially separated population groups of the same species that interact at a minimal level. This obligate talus lifestyle makes for some interesting physiological and behavioral properties of pika. In a meta-population, males are usually monogamous and females generally give birth to two litters per year. A yearling female can breed within its population or another meta-population. In addition to eating and gathering food for survival, pika mothers bear an increased burden. They must produce and care for two litters during the short spring-summer season. Each litter, on average, contains only two to three young. The burden of reproduction usually permits only the early litter to survive. If the first litter falls to predation, or does not survive an unusually cold spring period, the mother will attempt to foster the second litter. The young are born with patchy fur, closed eyes and fully developed teeth. Studies show that the mother must immediately leave the nest to feed. She must revisit the nest every two hours to nurse the young. Pika young grow quickly, with weaning occurring in three to four weeks. They reach adult mass of four to six ounces within three months. By four months, pika become intolerant of their siblings and begin to display territorial behavior. Young pika must establish themselves in an acceptable area within a meta-population or find another talus habitat with available space. Establishing an adult territory is difficult for young pika since they are poor dispersers. Average mortality has been shown to be as high as 50 percent. They are bound to their alpine talus islands and must immediately begin to eat and stockpile food to ensure winter survival. If they are diligent and lucky to avoid predators, they can live to four years, but individuals up to seven years of age have been documented.

Pika work to establish and defend their territory in several ways. They can produce a long whistling sound, which is usually given by the male. This sound signifies that he is defending his territory. Despite the danger faced from predators, pika can be observed perched atop a high rock amid the talus, surveying their territory for predators, as well as other pika identified as intruders or potential mates. Males are ready to defend their territory against competing males. Good talus is hard to find. In addition, pika have a scent gland in their lower cheeks which they use to rub against rocks as they go about their daily business. This scent marking identifies territory boundaries, warning others to stay away. Pika may be aggressive when defending their territory as adults, and they will tolerate their offspring only if food supplies are plentiful.

Using sophisticated genetic testing methods, American pika have been classified into several subspecies. *Ochotona princeps princeps* is the one found in RMNP. The Colorado Division of Wildlife has documented at least forty occupied sites in the northern part of the state. Spending several hours among a talus colony off Trail Ridge Road is a pleasurable experience.

## GLOBAL CLIMATE CHANGE IS THREATENING THE SURVIVAL OF THE AMERICAN PIKA

As previously mentioned, many scientific publications have focused on the American pika as a key sentinel species to document the negative effects of a warming climate. The higher elevation regions of the West have experienced rapid warming over the past thirty years. Both the International Panel on Climate Change (IPCC) in its fourth assessment report "Climate Change 2007," and the National Oceanographic and Atmospheric Association (NOAA) station in Boulder, Colorado, have collected temperature data. Their observations document that the western United States has warmed about 2°F during the past thirty years.

Scientists have documented that the rapid increase in mountain temperatures observed over the last decades has had negative effects on temperature intolerant animals such as the pika. As a result of this work, on October 1, 2007, the US Fish and Wildlife Service (USFWS) received a petition from the Center for Biological Diversity in San Francisco, requesting that the American pika be listed as threatened or endangered under the Endangered Species Act.

Combined observations from the studies at the Great Basin and the Southern Rocky Mountain region indicate that alteration of pika habitat caused by climate change is a threat to pika populations across the West. Depending upon the habitat, higher summer temperatures, drier conditions, and a loss of insulating snow cover in the winter can all lead to extinction of the pika. This is particularly true when the habitat is fragmented, because pika are not able to transition easily to higher elevations that may provide more favorable habitat. Studies from Yosemite National Park indicate that over a century of observed climate warming, small mammals living at low elevations expanded to higher elevations, and those from high elevations contracted their ranges to compensate for warming temperatures.

Concern over the survival of the pika across many western states has prompted more detailed studies to evaluate the stability of pika in their habitats. The National Park Service funded the "Pikas in Peril: Multiregional Vulnerability Assessment of a Climate-sensitive Sentinel Species" study. This three-year study (2010–2012) was aimed at determining the distribution of the pika across their habitat under a range of climate projections in eight national parks (four in the Rocky Mountains, including RMNP, and four in the Northwest). The study also examined gene flow and connectivity among pika populations in five parks and predicted the impact of climate change on future distribution and vulnerability of pika across the eight parks studied. Key goals of the study were to utilize consistent protocols among the researchers in order to define sample survey plots by GIS methodology, and to document pika presence by sound, sight, and detection of fresh caches and/or fecal pellets, employing pairs of independent observers.

In RMNP, fifty-eight and sixty-eight plots were examined in the study years 2010 and 2011, respectively. Pika or fresh pika signs, were found within twenty-nine (43%) plots in 2011, compared with thirty-nine (67%) in 2010. Of the twenty plots surveyed both years, seven (35%) changed occupancy status, all losing pika sign in 2011. A total of seventy-three fecal samples were collected for genetic analysis. A final report and genetic analysis information gained from the pika fecal samples from RMNP will be published in 2014.

Results from the "Pikas in Peril" program have confirmed the importance of local site characteristics in determining pika occupancy rates. The report showed that it was difficult to identify general characteristics associated with pika occupancy across large regions. Rather, it was the "idiosyncrasies of place," creating a favorable habitat for pika, that was most important for pika survival. Pika occurrence probabilities increased with decreasing potential solar insolation on cooler north-facing slopes. Pika occurrence probabilities were negatively associated with the presence of grasses and absence of forbs.

## THE PIKA GOES TO WASHINGTON

The accumulation of climatic data and decreasing numbers of pika observed in long-term studies from the Great Basin region did not go unnoticed by the scientific community and environmental watchdog groups. These data formed the basis for the Center for Biological Diversity's petition to add the American pika to the endangered species list.

How did the pika fare? In the decision published by the USFWS in the *Federal Register* on January 29, 2010, the government acknowledged published information documenting the decline of pika across the West. An accompanying climate report from NOAA conducted specifically for the pika petition supports the conclusion that rising temperatures are contributing to the decline of pika numbers. However, the final USFWS report states on page 15, that while the warming trends identified in the NOAA report are probably enough to harm some pika in certain habitats, *"every* pika is not at risk for extirpation by increasing temperatures across the West." Based on this statement, the USFWS denied the pika endangered or threatened species status. The available data indicate that temperatures have a very high likelihood to continue to rise through the year 2050 in the West. This will have lethal effects on pika in certain habitats, although some pika will likely survive in others.

## TALUS WITH ROCK ICE FEATURES:
## COULD THEY BE THE PIKA'S LAST STAND?

One of the recent studies referenced in the endangered species report, has added another twist to the pika's story. These investigators conducted an ambitious survey of over 400 potential pika habitats in the Sierra Nevada, Great Basin, and Oregon Cascades. They employed a rapid assessment method, in which the presence of pika were scored either visually, finding pika scat, or by locating their hay piles. Results showed a surprisingly high pika occupancy rate of 67 percent. This is a higher incidence than those encountered in other studies. While sub-talus temperatures were not recorded in this study, the authors explained that their high occupancy rate was related to the frequency of rock-ice-features (RIF) found along the occupied talus fields. RIF characteristically contain talus and boulder fields with streams fed by glaciers, located above the talus. The topographic contexts of rock-glacier and boulder–stream landforms are such that climatic conditions tend to be cooler than the temperature averages expected for their elevations. In addition, the authors describe the RIF environments as containing dense wetland with rich herbaceous vegetation below the boulder streams. Such habitat provides a diversified food source for pika. The down-slope flow of cold melt water creates a microclimate of cold air pools that circulate back up the slope. This maintains a talus habitat for the pika cooler than those habitats lacking this structure. These scientists found that 83 percent of the sites where they found pika contained RIF. They suggest that this feature may well account for why they documented such a high occupancy rate overall. Hopefully, Forest Service professionals will focus additional studies at RIF locations and prioritize them as protected pika habitats.

Much has been learned about the diminutive pika over the last decade. Only through scientific research, and public awareness, can humans begin to understand the climate forces influencing this tiny creature's life and future. High elevations in the Southern Rocky Mountains of Colorado contain a good deal of suitable habitat for the pika. It is hoped that more people who travel through Rocky Mountain National Park will learn about the pika's situation and become advocates for this wonderful species. The pika's "eeep" call should be a warning to us all of the dangers of global warming.

# TIMELINE OF HUMAN HISTORY

ESTES PARK–ROCKY MOUNTAIN NATIONAL PARK

| | |
|---|---|
| c. 1200–1850. | Ute Bands roam the central mountains of the future park. |
| c. 1790. | Arapaho begin to arrive in region. |
| 1820. | June—Major Stephen H. Long, traveling along the plains, makes first recorded sighting of the peak that will be named in his honor. |
| 1859. | October—Joel Estes and one of his sons first visit the valley that will bear the family name. |
| 1868. | August—Major John Wesley Powell and party make first recorded ascent of Longs Peak. |
| 1871. | August—Addie Alexander becomes first woman to reach summit of Longs Peak. |
| 1872. | December—the Earl of Dunraven visits on a hunting trip. |
| 1873. | October—English travel writer Isabella Bird arrives. |
| 1874. | May—Estes Valley surveyed and opened for settlement. |
| 1875. | Pioneer families arrive: among them the Spragues, Jameses, MacGregors, Fergusons, Hupps, and Lambs. |
| 1876. | August—Colorado becomes a state. |
| 1877. | July—Dunraven's Estes Park Hotel opens. |
| 1879. | Isabella Bird publishes *A Lady's Life in the Rocky Mountains*. |
| 1884. | Enos Mills arrives in the Tahosa Valley; Carrie Welton becomes the first recorded death on Longs Peak. |
| 1889. | William Allen White and KU friends summer in Moraine Park. |
| 1900. | Bear Lake fire sweeps Glacier Gorge region. |
| 1903. | June—F. O. Stanley comes to Estes Park in search of his health. |
| 1904. | Big Thompson Canyon road opens. |
| 1906. | Estes Park Protective and Improvement Association formed to promote tourism. |
| 1907–1909. | F. O. Stanley builds the Stanley Hotel complex; June 1909—hotel opens. |
| 1909. | October—Enos Mills begins his campaign for a national park. |
| 1912. | April—Colorado Mountain Club formed. |
| 1913. | Small band of elk from Wyoming reintroduced into future park; first park bill introduced in Congress; work begins on Fall River Road using convict labor. |

| | |
|---|---|
| 1914. | July—Arapaho revisit area on week-long pack trip. |
| 1915. | January—third park bill is passed by Congress and signed into law by President Woodrow Wilson. Dedication takes place on September 4. |
| 1916. | August—National Park Service created. |
| 1917. | April—town of Estes Park incorporated. |
| 1920. | September—Fall River Road opens. |
| 1922. | September—Professor James Alexander makes first ascent of Longs Peak's East Face. |
| 1925. | January—Agnes Vaille dies during winter ascent of Longs Peak. |
| 1926. | Boulderfield Hotel opens. |
| 1929. | October—work begins on Trail Ridge Road. |
| 1930. | Never Summer Range added to RMNP. |
| 1931. | Horseshoe Inn is purchased and removed (the first of the lodges within the park). |
| 1932. | July—Trail Ridge Road opens to Fall River Pass—completed to Grand Lake in 1938. |
| 1933. | May—first CCC camp opens in Little Horseshoe Park. |
| 1939. | June—work begins on thirteen-mile Alva Adams Tunnel as part of the Colorado–Big Thompson transmountain water project; park begins to charge an entrance fee. |
| 1944. | March—Alva Adams Tunnel holed through. |
| 1948. | RMNP visitors reach one million. |
| 1955. | December—Hidden Valley Winter Use Area opens. |
| 1960. | August—first ascent of the Diamond on Longs Peak's East Face. |
| 1965. | Current Alpine Visitors Center opens. |
| 1967. | Beaver Meadows Visitors Center completed as part of Mission '66 program. |
| 1968. | Kawuneeche Visitor Center opens; RMNP visitors reach two million. |
| 1976. | July—Big Thompson Canyon flood, the worst natural disaster in Colorado history. |
| 1978. | RMNP visitors reach three million. |
| 1982. | July—dam at Lawn Lake is breached causing massive flooding of the town of Estes Park. |
| 1991. | Hidden Valley ski area closed. |
| 2000. | Fall River Visitors Center opens as public-private partnership. |
| 2013. | September—RMNP and Estes Park suffer widespread flood damage. |
| 2015. | RMNP celebrates its centennial. |

# FURTHER READING

Buchholtz, Curt W. *Rocky Mountain National Park: A History*. Boulder, CO: Colorado Associated University Press, 1983.

Butler, William B. *Rocky Mountain National Park: Historic Places*. Estes Park, CO: Estes Park Museum Friends & Foundation Press, 2008.

Chapin, Frederick H. *Frederick Chapin's Colorado: The Peaks About Estes Park and Other Writings*, edited by James H. Pickering. Niwot: University Press of Colorado, 1995.

Drummond, Alexander. *Enos Mills: Citizen of Nature*. Niwot: University Press of Colorado, 1995.

Foster, Lisa. *Rocky Mountain National Park: The Complete Hiking Guide*. Englewood, CO: Westcliffe Publishers, Inc., 2005.

Frank, Jerry J. *Making Rocky Mountain National Park: The Environmental History of an American Treasure*. Lawrence: University Press of Kansas, 2013.

Gootz, Thomas. *Transformation in Rocky Mountain National Park: The Effects of Climate Change and Human Intervention*. Estes Park, CO: Estes Park Museum Friends & Foundation Press, 2014.

Pickering, James H. *America's Switzerland: Estes Park and Rocky Mountain National Park: The Growth Years*. Boulder, CO: University Press of Colorado, 2005.

———. *"This Blue Hollow": Estes Park, The Early Years, 1859–1915*. Niwot: University Press of Colorado, 1999.

Pickering, James H., Mic Clinger, and Carey Stevanus. *Estes Park and Rocky Mountain National Park: Then and Now*. Englewood, CO: Westcliffe Publishers, Inc., 2006.

Sprague, Abner E. *My Pioneer Life: The Memoirs of Abner E. Sprague*. Estes Park, CO: Rocky Mountain Nature Association, 1999.

Young, Mary Taylor. *Rocky Mountain National Park: The First 100 Years*. Helena, MT: FarCountry, 2014.

# SOURCES AND PERMISSIONS

## CHAPTER SOURCES

Chapter 1. Enos A. Mills. "The Rocky Mountain National Park." In *The Rocky Mountain Wonderland*, 335–53. Boston: Houghton Mifflin, 1915.

Chapters 2 and 3. Oliver W. Toll. *Arapaho Names & Trails: A Report of a 1914 Pack Trip*. Estes Park, CO: Rocky Mountain Nature Association, 1962.

Chapter 4. James H. Pickering. "The 1914 Arapaho Trip: The True Significance." *Rocky Mountain Conservancy Quarterly* (August 2014): 1–2.

Chapter 5. Milton Estes. "Memoirs of Estes Park." *Colorado Magazine 16* (July 1939): 121.

Chapter 6. Lewis W. Keplinger. "The First Ascent of Long's Peak, 1868." *Collections of the Kansas State Historical Society* 14 (1918): 159–61.

Chapter 7. Earl of Dunraven. "A Colorado Sketch." *Nineteenth Century* 8 (1880): 445–57.

Chapter 8. Isabella Lucy Bird. *A Lady's Life in the Rocky Mountains*, 97–118, 121, 122–23, 126–29, 130–32. London: John Murray, 1879.

Chapter 9. Lewis B. France. "The Lure." In *Fishing with the Fly, Sketches by Lovers of the Art*, 131–41. Manchester, VT: C. F. Orvis, 1883.

Chapter 10. Abner Sprague. "My First Winter in Estes Park." *Estes Park Trail* 2 (November 24, 1922): 3; (November 30, 1922): 3.

Chapter 11. Carrie Adell Strahorn. *Fifteen Thousand Miles by Stage*, 65–69, 70–72. 73–74. New York: G. P. Putnam's Sons, 1911.

Chapter 12. S. Anna Gordon. *Camping in Colorado*, 103–11, 113–19, 121, 136–37, 138–45, 148–50, 151–52. New York: The Author's Publishing Company, 1879.

Chapter 13. James H. Pickering. "'Alone Amid the Wind's Mad Revelry': The Death of Carrie Welton." *Colorado Heritage*, (Summer 1998): 3–13.

Chapter 14. Frederick H. Chapin. *Mountaineering in Colorado: The Peaks About Estes Park*, 69, 70, 71–75, 76–80, 83, 85, 86, 97–100, 101–4, 111–14, 119, 120–21, 124–27, 128, 129–31, 132, 134–35. Boston: Appalachian Mountain Club, 1889.

Chapter 15. James H. Pickering and Nancy Pickering Thomas. "'If I Ever Grew Up and Became a Man ...' The Boys of '89: A New Glimpse at William Allen White's First Summer in Estes Park." *Colorado Heritage* (July–August 2009): 12–22.

Chapter 16. Frederick Funston. "Storm-bound Above the Clouds." *St. Nicholas Magazine* (1891): 657–60.

Chapter 17. William Skinner Cooper. "Mountains" (1971), unpublished typescript manuscript, William Skinner Cooper Papers, University of Minnesota Library Archives. Published in James H. Pickering, "Exploring and Mapping Wild Basin," *Colorado Heritage* 2 (1989): 34–46.

Chapter 18. Enos A. Mills. "The Beaver's Engineering." In *Beaver World*, 139–50. Boston: Houghton Mifflin, 1913.

Chapter 19. James H. Pickering. "Vanished in the Mountains: The Saga of the Reverend Thornton R. Sampson." *Colorado Heritage* (Summer 2000): 14–19, 24–29.

Chapter 20. Charles Russell Trowbridge. *Superintendent's Monthly Report*, October, 1915. Rocky Mountain National Park Library.

Chapter 21. Clark Secrest. "Squeaky Bob Wheeler's Place: Way Station in the Rockies." *Colorado Heritage* (Summer 2000): 20–22.

Chapter 22. Julia Prouty. "The Tourist on the Trail." *Little Nature Studies of Estes Park*, 69–75. Estes Park Women's Club, 1916.

Chapter 23. James H. Pickering. "The Eve of Estes." In *America's Switzerland: Estes Park and Rocky Mountain National Park, the Growth Years*, 151–60. Boulder: University Press of Colorado, 2005.

Chapter 24. James H. Pickering. "Tragedy on Long's Peak: Walter Kiener's Own Story." *Colorado Heritage* 1 (1990): 18–28.

Chapter 25. Merrill J. Mattes. "The Boulderfield Hotel: A Distant Summer in the Shadow of Longs Peak." *Colorado Heritage* 1 (1986): 30–40.

Chapter 26. Dougald MacDonald. *Longs Peak: The Story of Colorado's Favorite Fourteeeener*, 93–96. Englewood, CO: Westcliffe Publishers, 2004.

Chapter 27. Jack C. Moomaw. "Winter Patrol." In *Recollections of a Rocky Mountain Ranger*, 48, 51, 54, 57, 60. Longmont, CO: Times-Call Publishing Company, 1963.

Chapter 28. Dorr G. Yeager. *Bob Flame: Rocky Mountain Ranger*, 73–87. Estes Park, CO: Rocky Mountain Nature Association, 2010.

Chapter 29. Stephen Trimble. *Longs Peak: A Rocky Mountain Chronicle*, 92–94. Estes Park, CO: Rocky Mountain Nature Association, 1984.

Chapter 30. Anne Zwinger and Beatrice H. Willard. *Land Above the Trees: A Guide to American Alpine Tundra*, 377–383. New York: Harper and Row, 1972.

Chapter 31. SueEllen Campbell. "The Edge of Winter." In *Even Mountains Vanish: Searching for Solace in an Age of Extinction*, 40–43, 45–47, 67–75. Salt Lake City: University of Utah Press, 2003.

Chapter 32. Michael Coughenour. "Elk in Rocky Mountain National Park—Dynamics and Management." Commissioned essay, 2014.

Chapter 33. Thomas D. Gootz. "The Pika's Last Stand." In *Transformation in Rocky Mountain National Park: The Effects of Climate Change and Human Interference*, 55–65. Estes Park, CO: Estes Park Museum Friends & Foundation, Inc., Press, 2014.

## ILLUSTRATION CREDITS

Map of Rocky Mountain National Park, 1948. Courtesy David Rumsey Map
Collection, www.davidrumsey.com

Cooper-Babcock map of Wild Basin. Courtesy Estes Park Museum.

Carrie J. Welton marker. James H. Pickering Collection.

Early day campers in what would become Rocky Mountain National Park. Courtesy
Lulabeth and Jack Melton.

Stead's Ranch and Hotel. James H. Pickering Collection.

1914 Arapaho Pack Trip. Courtesy National Park Service, Rocky Mountain National
Park.

Dedication: Rocky Mountain National Park. James H. Pickering Collection.

Goddess Colorado congratulates Enos Mills. James H. Pickering Collection.

Tourists on the trail. Courtesy National Park Service, Rocky Mountain National
Park.

Original park headquarters building. Courtesy National Park Service, Rocky
Mountain National Park.

Enos Mills and Superintendent L. Claude Way with the Eve of Estes. Courtesy
Lulabeth and Jack Melton.

Fall River Road. Photograph by William T. Parke. James H. Pickering Collection.

Thornton Rogers Sampson. James H. Pickering Collection.

Park Naturalist Dorr Yeager. Author: *Bob Flame Rocky Mountain Ranger*. Courtesy
National Park Service, Rocky Mountain National Park.

Colorado Mountain Club. Courtesy National Park Service, Rocky Mountain
National Park.

CCC Camp in Little Horseshoe Park. James H. Pickering Collection.

Chasm Lake. Photograph by Fred Clatworthy. James H. Pickering Collection.